MIR
IN THE
MAKING

in consultation with

Robert D. Auerbach, M.D., F.A.C.O.G.

Associate Clinical Professor
Department of Obstetrics, Gynecology and Reproductive Sciences
Yale University School of Medicine

Senior Vice President and Chief Medical Officer
Cooper Surgical, Inc.

ISBN Number 1-934052-00-0 • Printed in U.S.A.

This book does not take the place of your clinician. Different people react differently to the same treatment, test, or procedure. You should always consult your clinician before undertaking any course of treatment.

Neither the author nor the publisher take responsibility for any possible consequences of any course of action suggested in this book. Always call your clinician if you have a question.

NOTE: The terms clinician and healthcare provider/or professional are used interchangeably

Data on file at CooperSurgical, Inc.

Illustrator:
Amy Millar

Graphic Design:
Alicia Goff
Chris Rubino

Fill these in for easy reference:

Healthcare provider's name: ____________________

Office phone: ____________________

Home Phone: ____________________

Answering service: ____________________

Associate's name: ____________________

Phone: ____________________

Office nurse: ____________________

Phone: ____________________

Hospital: ____________________

Address: ____________________

Phone: ____________________

Pharmacy: ____________________

Address: ____________________

Phone: ____________________

Household help: ____________________

Phone: ____________________

Neighbor: ____________________

Taxi: ____________________

Partner's phone during the day: ____________________

Expected delivery date: ____________________

Blood type: ____________________

Chapter 1 Preconception

YOU HAVE TAKEN ON A MAJOR COMMITMENT with your decision to have a baby. Ideally, you will have the opportunity to read this book prior to becoming pregnant. If not, please take the time to refer to it regularly during your pregnancy. We hope you will find this book a good resource of information and help improve your communications with your healthcare professional.

Whether this will be your first pregnancy, or you are already an experienced mother, there are some facts you should be aware of.

If you have been using a barrier-type of birth control such as a diaphragm, a condom, cervical cap or spermicide (foam, jelly, cream), you are fertile as soon as you discontinue their use. This is also true if you have been wearing an intrauterine device (IUD) as your method of contraception. You can become pregnant as soon as your IUD is removed.

If you are using the Pill, Norplant or any hormone based medication, it may take some time to eliminate all of the drug from your system. You can ovulate soon after discontinuing the medication, or it may take months or longer to resume ovulation.

Ovulation must take place in order for you to conceive. Ovulation occurs when a mature ovum (egg) is released from the ovary and moves down one of the fallopian tubes. If the ovum meets up and is fertilized by a sperm, conception takes place (see page 15). Sperm can live inside a woman's body for 3 or more days. The life span of the egg is only 12 to 24 hours.

To improve your chances of becoming pregnant do not use K-Y Jelly or any other commercial lubricant which can impair the ability of sperm to fertilize the egg.

Plan your sexual activities around the time you ovulate.

- Ovulation usually occurs once during the menstrual cycle.
- Ovulation usually occurs about 14 days before the onset of the next menstrual period.

- A menstrual cycle is typically every 28 days but it may vary, a few days less or a few days more and still be normal.
- The exact time of ovulation is difficult to determine because it can be delayed by an infection or even stress.
- Clinicians advise having intercourse starting 5 days before and continuing a few days after you expect to ovulate.
- You can help determine ovulation by taking your temperature every morning before you get out of bed; this is your basal body temperature. Special thermometers for this purpose (basal body thermometers) are available at your pharmacy.
- Your temperature reaches its lowest point just before the pituitary gland releases a hormone (luteinizing) or LH, which triggers ovulation. Two days later your temperature rises above your baseline by as much as one half to one degree and remains elevated until you begin menstruating.
- The rise in basal body temperature occurs after you ovulate, it does not indicate when you will ovulate.

A urine ovulation kit, available from your pharmacy, can also be used to help determine the time of ovulation. The test works by measuring the LH surge in your urine 1 to $1^1/_2$ days before ovulation.

Should you have any questions regarding your pregnancy or information found in this book, ask your clinician or other health professional.

Though there are some aspects of pregnancy that you cannot control, one very important area where you can have a major impact is in following a healthy life style.

You should consider two major adjustments to your health prior to becoming pregnant. They are, increasing your daily intake of folic acid and achieving your ideal weight. Obesity is one of the most common high-risk problems of pregnancy in the United States and Canada. Under the supervision of your clinician, a pre-pregnancy weight loss program and appropriate prenatal care will help keep complications during pregnancy to a minimum in overweight women.

Overweight, as well as underweight, women should strive to reach an appropriate weight before becoming pregnant. Pregnancy is not the time to limit or greatly increase food intake. The early weeks of pregnancy, even before a pregnancy is verified, are crucial ones for the embryo/fetus (the first eight weeks after conception the fertilized egg is called an embryo, thereafter it is called a fetus). It is during these early weeks that the organs are being formed. At this stage, as well as later on, substances such as alcohol, nicotine, illicit drugs and certain medications can be most damaging to the embryo/fetus.

If you are planning to become pregnant, it is a good idea to schedule a visit with your healthcare provider. They will take a detailed family and medical history to determine any risk factors which may require special care should you become pregnant. Their evaluation will include questions regarding any medications or drugs you are currently taking, or have taken in the past. It is very important that your answers be honest and forthcoming to accurately determine your situation. Patients taking medication for diabetes, heart disease, epilepsy or other pre-existing conditions should not discontinue their medication. Instead, notify your clinician of your pregnancy and see if he/she wants to adjust your dosage or change your medication.

There are other drugs which are known to be teratogens (agents that can cause birth defects). A consultation with your physician prior to pregnancy is strongly encouragred. Some examples of thes drugs include:

- Contraceptive drugs: discontinue one to two months prior to becoming pregnant
- Accutane® (isotretinoin), Retin A (prescribed for cystic acne): discontinue at least one month prior to conception. The Food and Drug Administration (FDA) recommends a woman provide documentation of a negative pregnancy test to her pharmacist before a prescription for Accutane is filled.
- Preformed vitamin A: Large doses of vitamin A before conception are also known to increase the risk of birth defects. Studies at Boston University School of Medicine indicate that women who take large amounts of vitamin A prior to becoming pregnant or during the first few months of pregnancy, appear more likely to bear children with birth defects. Routine supplements of vitamin A during pregnancy are not recommended according to medical publications. See page 83 for recommended daily vitamin needs.
- Soriatane prescribed for psoriasis should be discontinued at least three years before becoming pregnant.
- Any vaccine made from live viruses, such as measles, mumps, chicken pox, etc. should be avoided for at least three months before becoming pregnant or during pregnancy. A new report from the Centers for Disease Control and Prevention (CDC) shortened the recommended waiting period from three months to twenty-eight days for rubella (German measles) vaccination. See pages 68-70 for more information on rubella.

- Prednisone or prednisone-like products
- Anticoagulants, for example, coumadin/warfarin, used to prevent blood clots
- Antithyroid medication which suppresses thyroid gland function
- Tetracycline (antibiotics) used to treat acne
- Cancer treating medications

A list of other harmful agents can be found on page 229

If you have a history of a sexually transmitted disease (STD), it should be reported to your healthcare provider. Some STDs can affect your ability to become pregnant. Should you become pregnant, a sexually transmitted disease could also infect and harm your baby. If you or your partner think you may have a STD, you should be tested and if necessary treated, preferably before becoming pregnant. For more information on sexually transmitted diseases, see pages 10-12.

Avoid hot baths, saunas, hot tubs or other facilities that elevate maternal body temperature particularly during the first trimester (see pages 141-142).

Radiation is used in some jobs and in the form of X-rays to diagnose and treat disease. High doses of radiation can lower fertility in men and women and can affect the fetus. While the amount of radiation for most X-rays is small, you should advise your healthcare provider of your pregnancy, or your desire to become pregnant, prior to having these procedures. For more information on radiation see page 121-123.

Because most women are not aware immediately that they are pregnant and neural tube defects occur during the first month of pregnancy, the Centers for Disease Control (CDC) in Atlanta, Georgia, issued a recommendation that all women of childbearing age in the United States take 0.4 mg of folic acid per day to reduce the risk of having a baby affected with spina bifida or other neural tube defects. A study reported in the August 1995 issue of Lancet, an English medical journal, found that women who took multivitamins containing folic acid at the time they conceived, substantially reduced their infant's risk for oral or facial defects such as cleft palate or hare lip.

Women who have given birth to a baby with a neural tube defect are at higher risk of it recurring in a subsequent pregnancy. For this reason they are advised to take 10 times more folic acid than is routinely recommended, 4 mg daily for 1 month before becoming pregnant and during the first 3 months of the pregnancy. These women should take a folic acid vitamin alone rather than a multivitamin containing folic acid. In order to get enough folic acid from a multivitamin, a woman would get an overdose of other vitamins. It is important to discuss this with your physician before taking any vitamins or other medication.

The National Institutes of Health sponsored a study which found that women who took a daily folic acid supplement of at least 400 micrograms during the first six weeks of their pregnancy, reduced their risk of having a baby with a congenital heart defect. A mandate by the Food and Drug Administration (FDA) to fortify grain products (breads) with folic acid may prevent miscarriages as well as lowering the risk of neural tube defects.

It is also important to obtain your partner's personal and family history to help identify any genetic history which could affect the fetus.

A study by scientists at the University of California at Berkeley and the Western Human Nutrition Research Center in Davis, California reported that enough folic acid in the diet may be as important for the prospective father as it is for the mother-to-be. The studies found that low levels of folic acid are associated with decreased sperm count and sperm mobility.

Researchers have found that men who do not eat enough fruits and vegetables rich in vitamin C were more likely to have damaged DNA, the genetic material found in chromosomes. This could increase the risks of birth defects, genetic diseases and/or cancer in their children. It is therefore prudent for a man to follow the governments dietary guide (see food pyramid page 80). This is even more important in smokers because vitamin C in the body is dissipated by tobacco use.

Recently published research, spanning 12 years of study, suggests the alcohol intake of men prior to mating can result in abnormalities of the fetus even if the woman does not drink any alcohol.

Two separate studies revealed that males who were exposed to the drug phenobarbital before birth (in utero), had long-term lower scores on intelligence tests and that exposure in late pregnancy to this drug had an even more profound effect. However, since this drug is used for seizure disorders it is important not to discontinue using this medication until your physician has evaluated your medical condition. The use of this medication, like certain others, requires a balanced decision based on evaluating the risks to both mother and baby.

Exposure to lead or certain solvents, pesticides or other chemicals can reduce a man's fertility by destroying or damaging his sperm.

Ideally, the time to evaluate your lifestyle habits, and eliminate or at least decrease risky behavior, is the time before you become pregnant.

Chapter 2 Examination for Pregnancy

CONGRATULATIONS ON YOUR PREGNANCY! You are about to experience one of the greatest adventures and miracles that any human being can have. In the months ahead, you will be undergoing a variety of changes—changes in the way your body looks, changes in the way you feel, changes in your daily activities, and changes in your wardrobe. These changes will be exciting ones, but they may also be cause for concern and anxiety.

The purpose of this book is to help you understand these changes so that you can eliminate as much of that anxiety as possible. The more accurate and detailed the information you have about your changing body, the more confident you will become about the adventure ahead. In this book you will learn about specific symptoms—what they mean and what you can do about them. You will also learn about personal reactions and feelings which may seem unusual to you. This book will help you to be well informed and confident so that your pregnancy will be as pleasant and safe as possible.

Modern medicine has made remarkable discoveries which have greatly reduced the discomforts and dangers which your great-grandmother faced. The years of medical research have greatly reduced the risks of pregnancy and have greatly increased the chances for a healthy normal childbirth.

But even though so much progress has been made in medical research, the March of Dimes, Birth Defects Foundation and Science Information Division still offer this caution: "Two to three percent of live births involve a significant congenital anomaly (abnormality) of some kind."

New information

In the great majority of cases, no cause can be ascertained that is attributable to actions or omissions by the parents or by healthcare providers involved in their cases. A report issued in January 2003 by the American College of Obstetricians and Gynecologists and co-authored by the American Academy of Pediatrics concluded that the majority of brain injury cases in newborns do NOT occur during labor and delivery. Most instances of neurologic abnormalities occur prior to labor and birth. A task force formed in 1999 and comprised of experts from multiple specialties, issued a 94-page report confirming that most brain injury cases are not due to events that occur during labor, delivery, resuscitation, or treatment immediately following birth. For example, cerebral palsy and encephalopathy (brain injury) in many cases are due to events occurring before labor begins. The condition could originate from developmental or metabolic abnormalities, auto-immune or coagulation defects, infection, trauma, or a combination of these factors.

This report was endorsed not only by the National Institute of Child Health and Human Development of the National Institutes of Health, and the Centers for Disease Control and Prevention, both world renowned government health institutions, but also by distinguished non-government health organizations such as the March of Dimes Birth Defects Foundation, the Society for Maternal and Fetal Medicine, and the Child Neurology Society. International endorsements were given by the Australian and New Zealand Obstetricians and Gynaecologists, and the Society of Obstetricians and Gynaecologists of Canada.

The point of this book is to help you as much as possible to be among the 98 percent of healthy mothers who have confidently reduced their risks.

As your body changes, you will have many questions about what is happening to you. The best person to answer these questions is, of course, your clinician. He/she needs as much information from you as possible in order to make the right decisions. But it will also be very helpful for you to read this book thoroughly and keep it handy in the months ahead. You will find many answers to your questions in the pages that follow, and you will probably also find many other questions and answers which you have not even thought about so far.

New studies indicate that inadequate prenatal care affects a person's intelligence. The implication would be that in-utero environment has a profound effect on IQ in the general population.

Information your healthcare provider (clinician) needs

While your clinician will be your main source of information throughout your pregnancy, you will also need to provide him or her with a great deal of information

as well. He or she will need to know basic facts such as your age, your weight, and whether you have been pregnant before. There will be a physical exam and perhaps lab tests. You will need to provide a urine sample, and you may need to have a Pap test. And you should objectively try to describe your working conditions and any potential stress that exists at work or at home. There are also additional facts your clinician will need to know. Let's look at some of those to understand why they are important.

For example, you will need to recall the exact date of your last menstrual period. This date will help your clinician to decide approximately when your baby will be born. Here is a simple formula for determining the date your baby is due: count back 3 months from the first day of your last period and then add 7 days. So, if your last period began on August 1, then you can count backwards 3 months to May 1 and then add 7 days. Thus, your baby's due date is May 8th. This formula is based on studies which show that the baby will be born approximately 280 days after the last menstrual period.

Accurate family medical history is important.

However, it's important to keep in mind that nature does not always cooperate with our formulas! Most babies arrive within a week of the calculated due date, few babies arrive exactly on the due date. It is perfectly normal for your baby's birth to occur within 1 to 2 weeks of the expected date.

If your pregnancy extends beyond 1 week after the scheduled birthdate, the clinician may order additional tests. As you know, menstrual cycles vary and are not always exact. Sometimes stress or some physical factor can affect your menstrual cycle. In fact, some women even have some bleeding after they become pregnant. Be sure to report any irregularities in your menstrual cycle.

Another piece of information that you will need to provide your clinician is your medical history. Think about your own family and the father's family. Is there any family history of chronic diseases such as high blood pressure, diabetes, heart or kidney diseases or allergies, including allergies to drugs? Have you ever had mumps, chickenpox, measles, hepatitis, or any previous operations? In the pages that follow, you will discover the reasons behind providing such accurate information.

Another source of vital information will be your blood test. This is important for several reasons. First, your baby receives its oxygen from hemoglobin in your red blood cells. If laboratory tests show that your hemoglobin is low (anemia) then your provider may consider supplements that will help maintain your energy and optimize nutients transferred to the baby. The blood test will also show whether you are immune to Rubella (German measles) or are Rh negative (see pages 46-48).

Hepatitis B screening

The hepatitis B virus is the major cause of acute and chronic hepatitis and cirrhosis of the liver. If the mother carries this virus or has one of these diseases, the baby can become infected. Clinicians need to know this early in the pregnancy so that the baby can be vaccinated within 12 hours of delivery. According to a study by the American College of Obstetricians and Gynecologists (ACOG) in September of 1986, certain women are in high-risk groups for this virus and should undergo prenatal screening. The following is a list of the main high-risk groups, though there may be others:

- Women of Asian, Pacific Island, or Alaskan Eskimo descent, whether immigrant or United States born
- Women born in Haiti or sub-Saharan Africa
- Women with histories of:
  - Acute or chronic liver disease
  - Work or treatment in a hemodialysis unit
  - Work or residence in an institution for the mentally retarded
  - Rejection as a blood donor
  - Blood transfusion on repeated occasions
  - Frequent occupational exposure to blood in medical or dental settings
  - Household contact with an HBV carrier or hemodialysis patient
  - Multiple episodes of sexually transmitted diseases
  - Percutaneous use of illicit drugs (by injection)

Because accurate medical histories are often difficult to obtain, some clinicians routinely screen all their pregnant patients for hepatitis B. In an article appearing in the May 1999 journal, *Contemporary OB-GYN*, it was found that 90 percent of infants infected with hepatitis B became carriers of the disease. It is estimated that 20,000 infants are born to mothers who tested positive to hepatitis B in the United States. Safe and effective vaccines are available to prevent the fetus from becoming infected with this virus. If all pregnant women were tested for hepatitis B at one of their early prenatal visits, babies could be given hepatitis B immune globulin and the hepatitis B virus (HBV) vaccine if the mother had tested positive. The Centers for Disease Control and Prevention (CDC) and the American College of Obstetricians and Gynecologists (ACOG) now recommend that screening for hepatitis B be added to the routine prenatal testing procedures. Hepatitis B is transmitted through sexual contact, intravenous drug use or via blood transfusion.

Other types of hepatitis which may affect the mother and the baby include hepatitis A and hepatitis C.

Hepatitis A is spread by person-to-person contact or by exposure to contaminated food or water. The virus that causes hepatitis A is rare in pregnancy. Hepatitis A is not passed on to the fetus. If you should be exposed to hepatitis A during your pregnancy you should take immune globulin within two weeks of exposure.

Hepatitis C is transmitted through sexual contact, intravenous drug use and blood transfusions. Only a small percentage (less than 10 percent) of women testing positive for hepatiti C pass the infection to their baby. A woman testing positive for hepatitis C should not breastfeed.

Sexually Transmitted Diseases (STDs)

According to the Centers for Disease Control and Prevention in Atlanta, Georgia, sexually transmitted diseases have been linked to a marked increase in the number of ectopic pregnancies and infertility.

A mother infected with a sexually transmitted disease can pass the disease on to her unborn baby.

Syphilis, in almost all cases, is spread through sexual activity with an infected partner or a carrier of the disease. Occasionally it can be transmitted by kissing if there is an open sore in the mouth of the infected person. An infected mother can also pass the disease on to her child. One of the problems with syphilis is that you may be unaware that you have the disease because symptoms may take years to surface. A blood sample is taken to test for syphilis.

But even if you have no symptoms, the disease can still be very dangerous, even deadly, to your baby. In the middle trimester of a pregnancy, the disease can pass through the placenta to the fetus. Consequences include structural birth abnormalities and possibly death of the developing baby. However, treating the infected mother for the disease can also help the child, and if the treatment is started early enough, chances are good for a healthy baby free of the disease.

At a recent conference sponsored by Baylor College of Medicine in Texas, a professor and chairman of obstetrics and gynecology from Rush Medical College in Chicago recommended that every woman be tested during her first prenatal visit for the two most common STDs, gonorrhea and chlamydia.

Gonorrhea, if left untreated in the mother, may attack the eyes of a newborn as it travels through the birth canal. This is why antibiotic ointment or eye drops are placed in almost all newborns' eyes, to prevent blindness caused by a gonorrheal infection. Like syphilis, gonorrhea can be treated and cured in most cases, thus helping to prevent complications compromising the health of the newborn.

Chlamydia is another sexually transmitted disease that is very prevalent, particularly in younger women. It too can cause eye infections in the newborn as well as other illnesses such as pneumonia. Most clinicians now will test for chlamydia on the first prenatal visit and again in the third trimester. Chlamydia can be treated with antibiotics but you must consult with your clinician who is aware of your pregnancy, to determine which, if any, antibiotic to take during your pregnancy.

Genital herpes is caused by a virus called herpes simplex and is transmitted by direct contact during sexual activity. An active infection is characterized by blisters and open sores primarily around the sex organs. Genital herpes may be associated with miscarriage as well as potential physical and mental disabilities.

It is important to tell your clinician if you have ever had genital herpes or had sexual contact with anyone who had the disease. Although not common, it is possible for a baby to become infected with the virus during a vaginal birth.

If your doctor is aware of your history of genital herpes, he or she may want to do more frequent examinations and possibly treat you with medication to prevent an outbreak at the end of your pregnancy. Should you show signs of an active herpes infection at the time of labor, a decision to deliver your baby by cesarean section may be made. Women who had recently been infected with the genital herpes virus were more likely to pass on the infection during birth.

Human papilloma virus (HPV), (also known as genital warts or condyloma) is another STD. It affects the genital area and is easily passed from one person to another during sexual intercourse, or oral or anal sex. Treatment of HPV can sometimes begin during pregnancy. However, if the warts are extensive, your doctor may want to wait until after your pregnancy to begin treatment.

Acquired Immune Deficiency Syndrome and Human Immune Deficiency

Both Acquired Immune Deficiency Syndrome (AIDS) and human immune deficiency are caused by the HIV virus. Once this virus gets into the blood stream it destroys the cells of the immune system. The immune system is the body's natural defense against infection.

HIV infected women who are pregnant, including those who have no symptoms of AIDS, treated with medications against the HIV virus are much less likely to pass the AIDS virus on to the fetus. The drug should be given to the HIV positive woman during her pregnancy, labor and delivery, and the baby must take the drug during the first six weeks of life. There is a test called enzyme-linked immunosorbent assay (ELISA) available to detect if your blood contains HIV antibodies — a sign of infection. The American College of Obstetrics and Gynecologists (ACOG) is now recommending that HIV screening be included in the standard series of tests for pregnant women — not just for women considered at high risk for this disease. Some states require that all pregnant women be tested for HIV.

The Food and Drug Administration (FDA) has cleared for market use the first oral, fluid-based, rapid HIV test with results available within 20 minutes.

Nearly everyone knows about the deadly disease called AIDS (Acquired Immune Deficiency Syndrome) and how it destroys the body's immune system. Thus, it is very important that you tell your clinician whether you or the father have AIDS, or test positive for HIV — not only for your own health and treatment but also because it is possible for the fetus to develop this disease. Breastfeeding is not recommended for a baby whose mother is HIV positive since the baby could acquire AIDS in this way.

Home pregnancy tests

Pregnancy tests done in the home are considered by many to be as accurate as laboratory tests. These home tests use urine samples which are then combined with a chemical to see if a certain pregnancy hormone is present. Such tests are private, convenient, and inexpensive (though so are many laboratory tests). But you have to be very careful to follow directions and not knock or disturb the specimen—otherwise the results will be inaccurate. If the home test indicates you are pregnant, you should make an appointment to see your clinician as soon as possible.

Your initial visit

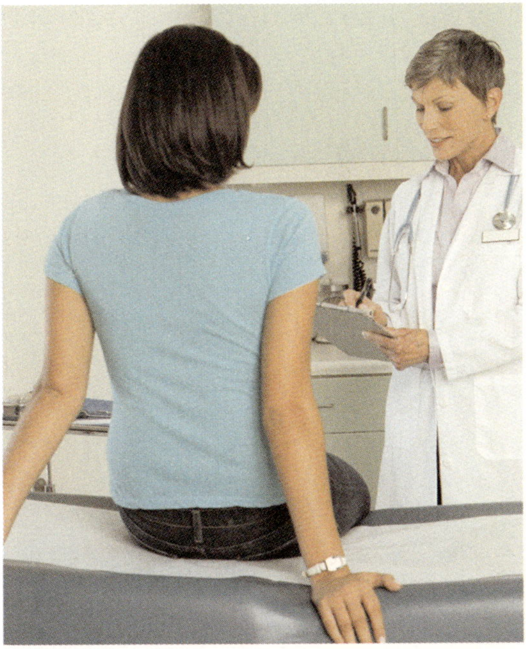

It is important to have a complete physical examination once you suspect you are pregnant. This will include taking your complete medical history. Your clinician will need to know if you had any previous pregnancies and, if so, whether there were any problems or complications. You will be asked questions about your family's medical history as well as that of the father and his family. This medical history is important; be sure to be completely forthright with your clinician.

Following your history, you will have a complete physical examination including having your eyes, ears, heart, abdomen, lymph nodes, breasts and lungs checked. This will be followed by a very thorough examination of your reproductive organs —vagina, cervix, uterus, ovaries and fallopian tubes.

If you are pregnant, there are several changes that the clinician will immediately notice. For example, shortly after conception, the uterus, cervix, and vagina begin to retain fluid. This causes the veins to become congested and dilated, causing a dusky bluish appearance to the cervix, vagina, and vulva. Your cervix and uterus will also become softened. In addition, your breasts will become slightly tender to the touch and fuller. The nipples and the areolas (the dark area around the nipples) will become dark and slightly puffy.

If it is not possible to confirm a pregnancy with only a physical examination, your clinician may recommend some type of pregnancy test.

Pregnancy tests

It is no longer necessary to wait until you have missed two menstrual periods before having a pregnancy confirmed.

One test for pregnancy uses a hormone in the woman's urine called human chorionic gonadotropin (hCG). This hormone is produced by the developing placenta and is excreted in the urine. Using an early morning urine sample, a clinician can determine pregnancy about a week after a missed period.

None of these tests will replace the physical exam, and your clinician may recommend various combinations of these tests, or perhaps some others. Whatever test you use, be sure to consult with your clinician as soon as you feel you are pregnant.

Fees

Once you are accustomed to the idea of being pregnant with all its ramifications, you should discuss the procedures and associated fees with your healthcare provider and your insurance carrier. Understanding the costs and anticipated reimbursements will enable you to better plan financially for your pregnancy and delivery. Below is a chart you can use to help with this process.

Estimate of obstetrical costs	**Normal**	**Possible**
Routine care, normal delivery	$	$
Postpartum checkup	$	$
Multiple birth	$	$
Cesarean	$	$
Circumcision	$	$
Anesthesia	$	$
Hospital costs per day_____ x _____ days	$	$
Baby's doctor	$	$
Totals	$	$
Less insurance reimbursement	$	$
Net to be budgeted	$	$

Chapter 3 The miracle of conception

WHETHER YOU ARE JUST PLANNING your pregnancy, or already expecting a child, you may be looking for more information on exactly how this miracle occurs. Fortunately, science has a great deal to share with you about how the act of conception takes place.

Not every act of intercourse can result in a pregnancy. This is because an egg, called an ovum, is needed from the female's ovary, and a woman usually produces only one each month. The egg or ovum is only ripe for a short period, which usually occurs midway between menstrual periods. Since this period is so short, it is surprising that there are so many pregnancies.

During intercourse, the male deposits millions of sperm in the vagina. These sperm are among the smallest cells in the human body, and it takes many thousands to equal one ovum in size. Each sperm has a small whiplike tail and is extremely active. The sperm, which can remain fertile for about 72 hours, swim up the vagina into the uterus and then into the fallopian tube searching for a ripe egg.

If the ovum is not fertilized during the short time it is ripe, the lining of the uterous breaks down and is expelled during menstruation.

When a fertile sperm reaches a ripe egg, the sperm penetrates the surface. The sperm loses its tail, and in an instant conception has occurred. At this stage, the lining of the uterus (endometrium) begins to thicken. The blood vessels to the endometrium enlarge in order to supply oxygen and nutrients to the fetus as it grows. The uterus continues to expand as the fetus grows.

The uterus is truly a remarkable organ. Located in the lower abdomen, and maintained at a constant temperature, the uterus serves as a "home" for the

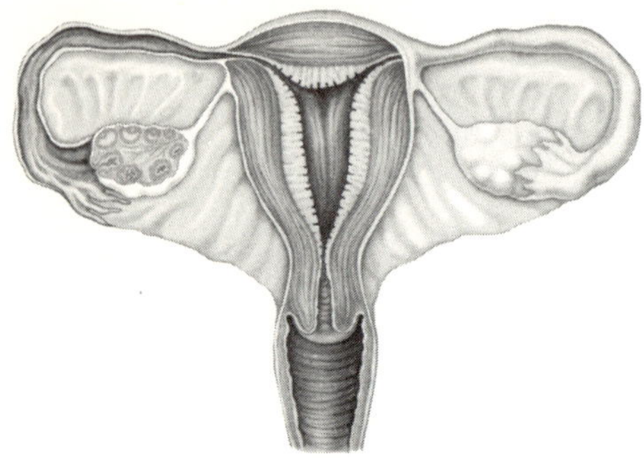

fetus for 9 months — allowing ample room for the fetus to grow without interfering with other organs in the region. A fallopian tube and one ovary extend from each side of the uterus, much like the branches of a tree (see drawing on page 16).

The uterus is a hollow pear-shaped organ weighing approximately 2 ounces. The lower, narrower end of the uterus, sometimes referred to as the "neck" of the uterus, is the cervical canal (the birth canal during a vaginal delivery) which extends into a tube-like structure called the vagina.

The placenta (afterbirth) begins to form by the time the embryo is 2 weeks old. Fetal blood is separate from the mother's blood, substances such as oxygen, nutrients, drugs, hormones, alcohol and almost everything else passes from the mother to the fetus through a semipermeable membrane. This route from the mother to the fetus also serves as a channel to remove all waste products from the fetus via the fetal vessels of the umbilical cord, to be excreted or disposed of by the mother's body. The placenta grows until it reaches its maximum size about 2 months before delivery. At this time it is about 8 to 9 inches in diameter. At birth the placenta weighs about 1 to 2 pounds.

Pregnancy is divided into 3 trimesters. Each trimester is approximately 13 weeks. Starting with the mother's last menstrual period, an average pregnancy lasts 280 days or 40 weeks. It is more accurate to calculate the gestational age of the fetus in weeks than in months.

If either the sperm or ovum is defective, nature frequently disrupts the pregnancy and the pregnancy ends in a miscarriage. This is nature's way of helping insure the survival of healthy future generations (see page 37).

Nourishment for the embryo

During the first eight weeks after conception the developing baby is called an embryo. The embryo produces small active cells called "trophoblasts" that are attached to the lining of the uterus (endometrium). These are the cells which seek out the food for the embryo. Everything that the mother takes in—food, air, liquid—the embryo gets a share of. This is an important fact to think about. For example, any drugs that you might take may be shared by the embryo. You need to be very careful because the side effects of many new drugs are uncertain or unknown. Even over-the-counter medications can be passed on to the embryo and be harmful (see pages 130-136).

Another thing that is happening in the uterus is the formation of amniotic fluid, which is contained in the "amniotic bag" (membrane) around the embryo. This amniotic fluid has several purposes. It provides a cushion against injury for the embryo; it gives the embryo some fluid; it keeps the temperature at a constant level; and it provides a liquid in which the embryo can move about.

Umbilical cord

As the embryo grows into the form of a baby, an umbilical cord grows from its navel. This long, semi-transparent, jelly-like rope is attached to the placenta and transports nourishment. The umbilical cord is really a continuation of the fetus' blood vessels. When the baby is born, the cord is cut.

The growth of the fetus.

Now that we have seen how the embryo gets nourishment from the mother, let's watch it grow through its various stages. After the first 8 weeks of gestation, the embryo is called a fetus. We have already noted the changes that take place during the first 3 or 4 weeks in the uterus—the time you discover you are pregnant.

The growth pattern discussed so far is for the average fetus. Just as children grow at different rates

What happens next?

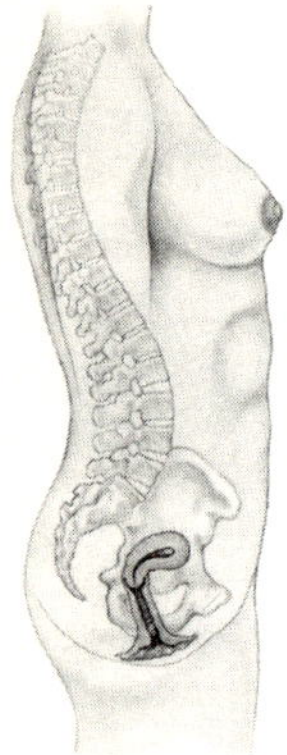

At 5 weeks the embryo is about 1 inch long and weighs less than an ounce. It has a two-lobed brain and a spinal cord. Tiny limb buds begin to appear which will eventually grow into arms and legs. The heart also forms, and though it is too faint to hear, it begins to beat on the 25th day.

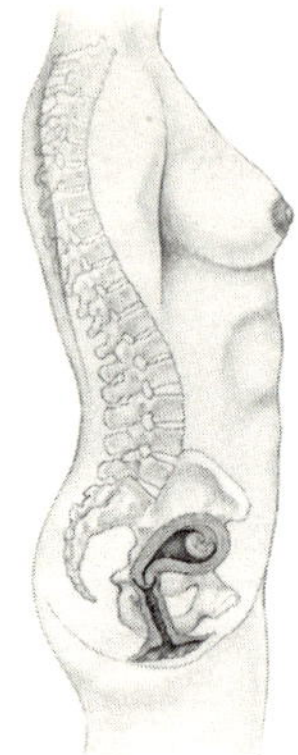

At 8 weeks the embryo is 1 inch long and still weighs less than an ounce. All major organs and ystems are formed but not yet fully developed. By the end of the second month of a pregnancy, the embryo is called a fetus.

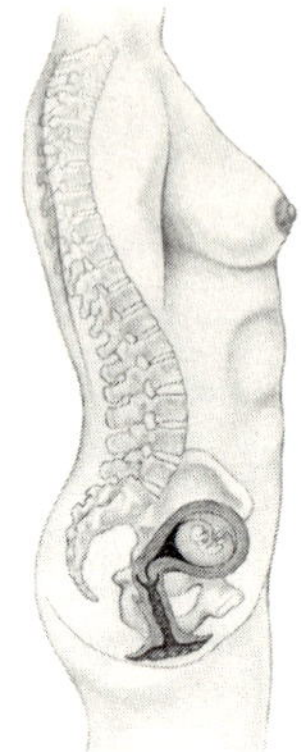

By the end of 3 months the fetus is 4 inches long and weighs just over one ounce. Buds for future teeth, soft finger and toe nails, and hair appear on the fetus' head. The kidneys begin to secrete urine and there is further development of organs. An electronic stethescope (doppler) can detect a heartbeat. From this time on the fetus begins to gain weight.

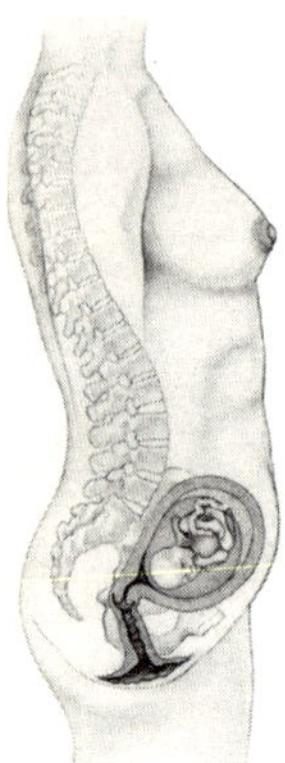

In the 4th month the fetus grows to 6 to 7 inches long and weighs about 5 ounces. Its own sex is developing. The fetus moves, kicks, sleeps, swallows, can hear and pass urine. The skin is pink and transparent and eyebrows have formed.

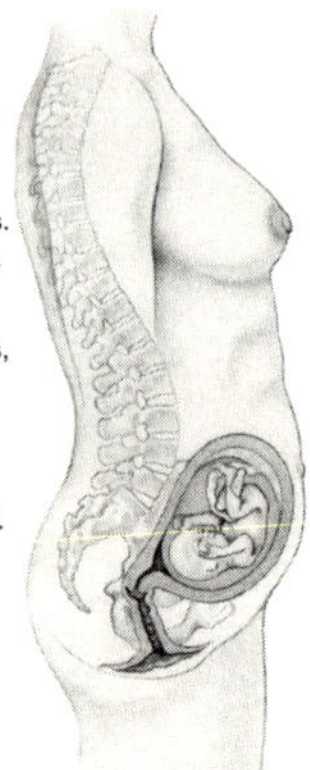

At 5 months the fetus will have a spurt in growth. The internal organs continue to mature. The fetus is much more active—turning from side to side and even flipping over. This is the month when movement is usually first felt by the mother. A stethescope can detect a heartbeat. By the end of this month the fetus has grown and is 8 to 12 inches long and weighs from 1/2 to 1 pound.

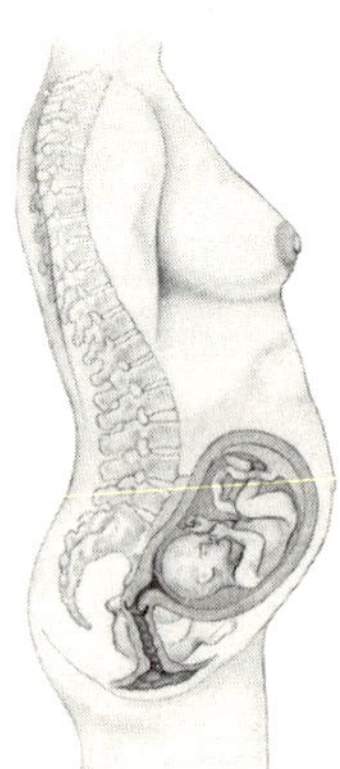

In the 6th month the fetus continues to grow rapidly. There is continued development of organ systems. The skin is red, wrinkled and covered with fine hair. By the end of this month, the fetus will weigh 1 to 1 1/2 pounds and be 11 to 14 inches long. The lungs are still not fully developed and as a rule the fetus cannot live outside the uterus without specialized, high-tech support systems.

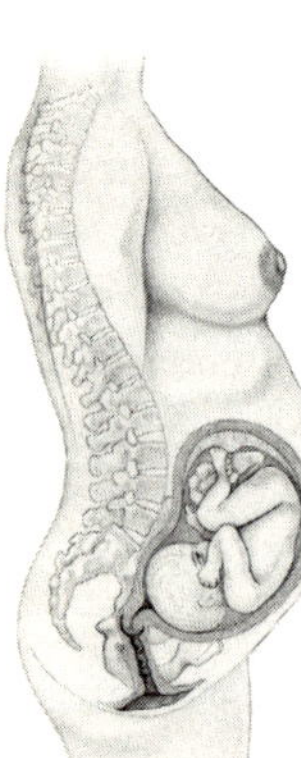

The 7th month is another rapid growth period. The fetus sucks its thumb, the eyes open and close, and fetal bones are hardening. The fetus now weighs about 3 pounds and is approximately 15 inches long. It now has a better chance of surviving if it is born.

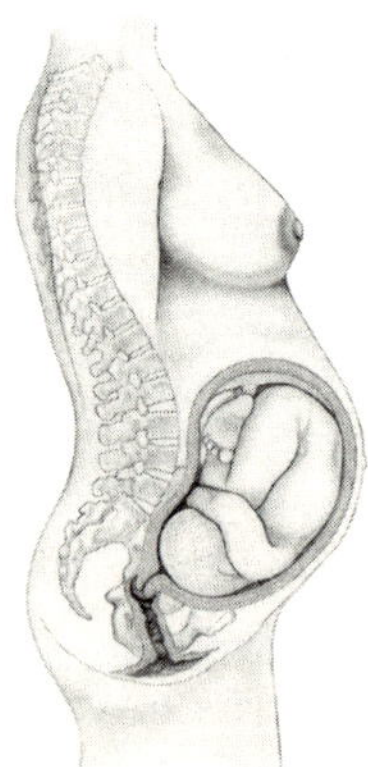

The 8th month shows continuing growth in the size and weight of the fetus. Though there is less room to move about, the kicks are felt more strongly. The fetus is now about 18 inches long and weighs about 5 pounds.

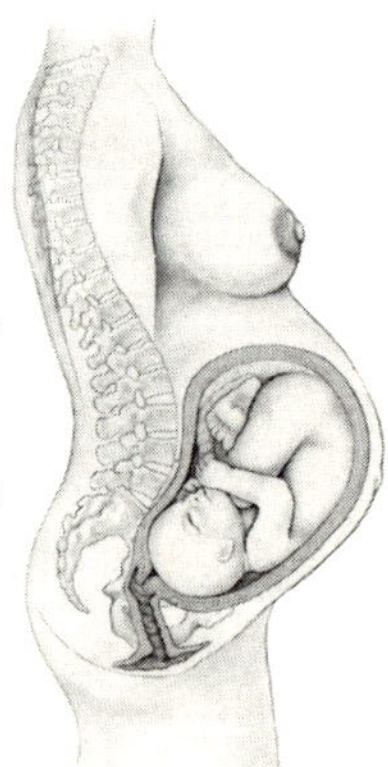

During the 9th month the fetus gains about 1/2 pound a week. The bones in its head are soft and flexible for delivery. Usually the fetus turns so as to settle into the optimal position for delivery. The fetus is considered full term at 40 weeks, weighing between 6 and 9 pounds with an average length of 19 to 21 inches.

once they are born, so too, fetuses develop at different rates. And only slightly more than 10 percent of pregnancies end exactly 280 days after the beginning of the last menstrual period. Your delivery will probably occur before or after the projected date.

As the time for delivery approaches, the cervix starts to "ripen." In other words, it thins out, softens, and may start to dilate. Your labor will be easier if these changes occur before labor. Your progress will be slower if they do not.

The period when the fetus is most vulnerable to birth defects is during the first trimester. However, even after the first trimester, many organs, even the brain, continue to develop and can be affected.

Fetal growth is affected by a number of factors including:

- Smoking, which can reduce birth weight
- Illicit drug use which can slow fetal growth
- Multiple pregnancy, babies usually smaller
- Diabetes in mother can result in larger or smaller baby

Chapter 4 Changes to expect during pregnancy

YOU SHOULD HAVE A PRETTY CLEAR PICTURE by now of what changes you can expect in the development of your baby at various times. But what additional changes will occur in your own body during this time? You know of course, that your menstrual period will stop for 9 months and resume after your baby is born. But what else can you expect in terms of physical and emotional changes?

Changes in your breasts

Because they are designed to produce milk, your breasts will be one of the first areas of your body where you will notice a change as they prepare for your baby's birth. They will become larger, firmer, and more tender, and in the first months you may experience a tingling, prickly sensation near the nipples. Around the nipple is a pinkish area called the areola. This areola will become darker, and you will notice small "bumps" which are a normal part of the development of the glands that produce the milk. After 4 months, your breasts may start to exude some moisture, and in the last stages of your pregnancy, you may have to place absorbent material between your nipples and bra to absorb leakage. The moisture is caused by a fluid called "colostrum," which is a forerunner of your milk supply. It may also be necessary to wash away any dried substance so that your nipples will not be itchy, sore or irritated. Wash nipples with warm water. Do not use soap which can cause dryness and irritate the skin.

Do not be alarmed if you notice the veins on your breasts becoming larger. This is normal. The veins are simply working harder to convey a richer blood supply to your developing breasts.

Nausea

There are many hormonal changes taking place at this time and some, but by no means all, pregnant women complain of nausea during the first trimester of their pregnancies.

The nausea, commonly referred to as "morning sickness," can occur at any time of the day, though it does seem to be more common in the morning, and usually ends after the third month. It may, however, return late in the pregnancy when there is increased pressure by the fetus on other abdominal organs, particularly the stomach.

There are a few simple steps you can take to relieve the nausea and increase your comfort. Eat small, simple, frequent meals. Avoid fried and greasy foods. Cabbage, cauliflower, and spinach, which are hard to digest, should also be avoided. Do not avoid eating—this will make any nausea worse. If you have problems in the morning, try eating a dry diet such as a few crackers or dry toast. Stay in bed for 15 or 20 minutes, and rise slowly. You should then be able to have a normal breakfast in half an hour. At other times during the day, simply lying down for a few minutes can help. Other women find that nausea can be prevented if they lie down for 15 minutes after each meal. Acupressure, motion sickness bands and ginger have also been suggested as alternative treatments for nausea. Check with your healthcare professional before taking ginger or any anti-nausea medication.

If you are less than 6 weeks pregnant, you can take a folic acid supplement rather than your multivitamin containing folic acid because folic acid alone is less likely to upset your stomach and it is very important that you have sufficient folic acid early in your pregnancy (see pages 83; 96-97).

Severe nausea and vomiting may lead to dehydration and weight loss and may require intravenous fluids. This extreme form of nausea and vomiting is known as hyperemesis gravidarum.

Call your clinician if:

- You cannot keep liquids down
- You are urinating less frequently and/or in small amounts.

- Your urine is dark in color
- You feel dizzy or faint when you stand
- You vomit blood
- You feel your heart pounding (palpitations)

Frequent urination

One difference you will notice in your habits is that you will want to urinate more often. This is because the uterus which holds your fetus is expanding and putting pressure on the bladder. This pressure feels similar to having a full bladder. Like nausea, this condition should clear up in a few weeks, but it may also come back at the end of your pregnancy when a much larger fetus is being carried in the lower abdomen and again exerting pressure.

Despite this condition, it is important to keep drinking plenty of liquids. Clinicians recommend a minimum of two quarts of liquid a day. Remember that your growing fetus needs these liquids. You can however, prevent waking up in the middle of the night to urinate by avoiding liquids a couple of hours before going to sleep.

Another common problem which may occur is urine leakage when you cough, laugh or sneeze. This is called stress urinary incontinence. As the uterus grows it puts pressure on the bladder. In addition, the relaxation of the pelvic floor muscles compounds the problem particularly during the 2nd and 3rd trimesters. Kegel exercises (see page 127) will help strengthen the pelvic floor muscles. If the urine leakage continues after delivery, continue with the Kegel exercises.

Your waistline expands

Your waistline will expand because of the dramatic changes taking place inside of you. By the start of the 4th month, the fetus will have grown to more than 6 inches in length, and it may weigh 5 ounces. The fetus will also be encased in fluid within the uterus, and the walls of the elastic uterus will grow thicker to contain this extra load. These changes will cause your abdomen to distend, and you may notice stretch marks—pink horizontal lines—on your stomach. Some people may recommend rubbing lotion, cold cream, or oil on these marks. But the truth is there is not much you can do. You are either born to get them or not. You can however, control your overall weight by following your clinician's orders about diet (see Chapter 9).

Fetal movement

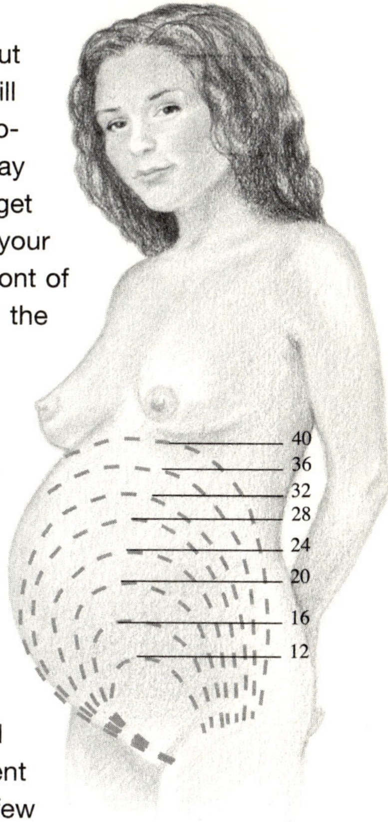

One of the most thrilling changes will occur about halfway through your pregnancy, when you will probably feel a faint, gentle fluttering in your abdomen, referred to as a "quickening." This feeling may not return for several days, but gradually it will get stronger and stronger. In fact, towards the end of your pregnancy, you will be able at times to stand in front of a mirror and watch your fetus' limbs poking at the walls of your abdomen.

Clinicians are aware that even embryos move, although women cannot feel them because their uteri are so well insulated. 8 weeks after conception, the embryo grows into a fetus. You can usually feel the fetus move by the 16th to 20th week. By the end of the fifth month fetal movements become distinct and strong. What is the fetus doing? It is probably stretching or turning its arms and legs. Or it may be moving its head from side to side. Sometimes you may feel a frequent rhythmic pattern of movement occurring every few seconds. These movements are probably the fetus hiccuping. The hiccups may even continue after baby is born. Feeling a fetus move for the first time is always a dramatic moment for a mother regardless of how many children she has had. It is especially surprising that the fetus can move around as much as it does in such a confined space. Remember, however, movement is not continuously felt, sometimes the fetus is asleep.

Changes in hormone levels may result in mood swings during your first trimester.

If you have not felt the fetus moving at all by twenty-two weeks, let your healthcare professional know. He or she may want to do an ultrasound. Sometimes the placenta is positioned on the front wall of the uterus and acts as a cushion, delaying the time when movement is first felt. If you have been feeling movement and notice the number of fetal movements has been reduced or you do not feel any movement for several hours, lie down on your left side and drink something sweet such as juice or soda. If you do not feel at least ten movements in the next two hours call your clinician. Depending on how far along you are in your pregnancy they may want to perform further tests.

Contractions

Irregular contractions, which can occur any time after the first trimester are called Braxton Hicks contractions after the doctor who first described them. For some women these contractions are like menstrual cramps. Because these contractions usually occur toward the end of pregnancy, they are sometimes the cause of what is called "false labor" — irregular contractions that occur without the dilation of the cervix. Mild menstrual-like cramps during the first mid-trimester are quite common.

Feelings and emotions

As we explained, your body will be undergoing some dramatic changes as it adapts to the needs of the fetus growing inside of you. There will also be changes in your hormones, and these changes can affect your feelings and emotions. You may experience periods of moodiness, but these shifts in emotions usually disappear by the 4th month; once hormone production levels off and comes into balance, your emotional well being will also come into balance.

Let's take a typical example. One morning you may wake up with no nausea, feeling great and full of energy. You have plenty to do in the day ahead, and you are looking forward to it. Then suddenly, during breakfast, your mood darkens and you start to feel depressed. Out of nowhere, you start to cry. Then, a few minutes later, you take a shower, get dressed, and are feeling just as energetic as when you got up. These are typical of the normal emotional changes that are caused by changes in your hormones.

There will also be a number of other questions which you will have about the dramatic changes that will be occurring in your life. But if you look at each question logically it will be much easier to deal with this anxiety. For example, you may worry about whether your baby will be born normal and healthy. The fact is that modern medicine has greatly reduced the risk of having an abnormal child. 60 years ago, the infant mortality rates in the U.S. and Canada were 100 deaths for every 1000 births. Today, that statistic has been reduced to 8.5 deaths per 1000 births. When you start to worry about a malformed child, remember that modern medicine has put statistics on your side for having a healthy baby. Don't let worry be a problem itself.

You may also be concerned about how a new human being will affect your relationship with your husband. Of course, there will be changes. Sexual activity is going to change somewhat in the next nine months. And as your pregnancy continues, you and your husband may become impatient for the pregnancy to end. This is perfectly normal. As adults, you can deal with this through tolerance, good will, common sense and open discussions.

Sometimes expectant parents have difficulty understanding their new roles. But the transition does not mean that you will go from being a young, active couple to old, inactive parents. The activities which you enjoyed before need not change very much or at all. In fact, one effect that your pregnancy may well have is to deepen the relationship between you and your mate.

Your love for each other may strengthen the bond between you as you focus your love on the new baby. This new focus in no way has to diminish the love you shared before the baby.

Finally, you need to remember that childbirth is no longer shrouded in mystery. It is a perfectly normal and natural function. There have been many myths about pregnancy. Most of them are silly. For example, if a pregnant woman attends a funeral, it will affect her baby; going to the zoo and viewing ugly animals can mark your child. Or, if you listen to good music while pregnant, your baby will have musical talent. These myths are so silly that they are almost comical. They have no basis in fact. Birthmarks are coincidental and genetic, and not caused by your baby looking at a baboon. There is no correlation between your thoughts and the fetus' development. The fetus does not know whether you are at a funeral or a supermarket. When you start to become worried or hear myths such as these, remember, that as a woman you were born to give birth to a new human being.

If your concerns and worries during pregnancy begin interfering with your daily life, speak with your healthcare professional. Help is available.

Chapter 5 Preexisting health problems and pregnancy

WITH NEW DEMANDS BEING PUT ON THE BODY, pregnancy can be stressful, even if no prior medical problems exist. However, there are some pre-existing health problems that can affect a pregnancy just as pregnancy can sometimes affect a preexisting health problem.

A pregnant women with a preexisting health condition will be followed more closely and may undergo additional tests to monitor her pregnancy as well as the preexisting condition.

The following chronic medical conditions are frequently seen in women of child-bearing age.

Diabetes

At one time diabetes was considered a major risk factor during pregnancy for both mother and fetus. With the increased knowledge of how to control diabetes, pregnancy today is much safer for most women with this condition. If kept under control before, as well as throughout the pregnancy, the risks for pregnant women with diabetes are almost as low as those of pregnant women without diabetes.

It cannot be emphasized enough that women with diabetes should have their diabetes under good control before they become pregnant. Studies have shown that the incidence of fetal abnormalities in diabetics is directly related to control of a woman's glucose level before she becomes pregnant and during the first trimester.

The more common risks associated with diabetes— particularly if the diabetes is not kept under good control, include:

- Birth defects

- Hydramnios— too much amniotic fluid in the sac surrounding the fetus which may precipitate premature labor and delivery (see pages 39-40)
- Macrosomia— larger-than-normal baby, making delivery more difficult
- Miscarriage, more common in diabetic women (see pages 37-38)
- Preeclampsia or high blood pressure (see page 42)
- Respiratory distress syndrome (RDS), the result of the baby's lungs not being fully developed and affecting the baby's ability to breathe
- Stillbirth, though not common, occurs more frequently in babies of diabetic mothers.

Asthma

Asthma is a chronic disease of the respiratory system that causes wheezing, difficult breathing and coughing. Asthma is unpredictable during pregnancy. In some pregnant women the asthma gets better, in some women worse or it may be the same.

Most medications for asthma are safe during pregnancy but always let your doctor(s) know what medication you are taking and that you are pregnant. Asthma could pose a problem if the fetus does not get sufficient oxygen. An asthmatic attack in the mother will lower the oxygen available to the fetus so it is very important to try and keep your asthma under control.

- First and foremost if you smoke, STOP!
- Recognize environmental triggers and avoid them if at all possible. If animal dander is the offender, find another home for your pet. Do not allow anyone to smoke in your home and avoid places where there is a lot of smoking. Keep your home as dust free and mold free as possible.
- Your clinician may recommend flu immunization after your first trimester if you will be pregnant during the flu season.
- Notify your clinician if your asthma begins to worsen. Do not wait until it is a full-blown attack, if at all possible.
- Do not delay treatment of any early symptoms of infection or pending asthmatic attack—call your clinician promptly.
- Go to the emergency room if an acute asthmatic attack does not respond to the first medication tried.

Systemic Lupus Erythematosus (SLE)

Systemic lupus erythematosus (SLE) is an autoimmune disease, a disease that results in the production of antibodies against the body's own cells, and can affect the entire body including the skin, kidneys, joints and nervous system.

SLE tends to occur in young women of childbearing age. It does not seem to affect fertility but it does seem to increase the risks of miscarriage, premature birth and stillbirth.

SLE has periods of remission and flare-ups. The woman who is symptom free for six months and has no kidney damage prior to her pregnancy, has the best pregnancy outlook. SLE is treated with corticosteroids. Always check with your clinician before taking any medication. If you are taking medication for any chronic medical condition prior to becoming pregnant, do not discontinue your medication until you consult your clinician. He or she may want to adjust your dosage. Your clinician may also prescribe low doses of aspirin or similar type of drug to control joint pain, but do not take aspirin unless recommended by your clinician. You will be followed more closely and additional tests may be recommended.

Breastfeeding is usually not affected by SLE. Discuss this with your clinician.

Hypertension (high blood pressure)

The arteries are the blood vessels in the body that carry oxygen-rich blood from the heart to all parts of the body. The blood vessels that carry the blood from the body back to the heart are called veins. When the force of the blood in the arteries reaches higher-than-normal levels, it is called hypertension or high blood pressure.

Hypertension can be chronic (existing before the pregnancy) or it can develop during pregnancy. Preeclampsia is a specific condition that causes high blood pressure in the mother along with other conditions such as kidney malfunctions (see page 42). Hypertension, whether chronic or first occurring during pregnancy, can, depending on the severity, affect the mother and the fetus.

If you have chronic high blood pressure, it should be brought under control before you become pregnant. Diet, life-style and heredity can affect your blood pressure. High blood pressure can put you and your fetus at higher risk for preeclampsia (see page 42). This is why it is so important to have your blood pressure checked at each office visit.

High blood pressure can put you at higher risk for a heart attack or a stroke. It can also cause problems for your fetus. This can include intrauterine growth restriction (IUGR), resulting in a too small for age baby (see pages 38-39).

Thyroid problems

- Hyperthyroidism (an over-active thyroid gland)
- Hypothyroidism (an underactive thyroid gland)

Both hyper- and hypothyroidism can be harmful to the fetus. Ideally thyroid disease should be under control before a woman becomes pregnant. Control of this disease must be maintained during pregnancy to avoid complications in the mother and the baby.

Hyperthyroidism occurs when the thyroid gland produces too much thyroid hormone. Graves disease, which is characterized by an enlarged thyroid gland and protruding eyeballs (exophthalmos), is one of the most common symptoms of hyperthyroidism. Blood tests are performed to determine and monitor the dose of medication needed. Treatment of hyperthyroidism with radioactive iodine must be avoided during pregnancy and breastfeeding.

Hypothyroidism is due to an underactive thyroid gland. It can be treated with thyroid hormone pills. Blood tests are also done periodically to determine if enough of the hormone is being taken.

Seizure Disorders (Epilepsy)

Most women with seizure disorders (epilepsy) are already on medication to control their seizures and go on to have uneventful pregnancies. Usually the same medication is continued during pregnancy, though the dosage may change. The lowest effective dose of a single therapy is recommended by the American Academy of Neurology. It is important to use the lowest dosage necessary to control seizures because the medication itself may cause a problem. Seizures can harm both the mother and fetus, so it is important to keep seizures under control. Never discontinue your medication unless specifically advised by your clinician to do so. If possible, it is better to take one single medication at the lowest effective dose rather than several different medications.

Because all medications used to treat seizures pose some risk of birth defects, your clinician may order more frequent ultrasound examinations to observe and evaluate the condition of the fetus.

Pregnant women who take the antiepileptic drug sodium valproate may be at greater risk of delivering a child with fetal malformation(s), according to a preliminary analysis of an ongoing study in Australia. Discuss this with your healthcare professional.

Medications prescribed for seizures use up folic acid. For this reason, it is suggested that women should begin taking folic acid supplements about three months before trying to get pregnant and continue during pregnancy.

Tuberculosis (TB)

Tuberculosis, a disease that affects the lungs, can spread to other parts of the body such as the brain, bones and kidneys. TB is caused by a bacteria that is carried through the air, most often by the sneezes and coughs of someone infected with the disease.

For years the number of cases of active TB has decreased. Now the number of people with TB has started to increase.

Pregnant women with TB can be treated. An infected mother can infect her fetus with TB through her blood. The baby can also be infected with TB by breathing in the bacteria at birth and through contact with the mother. Women with TB should not breastfeed without first consulting their doctor.

Chapter 6 Reporting to your clinician

THROUGHOUT YOUR PREGNANCY you will be visiting regularly with your clinician. These appointments are usually short but they are very important. In the first 4 months you will visit the clinician once a month. In the next 4 months your visits will occur every 2 weeks.

In the 9th month your visits will be every week. Special concerns or circumstances may increase the visits. Throughout this time, your clinician will be monitoring your progress with routine information. He or she will check your weight, your blood pressure and your urine. Monitoring the position of the baby, its size and progress are especially important during the last month.

Always keep the lines of communication open between you and your clinician. Such communication is the best way to insure a pleasant, comfortable pregnancy. At every stage of your pregnancy, the clinician will need to know exactly how you feel. Also remember that, as an experienced, well trained professional, the clinician's nurse is an excellent source of information. The nurse can help answer many of your questions.

This book is an additional source of information that focuses on questions most frequently asked by pregnant women. In this chapter we will look both at common problems during pregnancy and how to remedy them.

Breast self-examination

It is very important that you continue doing breast self-examination every month throughout pregnancy, while nursing and thereafter.

About 2 percent of all breast cancers are diagnosed during pregnancy. Breast examination should be part of the prenatal visit and appropriate diagnostic tests should be performed if any abnormality is found, according to the American College of Obstetricians and Gynecologists (ACOG). This includes fine needle aspiration, ultrasound, open biopsy under local anesthesia and, in selected cases, mammography with proper shielding of the fetus. According to the American College of Radiology, no single diagnostic X-ray procedure results in radiation exposure to the extent that it is a threat to the well-being of the developing embryo or fetus. Therefore, exposure to X-ray during pregnancy is "not an indication for therapeutic abortion." However, because a woman's breasts during pregnancy are so dense, it is almost impossible to screen the breasts visually, making diagnostic imaging an unreliable method of finding or evaluating breast cancer during pregnancy. Prompt diagnosis and appropriate treatment are as essential in the pregnant woman as in the non-pregnant woman.

For more information on breast self-examination read, *A Guide to Breast Health Care—How to Examine Your Breasts*, also published by Budlong Press Company and available through your physician.

Depression during pregnancy

Depression can occur during pregnancy. There has been much publicity about postpartum depression or "baby blues" but little has been said about depression during pregnancy. It is estimated that more than 1 in 4 mothers-to-be, experience depressive symptoms during pregnancy.

It is normal to occasionally feel sad, but if you feel sad most of the time you should report this to your healthcare professional and ask for help. Pregnant women who are depressed may not take care of their health and this could affect the fetus. Sadness that lasts for at least two weeks and has more than one of the following symptoms are signs of depression:

- Feeling depressed or "down" most of the day, almost every day
- Feeling guilty, hopeless or unworthy
- Lacking interest in work or other activities
- Thinking about death or suicide
- Feeling very tired most of the time. Loss of energy
- Sleeping more than usual or not being able to sleep at night
- Eating much more than normal and gaining weight, or loss of appetite and losing weight

- Being unable to make decisions or pay attention
- Experiencing aches and pains not relieved by any treatment

Some studies have suggested that a mother's depression and anxiety can have a strong impact on the pregnancy and the baby. Keep the clinician up to date on how you feel. This book presents answers to questions and situations most often asked by pregnant women. Yet there will be times when, as an individual, you present unique problems. The majority of your questions can be answered during your routine office visits. Routine office visits usually range from once a month up to week 28, then every 2 weeks until the 9th month, and every week during the 9th month. Of course, special circumstances or conditions can alter this schedule. At different times the fetus' growth and position may be determined. During each visit it is important to check your weight, blood pressure, urine, the position of the fetus and its size. Prenatal visits are not time consuming, but they are vital. This is a period when you and your clinician are working together. Be sure to use this time to discuss problems that relate to your pregnancy, whether physical or mental.

Remember, your clinician's nurse is an excellent source of information and support. Don't hesitate to discuss your concerns with the nurse who is an experienced professional trained to help you and to answer questions.

Keeping the lines of communication open between you and your clinician is one of the surest ways to guarantee a pleasant, comfortable pregnancy.

Other common disturbances of pregnancy, along with some suggested remedies, are included here to ease your concerns until you see your clinician.

Dizzy spells and fainting

It is not unusual in the first four months of pregnancy to occasionally feel dizzy and light-headed. Usually, you can remedy this by lying down on your side. It is not a serious condition and will stop in time, but if it persists, you should tell your clinician.

Breathing difficulties

By the end of your pregnancy, the fetus will have grown large enough to press on the rib cage, and interfere somewhat with your breathing. You may get winded climbing stairs or in other activities. Try to move more slowly and practice deep chest breathing. If you have trouble sleeping, prop yourself up in a semi-sitting position with some pillows. You should tell your clinician during your routine visits about any breathing difficulties. If shortness of breath and/or chest pain develop suddenly, call your clinician promptly.

Nosebleeds

During pregnancy hormone levels increase. This change increases the amount of blood your body makes to meet the needs of the growing fetus. A result of the increase in your hormone level is that the mucous membranes inside your nose may swell, become dry and bleed easily. To relieve these symptoms try:

- Increase your fluid intake.
- Use a humidifier to moisten the air in your house. Be sure the humidifier is cleaned daily.
- If you must, use saline nosedrops to help open your nasal passages. Do not use any decongestants unless your healthcare professional specifically advises you to do so.

Heartburn

After eating it is not unusual to experience some stomach discomfort, gas or belching. You may even have a slight burning sensation in your chest. To help avoid or minimize heartburn you should:

- Avoid eating spicy and greasy foods.
- Take a tablespoon of cream before meals. This will coat your stomach lining and cause better activity in the intestines.
- Eat more slowly.
- Avoid lying flat, particularly after eating; an extra pillow at night may give you some relief.
- If heartburn persists, call your clinician.

Recently, doctors at the University of Alabama, Birmingham Medical Center reported that chewing gum can help and even prevent symptoms of heartburn. Their recommendation was to chew gum for about 30 minutes immediately after eating.

Do not take baking soda preparations. These tend to increase heartburn and may cause you to retain fluid, because baking soda contains sodium that stimulates the production of acid.

Regardless of whether or not you experience heartburn, you should always be particularly careful not to overeat during pregnancy.

Muscle cramps

Leg Cramps: Avoid standing in one place for prolonged periods whenever possible.

As your fetus grows larger, it may put pressure on the large blood vessels in your lower abdomen. This can slow up the blood circulation in your legs and cause cramps. To relieve the discomfort try putting a heating pad or hot water bottle under the cramped muscles. Gently massaging the legs may also bring relief, or try bending your foot upward with your hands. Wearing comfortable shoes with low heels can also help. Do not use liniment. It will not help. Sometimes, the baby's head can put pressure on some nerves and cause shooting pains in your legs. Try changing your position or doing a few minutes of knee-chest positioning. Before going to bed, try stretching your legs, this sometimes relieves leg cramps.

Pain extending from the lower back down to one or the other leg is called sciatica. It is due to pressure on the sciatic nerve. Heat applied to the painful areas can usually provide relief. If the pain is severe, contact your healthcare professional.

Varicose veins

Varicose veins occur during pregnancy when certain veins become weakened and enlarged due to the increased pressure from the growing uterus. These enlarged veins occur most frequently in the legs but may also appear in the region of the vulva and vagina. Varicose veins can be quite uncomfortable. You cannot completely prevent varicose veins, but you can stop the painful throb that accompanies them. Try not to stand or sit for long periods of time without moving. Keep the blood circulating by walking and moving. You can also elevate your legs when you are sitting down to help the blood flow back from your feet through the rest of your body more efficiently. Do not cross your legs when sitting and avoid wearing knee highs or stockings with a tight elastic band. Support hose can provide comfort, especially if you put them on before you get out of bed.

Sleeping patterns

During the first few months of your pregnancy you may feel constantly tired—as though you can't seem to get enough sleep. If this is the case with you, organize your time so that you can work in a midday nap—or even a nap in the morning and another in the afternoon.

By the end of your pregnancy, however, it may be the inability to fall asleep (insomnia) that is most troubling. Your increased girth may require a change in sleep positions. Try using an extra pillow or two to prop yourself up in bed If you have difficulty falling asleep. Try taking a walk before bedtime. Other relaxing techniques include a warm bath or shower before retiring; even a warm glass of milk before bedtime can help you relax. Do not take any sedatives (sleeping pills) or tranquilizers.

Vaginal discharge

Even when you are not pregnant, your vagina secretes a small amount of liquid, though it is hardly noticeable. But when you become pregnant, this discharge may increase. Such an increase is caused by the changes in the vaginal cells which are becoming softer, thicker, and more elastic so that the baby can be born. Some seepage of fluid comes from the cervix. You really cannot stop this discharge, but you can keep the area clean by washing frequently with mild soap. However, do not douche. Tell your clinician if the discharge is excessive, if there is itching, or if you experience a sudden gush of water or constant leaking. (See PROM on page 41.) The vaginal discharge that occurs after delivery is called lochia (see page 180).

Constipation

When your uterus grows larger, it will press on your lower intestines and may cause constipation. You can help this condition by avoiding constipating foods such as cheese, chocolate and rice. Simple adjustments in your diet can help relieve this condition. You may find that fruit, especially at night, is a good laxative. Prunes, figs, peaches, and cherries are effective and also nourishing. Increasing the roughage in your diet will also help your bowel movements. Roughage is found in green vegetables, either cooked or raw, and whole grain bread. For breakfast, eat whole grain or bran cereals. Begin each morning by drinking a glass of water and continue with a total of 8 glasses of water or juice throughout the rest of the day.

If the problem persists, do not be embarrassed to tell your clinician.

Hemorrhoids

Constipation can also cause hemorrhoids which are enlarged veins at the opening of the rectum. Eating fiber and roughage will soften the stool and make passage easier. Do not experiment on your own with over-the-counter drugs for this condition. Instead, tell your clinician. He or she may recommend a stool softener.

Lower abdominal pain

Bands of fibrous tissue, which are the round ligaments on each side of the abdomen, support the uterus. As the uterus grows, these bands are stretched. You may feel as if something is "pulling" or even have a sharp pain in the lower abdomen on one side or the other. The pain occurs most frequently between weeks 18 and 24 of pregnancy. Avoiding rapid changes in position will help prevent these pains. If you should feel sharp pain in the groin area, try bending toward the side of the pain. If the abdominal pain persists or becomes more acute, call your clinician.

In the microscopic examination of embryos and fetuses after a miscarriage, it was found that more than 80 percent revealed an abnormality that would prevent a surviving baby from living a normal life. A miscarriage in many cases, then, is one of nature's built-in checks that tries to assure the survival of healthy future generations.

Miscarriage

Miscarriage occurs most frequently during the first 3 months of a pregnancy, though it can occur any time during the first half of a pregnancy. As many as 20 percent of pregnancies end in a miscarriage. The fetus is unable to survive outside the mother's body at this stage of the pregnancy.

Recurrent miscarriage is 2 or 3 pregnancy losses in a row within the first 15 weeks gestation. It is distinct from an isolated miscarriage. The American College of Obstetricians and Gynecologists recently released a bulletin advising women suffering from recurrent miscarriages to consult their physician for specific testing.

Vaginal bleeding is the most common symptom of a miscarriage. Spotting early in a pregnancy does not always mean a miscarriage. Sometimes at the beginning of a pregnancy, when the fertilized egg first attaches itself to the lining (endometrium) of the uterus, spotting or staining can occur. This is called implantation. Should you notice any bloody discharge, however, report it to your clinician immediately. He or she will probably prescribe bedrest.

Ectopic pregnancy

As we explained earlier, a fertilized egg implants itself in the lining of the uterus and develops into an embryo. But if the embryo attaches itself outside of the uterus (usually in a fallopian tube), this is known as an ectopic pregnancy, and such pregnancies do not survive

Because an ectopic pregnancy is very dangerous, even life-threatening, you should be alert for the symptoms. Dizziness, paleness, light-headedness, sweating, and rapid pulse may indicate internal bleeding leading to shock. Low abdominal pains and light vaginal bleeding are other signs. Sometimes there is pain in the shoulders. This pain is caused by blood escaping from a rupture into the abdomen and putting pressure on the diaphragm (the partition between abdominal and chest cavities) and in turn on the shoulders.

Current treatment can include medical therapy and minimally invasive surgery. Once a woman has an ectopic pregnancy there is an increased chance of another occuring each time she becomes pregnant.

You should also be aware that smoking can affect ectopic pregnancies. Researchers in France discovered that women who smoke have a two-thirds greater risk of an ectopic pregnancy than do nonsmokers. If you smoke at least half a pack a day, the risk is double.

Intrauterine growth restriction (IUGR)

In a low-risk pregnancy, fetal growth is determined by measuring the fundal height — that is, from the top of the pubic bone to the top of the uterus. This measurement in centimeters approximately equals the number of weeks gestation. If your clinician finds this measurement is smaller than expected, an ultrasound exam may be recommended to more closely determine the fetus' growth.

During the ultrasound examination, measurements are taken of various fetal body parts to determine the approximate weight of the fetus. This weight is compared with the average weight for fetuses at the same gestational age. The average percentile is 50, but anything between the 10th and 90th percentile is considered within normal range. In other words, 10 percent of the population are smaller than normal and 10 percentile are larger than normal. This is not to say that all fetuses above the 90th percent or below the 10th percentile are not normal— most are completely normal. It does indicate to your clinician that some may not be thriving and may need to be followed more closely.

The fetus whose estimated weight falls below the 10th percentile (small for gestational age) SGA may have intrauterine growth restriction. The following are some of the possible causes of SGA and possible IUGR:

- There may be multiple fetuses.
- Some genetic factors may result in less than average fetal growth.
- Certain infections such as cytomegalovirus, measles and toxoplasmosis may affect growth. (see pages 72-73; 68-70; 138-139)
- Chromosomal abnormalities are known to affect growth.
- The mother may have had poor nutrition, particularly in the third trimester.
- Smoking, alcohol, cocaine and other environmental toxins are also known to decrease birth weight.

The fetus estimated to be above the 90th percentile may have macrosomia, that is, being large-for-gestational-age (LGA). The possible causes of a LGA baby may be:

- The mother is a poorly controlled diabetic.
- The pregnancy goes beyond 40 weeks gestation.

Premature Rupture of Membranes (PROM)

The main symptom of premature rupture of membranes (PROM) is a sudden gush of water with a characteristic smell, before the 37th week of pregnancy. What has happened is that the membrane or bag of waters surrounding your fetus has ruptured (torn). PROM is the major cause of premature labor.

About half of preterm patients will go into labor within 24 hours of PROM and over 85 percent of preterm patients will be in labor within a week. If your clinician does diagnose PROM, you may have to be hospitalized so that you and your baby can be carefully monitored.

Other symptoms of PROM are increased vaginal discharge, menstrual-like cramps, backaches, and contractions, whether painful or painless. These symptoms are more common in women with PROM. If you notice any of these, call your clinician immediately, and in the meantime rest in bed.

There are many risk factors for PROM including in vitro fertilization, incompetent cervix, polyhydramnios (excess of amniotic fluid), multiple births, higher parity (four or more previous births), and viral disease. Additional risk factors can be a prior history of a low-birth-weight infant, prior preterm delivery, sexually transmitted diseases and smoking a half pack or more of cigarettes a day. Non-caucasians are also more likely to be at risk for PROM.

Premature labor

If your labor begins before the 37th week, it is called preterm or premature labor. A premature baby usually has more problems. Symptoms of premature labor include:

- Menstrual-like cramps which may be constant or intermittent (on and off)
- A feeling of heaviness or pressure on your rectum or perineum
- Lower back pain
- Cramps, with or without diarrhea
- Change in vaginal discharge (it may be heavier, watery or blood-tinged)
- Contractions

If you notice any of these signs, you should lie down on your side for an hour.

If the symptoms do not disappear, call your clinician and give him/her:

- Your name
- The date your baby is due
- Your symptoms
- The frequency of any contractions

Your clinician may take various actions. He or she may ask you to come to the office or go directly to the hospital. You may be given some drugs, called tocolytic (to-co-li-tic) agents to stop the labor. They can be given in IV fluids, by injection, or orally, and they work to relax the muscles of the uterus. Side effects may include nausea, vomiting, headache, tremors, flushing of the skin, and/or increased heartbeat.

Incompetent cervix

This describes a cervix which is unable to perform its required function of retaining a pregnancy, frequently resulting in miscarriage or preterm birth in the second trimester.

Cervical incompetence may be the result of previous cervical trauma due to surgery or a difficult vaginal delivery, or it may be due to a genetic malformation of the cervix. These factors make it more likely for a recurrence of this problem in subsequent pregnancies.

The primary symptom of an incompetent cervix in pregnancy is spotting or bleeding. The majority of miscarriages are due to an abnormality in the fetus (see pages 37-38). However, recurrent miscarriages, that is, 3 or more in a row, may be due to an incompetent cervix. Fortunately, today, with the aid of ultrasound (see pages 50-52), indications of an incompetent cervix can be determined and treated early-on. One such surgical treatment is called cerclage. In this procedure, 1 or 2 sutures encircling the cervical opening are taken. The purpose of the suture is to tighten the cervix to prevent it from dilating under the growing weight of the fetus. The suture is removed approximately 1 week before delivery.

Another treatment, a non-surgical approach, used alone or in conjunction with a cerclage, is the use of a pessary, which is precisely fitted to the individual patient. A number of different pessaries have been used during pregnancy.

With the aid of ultrasound, certain risk factors for premature labor can be identified early and treatment can begin prior to the onset of symptoms. Your clinician may also recommend bedrest and the administration of a tocolytic agent to relax the muscles of the uterus, if there are no contraindications for its use.

Preeclampsia (Toxemia)

If a patient develops high blood pressure combined with protein (albumin) in her urine for the first time during the second half of her pregnancy, it is called preeclampsia (also known as toxemia). This is why your blood pressure is taken and a urine sample tested at each office visit. About 7 percent of pregnant women develop preeclampsia.

Doctors do not know exactly what causes this condition. Signs of preeclampsia such as fluid retention (swelling of face, legs and hands) and headaches should be reported to your healthcare professional immediately. He or she will want to check your blood pressure and a urine sample. An elevated blood pressure and protein in the urine are symptoms of preeclampsia.

Warning Signs of Preeclampsia:

- *Edema (swelling) of the face, hands and feet*
- *Severe headaches*
- *Dizziness*
- *Blurred vision*
- *Sudden weight gain*

A study reported in the March 2002 issue of *OB-Gyn News*, found that women who were physically active during their first 20 weeks of pregnancy had a reduced risk for preeclampsia. This supports ACOG guidelines (see page 128) recommending pregnant women engage in moderate exercise on most if not all days, unless there are specific contraindications.

Preeclampsia is most common in first pregnancies. It is also seen more frequently in women who have a history of high blood pressure, heart disease, diabetes or other chronic disease prior to their pregnancies. Preeclampsia can develop rapidly at any time, and it is not self-limiting. If left untreated, the condition can progress to include convulsions and coma, known as eclampsia. But it can often be prevented or controlled if monitored carefully. This is why it is so important to have regular prenatal visits.

Post Maturity (Post Term)

As we said earlier, your due date is approximate, and you can deliver 2 weeks before or 2 weeks after that due date; babies born after 42 weeks of gestation are called post mature, and they may have problems that babies delivered at term do not have. Recent evidence has prompted some physicians to consider 41 weeks as the time to consider testing or the induction of labor.

Placenta Previa and Abruptio Placentae

Heavy bleeding occurring in the second half of a pregnancy suggests a problem

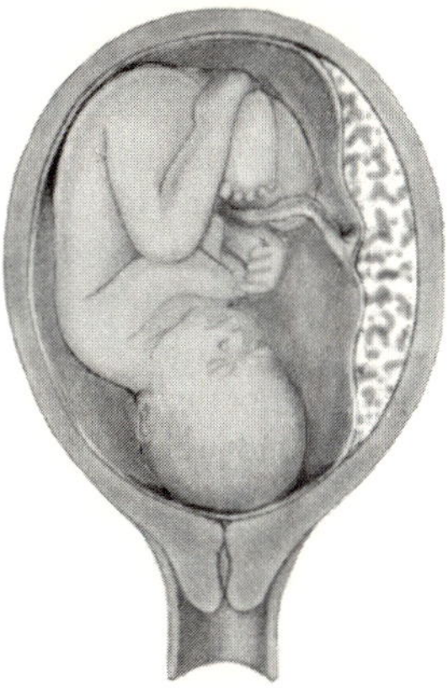

Normal Pregnancy

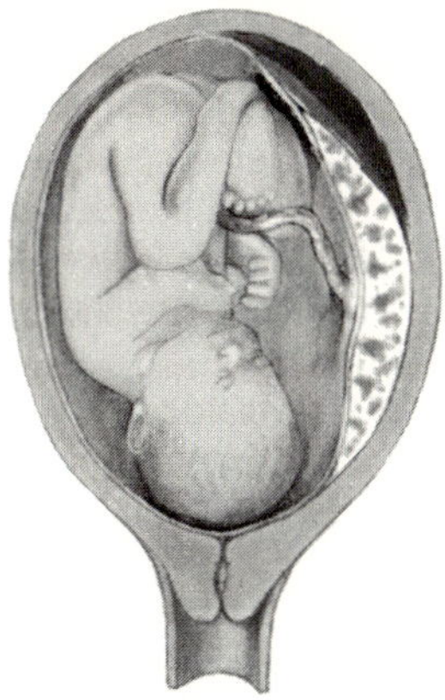

Abruptio Placentae

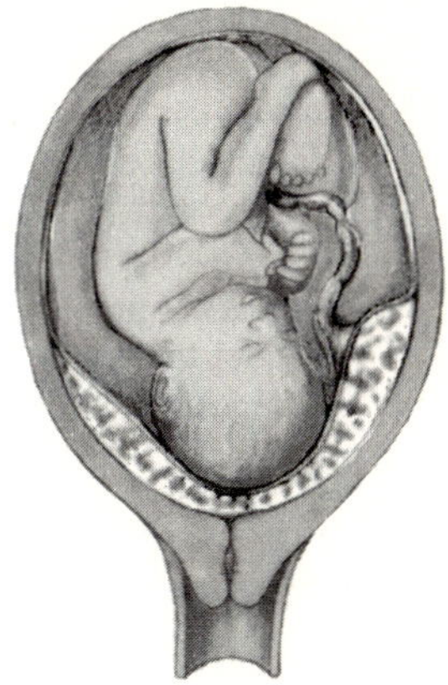

Placenta Previa

with the placenta. The two most common problems involving the placenta are placenta previa and abruptio placentae.

Placenta previa occurs when the placenta lies very low in the uterus, partially or completely covering the cervix, blocking the baby's exit from the uterus. When the cervix dilates (begins to open), bleeding occurs requiring immediate medical attention.

Abruptio placentae is the result of the placenta detaching or separating from the uterine wall either before or during birth, and is usually followed by heavy bleeding and constant and severe abdominal pain. The detachment and heavy bleeding may deprive the baby of oxygen. Maternal cocaine use has been associated with a marked increase in the risk of abruptio placenta.

It is, therefore, important that you notify your clinician immediately if you have any bleeding late in your pregnancy. Hospitalization for as long as several weeks may be necessary. Both placenta previa and abruptio placentae may require early delivery of the baby, sometimes by cesarean birth.

Phoning your clinician

About 4 A.M. one morning, Mrs. Brown stumbled back into bed, awoke her husband, and said, "Call the clinician, I'm spotting."

Mr. Brown hastily put on his robe, dialed the clinician's number, and the following conversation ensued:

"Hello, Dr. Greene speaking."

"Dr. Greene, this is Jim Brown. My wife is spotting."

Dr. Greene, awakened from a deep sleep, is desperately trying to determine which of the three Mrs. Browns in his practice it is. He asks, "How much is she spotting?"

"I don't know. I'll ask her. Just a moment."

The question is relayed from husband to wife. The answer is relayed from wife to husband to clinician, who is still not sure which Mrs. Brown is involved. The clinician's next question, "When did I see your wife last?" results in another round of relayed messages until finally the clinician believes he knows who the patient is.

Ongoing, accurate communication between you and your healthcare provider is extremely important during your pregnancy. This will make it easier to resolve any problems, or emergencies which might occur between office visits.

Except in extreme emergencies, you should be the only one speaking with your healthcare provider. Avoid relaying information to the clinician through your spouse or other family member.

Some simple procedures can help eliminate confusion:

1. Call during regular office hours whenever possible. With your records available at the office, it is easier for your clinician to manage your problems from there. Give information to the nurse. If it is a routine question, she may be able to give you an immediate answer, and she can always determine the necessity of your speaking directly to the clinician. If he/she can't come to the phone, she may relay the question or have the clinician return your call as soon as possible.

2. Any time you call, whether it is to the office during the day or directly to the clinician during non-office hours, give your full name, when you last saw the clinician, and your present month of pregnancy. Describe your situation in concrete terms. How much blood is being passed? How often? What does it

look like? When did you last urinate? About how much? A cup? A teaspoonful? How much water did you drink since then? How often are your headaches? If there is swelling, where? For how long? Being specific can facilitate treatment.

3. Make the call yourself if at all possible. Relaying messages through a third party may give your clinician misleading information.

4. Always have a pencil and paper at the phone before you call. Write down whatever you are told to do. Making an emergency phone call when you are upset may cause you to misunderstand your clinician's instructions.

5. Know the name, address, and phone number of your pharmacy. Your clinician may need to contact them to prescribe a medicine.

6. At the beginning of your last month, you should ask your clinician when he or she wants to be called after labor begins.

Clinician's phone number: ________________________________

Pharmacy's phone number: ________________________________

Chapter 7 Special pregnancy tests

THE MIRACLE OF BIRTH CONTINUES to inspire awe in each generation. And, with each generation, it is amazing to see how far science has progressed with more sophisticated testing and information available to the mother during her pregnancy.

By now you should be familiar with the routine tests that your healthcare provider will perform during your regular monthly and weekly visits. These tests of your blood pressure, weight, urine, and blood will provide valuable information so that he or she can monitor the progress of you and your fetus. Modern medicine has also developed several other more sophisticated tests which help to evaluate the health of both mother and fetus, especially those who are considered high risk. In this chapter, we will discuss several special situations and the tests which have been devised to analyze them. These tests are not standard procedure in all cases. You may or may not fit into these situations, but you should be aware of these tests. The more information you have, the more confident you will be.

You should be aware of the difference between a basic screening test and an invasive test. A blood or urine test would be an example of a screening test. These tests pose no risk to the pregnancy. Amniocentesis, a procedure in which a hollow needle is inserted through the abdomen into the amniotic sac, is an invasive test. Both screening and invasive tests will be reviewed in this chapter.

Reasons for testing

There are a number of special conditions that require special tests. In this chapter we will discuss these conditions.

The Rh factor

In order to understand the Rh factor, you need to know some basic facts about the structure of your blood. There are four blood types—A, B, AB, and O. These blood types are determined by antigens in the blood cells. Antigens are part of our immune system. They are proteins on the surface of the blood which produce the antibodies we need to fight off disease. There are a number of minor antigens, and the most common is called the Rh factor.

You are either Rh positive, meaning you have the factor or antigen, or Rh negative, meaning you do not have the Rh factor. 85 percent of Caucasians and a slightly higher percentage of African Americans are Rh positive. One of the routine blood tests that your clinician performs will determine whether you are Rh positive or negative.

If you are Rh negative and the father is Rh positive, the baby can acquire Rh factor from the father and be Rh positive. If this occurs, that is, the baby is Rh positive, and you are Rh negative, problems can arise. What happens is that a small amount of your blood will mix with the baby's blood. Since your blood does not have the Rh factor, it can respond as if it were allergic to the baby's blood by making antibodies to attack the foreign Rh positive blood of your baby. This condition is called *sensitization,* and it can cause serious illness or death to the fetus. This process usually occurs in subsequent pregnancies. The antibodies will attack the red blood cells in your fetus and cause it to be anemic. This type of anemia is a serious condition known as erythroblastosis fetalis, hemolytic disease or more simply, Rh disease.

This development of antibodies (from the mother) against an antigen (in the fetus) which comes from a person who is genetically different is called alloimmunization. In Rh iso-immunization, the red blood cell count of the fetus may be examined and evaluated in order to best determine how severe the destruction of these cells may be. If necessary, an intrauterine blood transfusion, using the umbilical vein, can be performed.

Rh alloimmunization of Rh negative women may occur after a transfusion of Rh-positive blood or during pregnancy with an Rh-positive fetus. This can occur when the mother is exposed to fetal blood during delivery, amniocentesis, miscarriage or abortion, and may result in the development of erythoblastosis fetalis in any future pregnancy with an Rh-positive fetus.

Fortunately, modern medicine can usually prevent the main cause, the sensitization to the Rh factor. Since the antibodies do not go away once they are formed, it is best to prevent the mother from originally becoming sensitized. If you have

Rh disease develops this way:

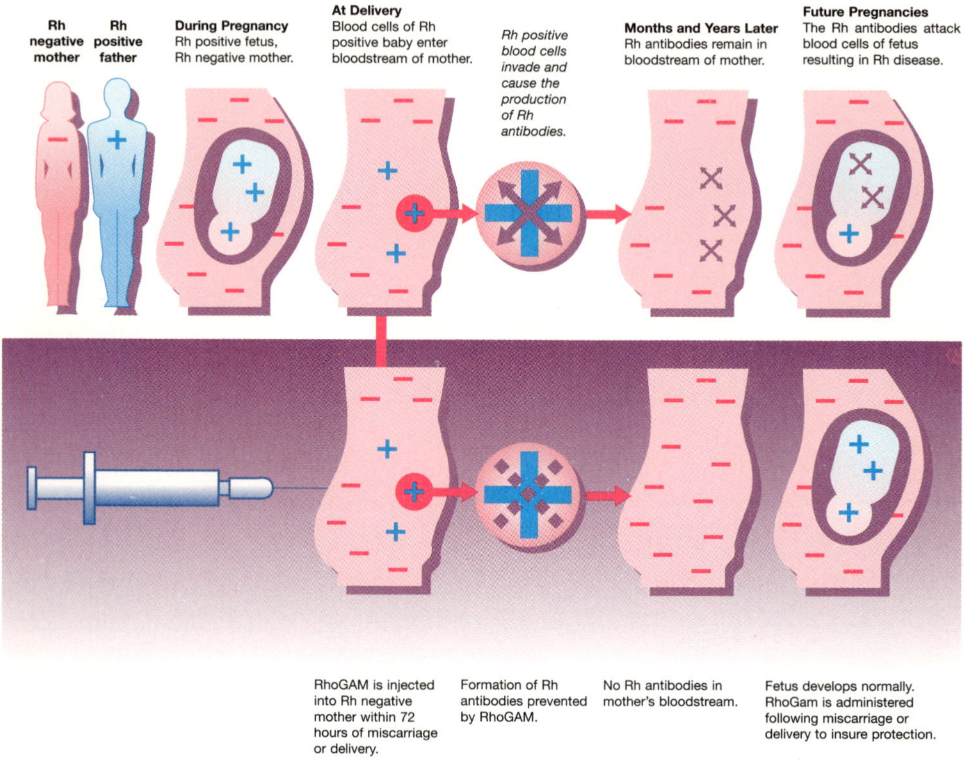

not been sensitized, your doctor may give you Rh immunoglobulin (RhIg or RhoGAM®) in about the 28th week of your pregnancy so that you will not produce antibodies for the remainder of your pregnancy. You will also be given another dose soon after delivery if the baby is Rh positive. The reason for this procedure is to prevent you from developing antibodies to any Rh-positive cells from your baby that might have occurred during labor and/or delivery. This would avoid the risk to your fetus in any future pregnancies. With each pregnancy and birth of an Rh-positive baby, the doctor would give you repeat doses of RhIg. RhoGAM should also be given following a miscarriage, abortion, ectopic pregnancy, or other situations presenting a risk of the fetus's blood entering the bloodstream of the mother.

According to the American College of Obstetricians and Gynecologists (ACOG) RhIg is safe for pregnant women. The only two known side effects are a slight fever or a temporary soreness where the drug was injected.

RhoGRAM® is a registered trademark of Johnson and Johnson

Maternal serum screening tests

There are a number of blood tests used to determine if a woman has a higher-than-average risk of giving birth to a baby with certain defects. If certain birth defects are present, substances in the mother's blood undergo changes which can be detected in the blood sample taken. These tests are performed on all pregnant women. If initial test results are abnormal, additional tests will be performed. The most common problems found through maternal serum screening are neural tube defects, Down's syndrome and abdominal wall defects. Maternal serum tests include alpha-fetoprotein (AFP) screening and multiple marker screening (MMS).

Alpha-fetoprotein (AFP) screening

A protein called alpha-fetoprotein is produced by a growing fetus and is present in fetal blood and in the amniotic fluid surrounding the fetus. A smaller amount of this protein crosses the placenta into the mother's blood. Abnormal amounts found in the mother's blood sample during pregnancy can be an indication of a neural tube defect (NTD).

> *Neural Tube Defects*
>
> ***Anencephaly***
> *Brain and head do not develop normally*
>
> ***Spina Bifida***
> *Lower part of the neural tube doesn't close during embryonic development*

The brain and spinal cord of the embryo are formed in the first month of gestation. If problems arise during the time the brain and spinal cord are forming, an infant may be born without a brain or with spina bifida (split spine). A fetus with central nervous system problems will secrete large amounts of alpha-fetoprotein. This AFP can be detected in the mother's blood and in the amniotic fluid, although this test is not 100 percent foolproof.

Multiple marker screening (MMS)

Multiple marker screening, also called triple screening, includes tests in addition to AFP which gives even more information about the risk of bearing a Down's syndrome baby. This MMS test measures levels of the hormones human chorionic gonadotropin (hCG), inhibin and estriol in the mother's blood. A simple blood test can also provide this information.

Levels of estriol are lower than normal when the fetus has Down's syndrome. Levels of hCG, a hormone made by the placenta, are higher than normal when the fetus has Down's syndrome.

Multiple marker screening is performed at 15 to 18 weeks of pregnancy with the results available within 1 to 2 weeks. Unless the results of the 3 substances (AFP, hCG and estriol) fall into the high-risk range, further testing will probably not be recommended by your clinician. These additional tests might include ultrasound and amniocentesis. Not all women whose multiple marker screening test show an increased risk for Down's syndrome will have a baby with this defect. This test only predicts how likely a Down's syndrome birth will be.

Researchers at the University of Alabama Medical College reported the addition of a test called inhibin A to the traditional triple marker maternal screening test in the second trimester. The quadruple test calculates the risk of Down's syndrome from maternal age and the concentrations of maternal serum alpha-fetoprotein, unconjugated estriol, human chorionic gonado-tropin and inhibin A. This test is performed between 14 and 22 weeks gestation and offers a more accurate means of detecting Down's syndrome than the triple multiple marking screening test. This test can improve the detection rate for Down's syndrome by 16 percent. However, the traditional triple marker screening test remains the most widely used test for Down's syndrome.

Both the AFP and MMS tests are routinely offered to all pregnant women.

Ultrasound

Doctors can display a picture on a TV-like screen of the fetus in your uterus using sound waves which humans cannot hear. While you lie on a table, a technician passes a scanner over your abdomen aimed at your uterus. This ultrasonic scanner sends out sound waves which create different echoes as they encounter different types and densities of tissues. These echoes are shown on a TV screen as various patterns of light called a sonogram.

What can the clinician see in the sonogram? For patients without a high risk indication, office ultrasound is used to observe the size and shape of the fetus. The clinician can also tell the gestational age and growth of the fetus, its position in the womb, and whether there are twins or more. This procedure is usually performed between the 16th and 20th weeks. Unlike X-rays, there is no proven risk in ultrasound. It is non-invasive and causes no pain. It is also accurate, detailed, and performed quickly.

During the first trimester, ultrasound is used vaginally to view the baby. Ultrasound can measure the fetus from the crown of the head to the rump to determine if the fetus is larger or smaller than the date your last menstrual period would indicate. Known as the crown-rump measurement, it can help your clinician adjust your due date if necessary.

Ultrasound can also detect abnormalities such as a thickening behind the neck of the fetus called increased nuchal translucency. Knowing this can help determine if there is an added risk for genetic or chromosomal problems. Increased nuchal translucency, even in a fetus with normal chromosomes, can indicate an increased risk of congenital heart defect, according to a study sponsored by the National Institute for Child Health and Development.

Some obstetricians recommend ultrasound as part of their routine diagnostic tests while others use ultrasound only if there are clinical indications to do so. It is most often used with those pregnant women for whom a detailed view of the fetus can help in caring for the mother and the fetus throughout the pregnancy.

Although regular office ultrasound examination may discover abnormalities in the fetus, this is not the primary purpose for doing such an examination. Unless a patient is identified as a member of a high risk group, referral to a specialist is normally not indicated.

There are special situations where multiple ultrasound examinations may be indicated. The following conditions may require more than one ultrasound exam:

- If your clinician suspects the fetus is too large or too small for its estational age
- If you are carrying twins or more
- If you are at increased risk for preterm labor (see pages 40-41).
- If you have any underlying medical condition such as diabetes or hypertension
- If your clinician suspects you have too much or too little amniotic fluid (see pages 66-67)
- If you are bleeding

As mentioned previously, an ultrasound examination called a transvaginal ultrasound or sonogram uses a scanner or transducer probe inserted into the vagina. This helps your doctor view your pelvic organs and can also be used to measure the length of the cervical canal. An ultrasound examination with a vaginal probe is not painful. A new form of ultrasound called Doppler velocimetry, views the uterus to check the blood flow.

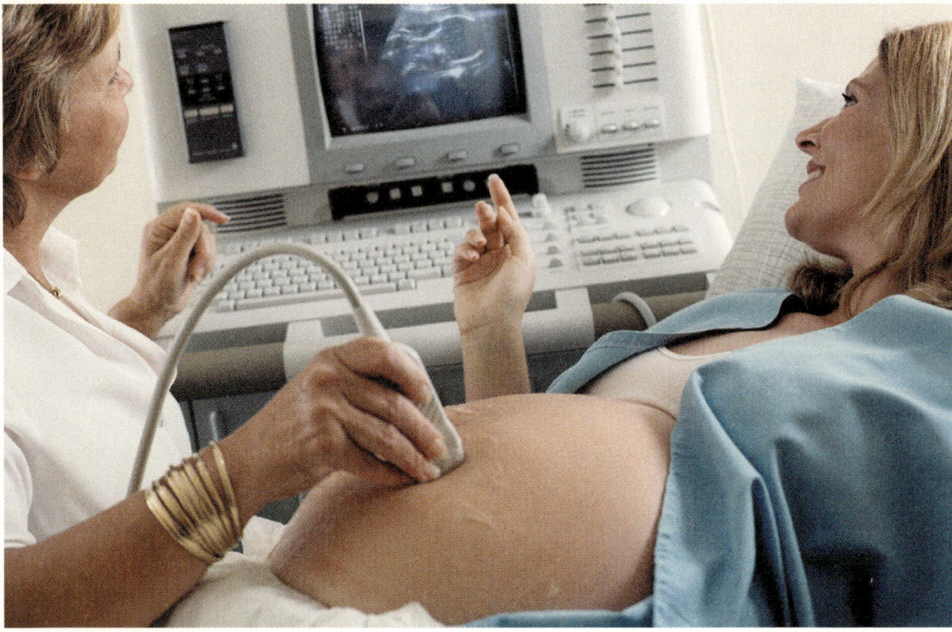

Amniocentesis

Amniocentesis is a test to help detect certain genetic disorders. It is performed by inserting a long hollow needle through the abdomen into the amniotic sac to obtain a sample of the amniotic fluid. This fluid contains cells generated by the fetus which are then analyzed for its chromosomal and chemical makeup. This procedure can detect several abnormalities and growth patterns such as Down's syndrome or fetal lung maturity. Researchers are making progress in detecting other potential problems through analysis of the amniotic fluid. The cells of the amniotic fluid will also indicate the sex of the fetus. This is very important when a sex-linked disease is suspected. (Hemophilia, for example, is a blood-clotting disorder found almost exclusively in males.) Amniocentesis is never performed simply to satisfy curiosity about a baby's sex.

When checking for genetic disorders, the cells from the amniotic fluid must be incubated. An amniocentesis performed to check for genetic problems primarily tests to see if the 23 chromosome pairs are present and are normal in structure. The test is usually performed between the 16th and 18th weeks of pregnancy, but results may take up to 3 weeks to complete This makes the waiting period the most difficult part of the test. The test should be no more painful than an injection.

A shift from testing for Down's syndrome in the second trimester from 13 to 26 weeks, to testing in the first trimester using the nuchal translucency measurement (see pages 55-56) is now being recommended by some obstetricians.

Although it is more accurate than ultrasound in detecting potential problems, there is a higher risk. The last studies were done in September 1987, by the American College of Obstetricians and Gynecologists (ACOG) and were reported in the *ACOG Technical Bulletin*. According to those studies, less than 1 in 200 of women who had amniocentesis had a miscarriage. A study of over 28,000 amniocentesis procedures reported at the 2002 annual ACOG conference, found a fetal loss of 1 out of 327 procedures performed by obstetricians/gynecologists, a much lower fetal loss rate. Ultrasound is helping to reduce this small risk by showing doctors where to insert the needle.

Some side effects following amniocentesis may include cramping, vaginal bleeding and leakage of amniotic fluid. The leakage, if it occurs, usually stops within 48 hours and the pregnancy continues normally. If the leakage continues or there is greater than 1 to 2 teaspoons of leakage, be sure to notify your clinician.

If you are RH negative, you will be given an injection of RhoGAM (see page 48) following the amniocentesis to help prevent Rh sensitization (see pages 47-48).

Chorionic villi sampling (CVS)

Another relatively new test for the early detection of some genetic disorders is called chorionic villi sampling or CVS. The chorionic villi are fingerlike projections attached to the outermost fetal membrane. In CVS, cells are taken from this outer layer of the amniotic sac. CVS can be performed by inserting a small catheter, guided by ultrasound, through the cervix to the villi where cells are collected from the developing placenta. This is called the transcervical approach to CVS. Another technique for performing CVS is called transabdominal CVS. In this approach, the skin is anesthetized locally and a needle is inserted through

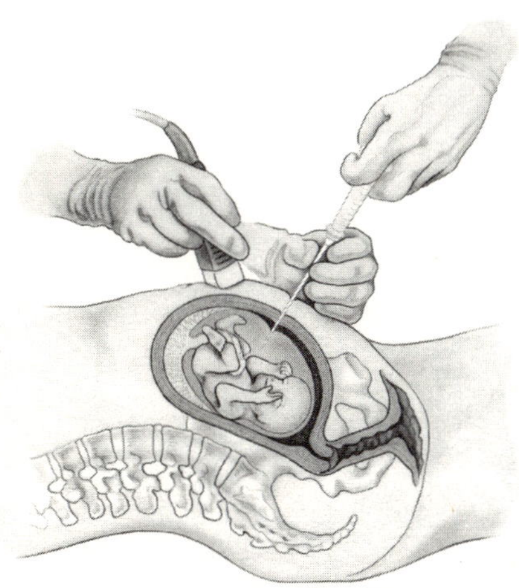

Amniocentesis

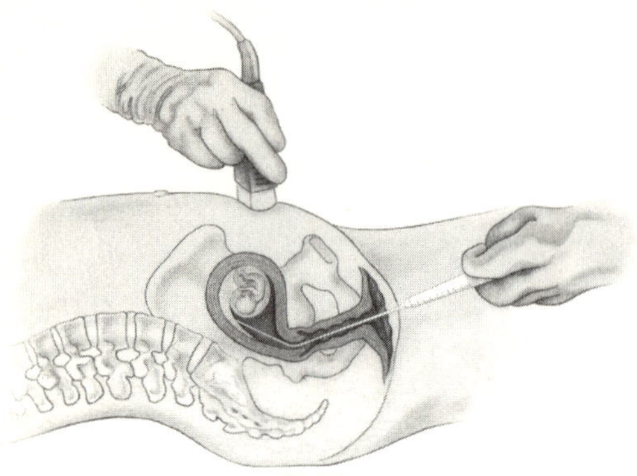

Transcervical CVS

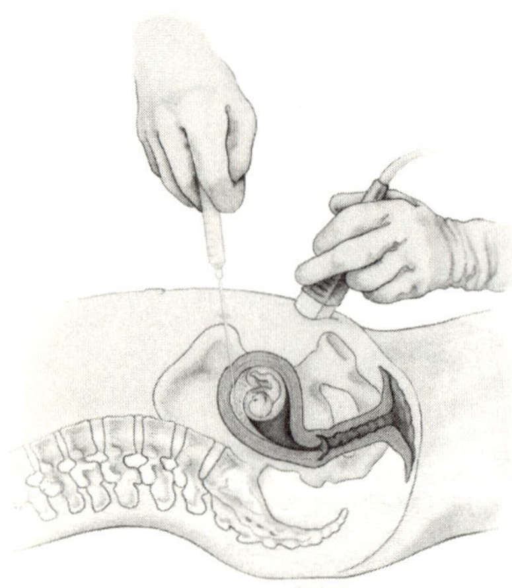

Chorionic Villi Sampling (CVS)
Transabdominal CVS

the abdominal wall (also guided by ultrasound) to the villi. This transabdominal approach is an important alternative in women with vaginal infections such as genital herpes, gonorrhea, chlamydia or other similar types of infection. Transabdominal CVS is also indicated when the position of the placenta makes it difficult to reach through the cervix.

As with amniocentesis, a woman who is Rh negative and undergoes CVS, should receive an injection of RhoGAM following the procedure (see page 48).

Although CVS reveals excellent information about many genetic disorders, it does not give any information about the development of the spinal cord.

CVS has two major advantages over amniocentesis. First, it can be performed at 10 to 12 weeks gestation, compared to amniocentesis which is performed later at 16 to 18 weeks. Second, the test results for CVS are available within 1 week while results from an amniocentesis may take 2 to 4 weeks. The anxiety of waiting to have an amniocentesis performed and the time it takes to get the results can be very difficult for the parents. An international randomized trial suggest that chorionic villi sampling may be safer and more efficient than early (11 weeks) amniocentesis. Discuss the advantages and risks of these procedures with your doctor.

When CVS is performed by a physician experienced in doing this procedure, the risk of miscarriage is slightly higher than it is for amniocentesis

Some of the tests that may be performed during your pregnancy, depending on your risk factors and your personal and/or family history, are summarized in the chart below.

Genetic problems

One of the normal concerns of new parents is whether their child will be born with any flaws, defects, or tendency toward inherited diseases, any of which may be passed on to future generations. This concern is especially great if the couple has already had a child with a condition such as Down's syndrome, hemophilia, Tay-Sachs disease, club feet, or cleft palate. The parents may also be concerned about the possibility that a genetic disorder may recur in other children they might have. For these reasons it is absolutely essential to obtain an accurate diagnosis of the problem and to give your clinician detailed family histories of both the mother and the father.

Additional prenatal tests are designed to detect certain genetic diseases or conditions. The need for additional tests may be determined by your age, medical or family history. Prenatal tests can include testing the chromosomes of the fetus. Chromosomes carry genetic information. Normally there are 46 chromosomes.

Gestational Stage	Test	Indication
10 to12 weeks	Chorionic villi sampling (CVS)	To examine placental tissue for chromosomal and genetic diseases (see pages 53-55)
15 to 18 weeks	Amniocentesis	To test amniotic fluid for chromosomal and genetic diseases. (see pages 52-53)
15 to 21 weeks	Alfa-fetoprotein (AFP screening	To check blood to determine risk for neural tube disorders or Down's Syndrome (see page 49)
16 to 18 weeks	Multiple marker screening (MMS)	To measure multiple markers and AFP levels as a check to determine risk of Down's Syndrome (see pages 49-50)
18 to 20 weeks	Ultrasound	To check the fetal growth, if a multiple pregnancy, some congenital abnormalities, as well as a check for the position of the fetus and the placenta. (see pages 50-52)
24 to 28 weeks	Glucose screening	To test for gestational diabetes (see pages 59-61)
35 to 37 weeks	Group B streptococcus (GBS) screening	To test for GBS in mother, who can pass it on to the baby during delivery (see page 73-74)

The fetus inherits 23 chromosones from the mother and 23 from the father. The 23 chromosones from each parent are paired inside the nucleus of each human cell.

Only one pair of chromosones among the 23 are related to gender. These determine whether the baby will be a boy or a girl. The XX chromosome is for a girl and the XY is a boy. The sex of the baby is determined by the father. A woman can only give an X chromosome while a man can give either the X or the Y chromosome. If he gives the X chromosome the baby will be a girl. If he gives the Y chromosome, it will be a boy.

Genes are the DNA molecules which determine the characteristics you inherit from your parents. Genes are located on chromosomes. Genes occur in pairs, one from each parent. For example, a gene that occurs on chromosome 7 in the mother, is paired with the gene on chromosome 7 from the father.

Each person carries a few abnormal genes. Most often they do not cause a defect. The abnormal gene is cancelled out by the normal gene.

Single gene abnormalities can be:

- Recessive (both of the same gene from each parent are altered or changed)
- Dominant (only 1 gene is altered but it overrides the normal gene)
- X-linked or sex linked (the gene on the X chromosome is abnormal)

A carrier is a person who has only one copy of a recessive gene for a specific disorder but has no symptoms of the disorder. The abnormal gene only causes the disorder if the same gene is altered or missing in the partner, and the child inherits both faulty genes. The chances that you and your partner have the same abnormal gene increases if you are blood relations.

Recessive disorders only occur when both partners contribute the same abnormal gene. When each parent is a carrier for the same chromosome recessive disorder, each of their children has one chance in four of having the disorder and one chance in two of being a carrier.

Dominant disorders are usually transmitted from parent to child through a single altered (abnormal) gene. The child of a parent who has this altered gene has a 50 percent chance of inheriting the disorder. It is also possible that there can be a mutation (change) in the child's genes even if neither parent is a carrier, that can cause a dominant genetic disorder. One factor that is associated with new mutations is advanced paternal (father) age.

X-linked (sex linked) disorders affect an altered gene on the X-chromosome. Normal men carry one X-chromosome and one Y-chromosome. Women carry two X-chromosomes. A woman can carry an altered gene, even though she is normal, that is, does not have the disorder. An X-linked disorder can be recessive or dominant.

As a general rule, X-linked recessive disorders are passed from normal women carriers to their affected male children. Female children will usually not have symptoms of the disorder but they can be carriers. If you are a carrier, each of your sons will have one chance in two of having the disorder while each of your daughters will have one chance in two of being a carrier. There are instances, however, where the female may have mild symptoms of the disorder.

There are now blood tests which can be performed at any time, even before pregnancy, to help determine whether parents carry a genetic mutation that would make their child more susceptible to disease. Higher resolution sonogram machines can detect more subtle defects earlier in the pregnancy to track the health of a fetus. Some couples who may be at high risk for a genetic problem can choose to undergo in vitro fertilization. The doctor can check a single cell within the embryo. If the cell shows no genetic defect it can be implanted.

A defect that is present at birth is called congenital disorder, whether the disorder is inherited or not. Genetic defects fall into three categories:

1. Chromosomal defect caused by a damaged, missing or extra chromosome

2. Inherited defect caused by a gene that is passed from a parent to a child. This can be a result of a dominant, recessive or X-linked gene

3. Multifactorial defect caused by a combination of factors

Certain couples have a greater risk than others, and if you are at increased risk of having a genetic disorder, it is recommended that you undergo genetic counseling. High risk couples include:

- Couples who already have a child with a birth defect

- Couples with a history of a genetic disorder

- Women aged 35 or over

In addition, some racial and ethnic groups are associated with specific disorders. For example, Tay-Sachs disease is associated with those of Jewish heritage.

Sickle-Cell Anemia is associated with African-Americans. Beta-thalassemia (which causes anemia) is common in persons of Mediterranean descent, for example, Italians and Greeks. Cystic fibrosis is most common among white persons of northern European descent. This last disease affects primarily infants, children, and young adults, and causes severe respiratory symptoms. The American College of Obstetricians and Gynecologists (ACOG) now recommends that DNA screening for cystic fibrosis be made available to all couples seeking preconception or prenatal care, not just to those who have a personal or family history of carrying the cystic fibrosis gene.

Another genetic disorder called hemophilia causes the baby to have trouble with blood clotting. As a result, an injury or internal bleeding can be life-threatening because the bleeding is difficult to stop. Hemophilia is carried by the X chromosome and is called a sex-linked or X-linked disorder. Mothers carry this recessive disorder, but it is rarely passed to the daughter. If the father is normal, there is a 50 percent chance that the son will be a hemophiliac.

Color blindness is a common X-linked trait. A woman may carry this gene on the X chromosome but the other X chromosome cancels out the recessive one. But if this X chromosome is passed on to her son, and he does not have a normal X chromosome he may be color blind. An X-linked disorder can be recessive or dominant.

So you can see the importance of giving your clinician a complete family history, even if you might be fearful or ashamed of revealing that history. Your child's health will depend on it, and you will need to consider what such a condition means and the realistic risk of having an affected child.

Certain tests, like amniocentesis, chorionic villi sampling or ultrasound, can help in the investigation. These tests can detect in advance some genetic problems or potential genetic defects, and will be discussed in the pages ahead. But do not expect your doctor to have all the answers at once. Genetics is a specialized field and will require some research and time. Your clinician may recommend that you see a geneticist or refer you to a genetics laboratory for more detailed evaluation. According to an April 1999 article appearing in the *OB-GYN News*, several new genetic tests, endorsed by the American College of Medical Genetics, are now available.

- **Familial Mediterranean Fever**: This is caused by a recessive mutation carried by 14 percent of people with Armenian ancestry, and is believed to be equally common in those of Arabic, Turkish and Sephardic Jewishback ground. Diagnosing this disease early in a newborn is important to help avoid a potentially fatal kidney disease. Screening for carriers of this disease is also useful to help prevent affecting children.

- **Canavan's Disease**: This is caused by a recessive mutation that results in mental retardation, and can be fatal. This disease is most prevalent in those of Ashkenazi Jewish ancestry. Screening for Canavan's disease mutation can be combined with screening for Tay-Sach's disease.
- **Congenital Deafness Caused by Connexin 26 Gene**: This gene is carried by 3 percent of people of European ancestry and nearly 5 percent of people of Ashkenazi Jewish background. Current screening procedures can identify 90 percent of mutations in the connexin 26 gene.
- **Fragile X Permutations Flagged by Premature Ovarian Failure**: A family history which includes any woman with premature ovarian failure, that is, menopause before the age of 40, is a signal to screen all relatives with learning or behavioral problems for the fragile X mutation. All females in the family that are of reproductive age should also be screened for a permutation.Fragile X is a recessive condition mostly affecting boys.

Remember, being a carrier does not mean you have the disorder. It means you carry the gene for it. Most genetics counselors recommend both parents undergo blood tests for carrier status, even if only one member of a couple is known to be a carrier of a specific disorder.

Though certain genetic problems are much more common in one ethnic or racial group, the problem can still occur occasionally in another group.

Gestational diabetes

This kind of diabetes develops during pregnancy and often disappears after delivery, but it is one of the most frequent complications of pregnancy today. High blood sugar can affect your fetus by crossing over to the placenta, so it is very important to follow your clinician's orders to keep your own blood sugar within normal limits. There is an increased risk of having a very large baby (macrosomia) if you have gestational diabetes.

Gestational diabetes often does not cause any symptoms. This is one reason why a urine specimen is checked at each prenatal visit. According to ACOG, your healthcare professional may order a test called a glucose screening test. This is often given at 24 to 28 weeks gestation. This is a simple test where the patient is given a special sugar mixture to drink. An hour later a blood sample is drawn from the arm and sent to the laboratory to be tested for glucose (sugar) level in the blood.

If the glucose level is high, a glucose tolerance test is ordered. This is similar to a glucose screening test but it lasts longer, about 3 hours, and requires 4 blood samples. The patient should have an empty stomach when a glucose tolerance test is given.

The American Diabetes Association now recommends selective screening. Pregnant women who are at increased risk for diabetes should be tested for gestational diabetes. Risk factors include women:

- over 25 years of age
- who are overweight or obese
- with a family history of diabetes
- who are member of an ethnic/racial group with high incidence of diabetes (Hispanic, African American, Native American, Asian)
- who have delivered a baby weighing over 9 pounds or who were diagnosed with gestational diabetes in a previous pregnancy

However, to be on the safe side, The American College of Obsttricians and Gynecologists (ACOG) recommend, and many healthcare providers routinely order, a glucose screening test at 24 to 28 weeks gestation.

Studies have shown that if you have gestational diabetes, you will have a greater risk of developing diabetes later in life. Having periodic checkups and keeping your weight within normal limits thus become essential.

New guidelines are being prepared to identify and manage gestational diabetes. The emphasis of these guidelines is to help prevent “very large” babies and the complications associated with them. The American Diabetes Association (ADA) stresses the need to lower the mother’s blood glucose (sugar) levels. The ADA feels the mother’s glucose level is related to the risks/complications during pregnancy for both the mother and the fetus.

Gestational diabetes is usually detected in the middle of pregnancy. Once identified, it is then essential that your blood sugar be brought to, and maintained at, normal levels so that your baby will not be affected. As a rule, if you have gestational diabetes, it will recur with each additional pregnancy. Sometimes controlling blood sugar can be done by diet alone. Other mothers need insulin for the remainder of their pregnancies. But remember that you will still need a balanced diet of sufficient calories and nutrients for your baby's nutrition and normal development, so do not limit your diet more than you are told. If you develop gestational diabetes, following your clinician's advice is essential. Ask your healthcare provider if you should monitor your blood glucose levels yourself to see if your diet is controlling your glucose level, or whether insulin is needed.

Kick count

Your clinician may ask you to monitor the movements of your fetus. A common way of keeping track of fetal movements is to do what is called a "kick count." Ask your clinician what time of day you should do a kick count, then time how long it takes for the fetus to move 10 times (movement may feel like a kick, flutter, or a roll). Fetal movement varies, so it is not a good idea to compare the activity of your fetus with that of someone else. If you have been advised to do a kick count, your doctor or other health professional will give you specific instructions, including how often it should be done and at what point you should call your clinician.

The purpose of doing kick counts is to help identify a potential problem at its earliest stage.

Non-stress and contraction stress tests

Two simple, inexpensive tests have been developed to help observe and monitor fetuses of post-date pregnancies who may be at risk.

The non-stress test is now the most widely used method of closely observing the fetus. In this test a monitor is placed over the woman's abdomen and the fetus's heartbeat is recorded. When the mother feels the fetus move or kick, she pushes a button to record the event. This test is based on the premise that the fetal heartbeat will increase with body movement, just as a healthy adult's heartbeat increases with exercise.

Sometimes the non-stress test is inconclusive or the clinician wants to see if the fetus can withstand the demands of labor. Then the contraction stress or oxytocin test may be performed. This test focuses on the fetal heartbeat as the fetus reacts to a uterine contraction, rather than to fetal movement. The mother is again hooked to a monitor, and the heartbeat is examined in relation to uterine contractions. Oxytocin is administered to stimulate contractions if there are no contractions, or, if they are not frequent enough. A pregnant women can also produce her own oxytocin by stimulating her nipples with hot towels or manually. Occasionally, clinicians will use this method to stimulate uterine contractions.

Biophysical profile

The biophysical profile is a combination of the nonstress test with ultrasound to examine the muscle tone, fetal movement, fetal breathing and the amount of amniotic fluid surrounding the fetus. Though the fetus gets oxygen through the placenta, there are chest wall movements that are also monitored in the profile.

Each of the preceding factors is given a numerical rating or score and this score is totaled. A score of 8 to 10 is normal. If the score is below this range, the test may be redone the following day. This nonstress/ultrasound test takes about 30 minutes. It is not harmful to the fetus and can be repeated as needed. The results of the biophysical profile will help your clinician determine whether you need special care or an early delivery.

Age as factor in pregnancy

In the past decades, it was normal for people to marry at a young age so that the woman had her first child in her early 20's. But life styles have been changing, and today many couples postpone having a family until the woman is in her late 20's, early 30's, or even 40's. But because medical science is so sophisticated and has made so many advances, most women, whatever their age, do not need to fear a

difficult pregnancy or birth. Still, clinicians do recognize that women under 18 and over 35 need additional care and observation before, during, and after their pregnancies in order to reduce the risks to themselves and to their babies. Though complications such as hypertension, diabetes and multiple births are more common in the older pregnant woman, a woman's health and level of fitness can affect her pregnancy more than does her age. There may be additional tests performed, such as an amniocentesis (see pages 52-53), to more closely monitor the fetus. Other tests may be used as well, especially for the pregnant woman who is older. A clinician who is familiar with you and your medical history can help you plan your family. Be sure to discuss your age with your clinician.

Twins or more

Twins occur naturally in 1 of every 90 births. Twins formed from a single fertilized egg which, for unknown reasons, splits in two are said to be identical twins. Identical twins come from the union of one egg and one sperm and are called monozygotic twins. Fraternal twins come from two eggs, which are fertilized by two different sperm and are implanted in the uterus at the same time. These are known as dizygotic twins. Identical twins are always of the same sex and may look so much alike that even their families can't tell them apart. Far more common than identical are fraternal twins. Fraternal twins each have their own placenta and amniotic sac. Because they are the result of two eggs being fertilized, they can be of the same sex or one boy and one girl. They would look no more alike than any other two siblings.

For some unknown reason, multiple pregnancies are more common in African-American couples and less common in Asian couples.

Triplets and quadruplets that are the result of one egg splitting are identical. When they are the result of multiple eggs being fertilized, they are fraternal. Identical multiple births are always of the same sex. Fraternal births can be of the same sex or of different sexes.

The use of fertility drugs to help stimulate ovulation frequently causes more than one egg to be released by the ovary, thereby increasing the incidence of multiple pregnancies.

Fetal reduction is most commonly used in women who have taken fertility drugs and are now carrying more than three viable fetuses. Because of the high risk of preterm delivery if all the fetuses are carried, some physicians reduce the number in order to improve the chances of delivering healthy babies. This procedure for multifetal reduction is performed later in the first trimester of the pregnancy at special centers where a physician, specifically trained in this procedure, is available.

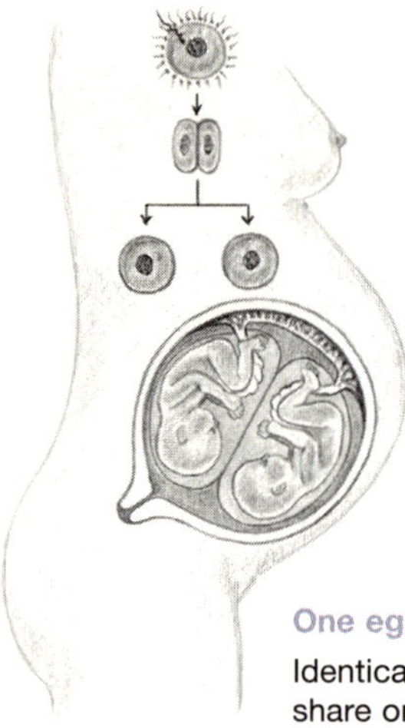

One egg fertilized
Identical twins share one placenta.

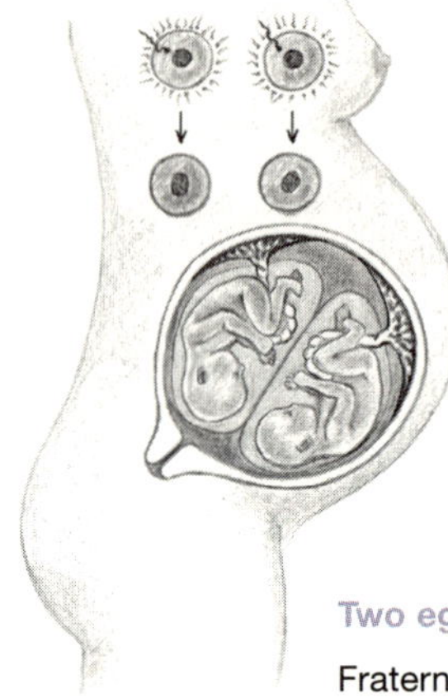

Two eggs fertilized
Fraternal twins have two placentas.

A mother who is carrying twins is often more uncomfortable than a mother carrying a single fetus. The presence of twins intensifies all of the conditions of pregnancy which we discussed in the last chapter—the indigestion, the backache, the varicose veins, the sleeplessness, the shortness of breath, and the swelling of the feet and ankles.

Since it is not unusual for twins to be born about two to five weeks before the calculated due date, special planning is necessary. The mother will need additional help when she returns from the hospital, and this should be arranged in advance. Plans should also include obtaining extra clothing, diapers, cribs, bedding, and other essentials.

Percutaneous umbilical cord blood sampling (PUBS)

This test is performed by using a very fine long needle, directed continuously by ultrasound, to obtain a blood sample from the umbilical cord close to where it is attached to the placenta. In this test, doctors check for some genetic diseases using a sample of the blood from the fetus. This test does have risks, and it is not available in every area.

Umbilical cord blood banking

As a result of years of research, a wonderful discovery was made. Umbilical cord blood has been found to contain the same disease-fighting stem cells as is found in bone marrow. These special cells can be used to treat a number of life-threatening diseases such as blood and immune disorders and leukemia as well as certain other types of cancer.

Unless you specifically request your baby's cord blood to be "banked," it will be discarded after birth. By using state-of-the-art procedures for preservation of the cells, research indicates these cells can last indefinitely.

Routine cord blood banking is not currently performed. Private, cord blood banks are available for a fee. For those interested in their services please consult your physcian for more information.

Fetal Medicine

The relatively new field of fetal medicine has made a great deal of progress in saving babies who at one time had little chance of survival. Conditions ranging from spina bifida to urinary tract blockage and tumors are examples of fetal problems which can be treated surgically. There are two types of surgery, open and closed. Open fetal surgery requires making an incision into the mother's abdomen and partially removing the fetus so the surgeon can correct the defect. In closed fetal surgery, the fetus remains in the uterus while the defect is being repaired. Currently, open fetal surgery is performed at only three medical centers in the United States, the University of California at San Francisco, Children's Hospital of Philadelphia and Vanderbilt University Medical Center in Marshall, Tennessee.

Risks vs Benefits

Always discuss risks versus benefits of any special test that is recommended during pregnancy.

Open surgery poses risks to mother and fetus. It increases the risk of premature labor and delivery and, as with any surgical procedure, exposes the mother to the usual risks of surgery such as infection. New and safer techniques using fiber-optic instruments are now being tested.

Fetal surgery, though the most dramatic example of the new field of fetal medicine, is not the only advance in treating high-risk complications of newborns. The use of prenatal injections of drugs called corticosteroids, to speed the development of the fetus' lungs and other organs, has reduced deaths of premature infants by about 30 percent. It has also reduced the rate from respiratory distress syndrome (RDS) by 50 percent.

Doctors can now diagnose an irregular heartbeat in a fetus of just 10 to 12 weeks of gestation. The mother can be treated with medication or, rarely, medication can be delivered directly into the fetus' blood stream via a procedure called cordocentesis. A blood transfusion directly to the fetus can be given in case of severe anemia in the fetus as a result of Rh disease (see pages 46-48).

Amniotic fluid volume

The fetus grows within the amniotic sac, what is commonly called the "bag of water." This sac contains amniotic fluid. The volume of fluid increases until it reaches its maximum level at 34 weeks gestation. After that the fluid level gradually decreases in volume. Either a little more or a little less amniotic fluid is not usually a problem. However, large variations in amniotic fluid volume may be a symptom of a problem.

Oligohydramnios is the medical term for too little amniotic fluid. This can be the result of a rupture or tear in the membranes, allowing the fluid to leak out. This can indicate a problem with the mother and/or the fetus. If this happens, and you are very close to your delivery date, your clinician may decide to delivery the baby, or the fetus may be very closely monitored and undergo tests to assure its well being. You may be advised to stay off your feet and get more rest in order to improve blood flow to the uterus and placenta, thus increasing the urine output of the fetus, resulting in an increase in amniotic fluid.

Polyhdramnios or hydramnios is the medical term for too much amniotic fluid. Larger increases in amniotic fluid volume may indicate a problem in the mother or fetus. Certain viral infections or diabetes in the mother can result in an increase in fluid. In rare cases, the increase may be due to a problem in the fetus such as a block in the gastrointestinal (GI) system. For example, if the fetus is having trouble swallowing fluid, more of it can accumulate in the sac.

In conclusion

You can see how the amazing developments in science have helped to reduce the risks involved in the miracle of birth. The tests which we have discussed here are certainly not the only screening procedures available. There may be other tests which your clinician will recommend for you instead of the tests discussed here or perhaps in combination with the tests discussed here. But it is also important for you to understand that the tests in this chapter are not all routine or performed automatically. They are another means of helping to evaluate any possible problems with your progress and to assess the growth and development of the fetus when a problem is suspected.

As we have said before, pregnancy is a healthy, normal bodily function, but it is also very complex. The health of both the mother and the fetus are so important that careful monitoring is needed throughout the gestational process. Certainly you will want to discuss the risks and benefits with your clinician if he or she recommends any of these screening procedures. Modern medicine continues to try and reduce the dangers and discomforts of pregnancy. These tests are a part of that process.

Chapter 8 Infections of special concern

HEPATITIS B and selective sexually transmitted diseases have already been discussed in Chapter 2. There are additional infectious diseases you should be aware of because they can affect your pregnancy.

First, it should be emphasized that no matter how minor you may think your infection may be, even a head cold or sore throat, do not take any prescription or over-the-counter medicine without first checking with your clinician. Many drugs cross over the placenta directly to the fetus, and some drugs taken during pregnancy may be harmful to mother and fetus. (See Chapter 13.)

If you have never had childhood diseases such as measles, German measles or mumps, and have not been vaccinated against these diseases, the best protection is to avoid exposure to them before and during your pregnancy. The common childhood diseases which may be minor illnesses in most children can be far more serious in adults and cause serious problems in a pregnant woman and her fetus. If you have had any of these childhood diseases or been vaccinated for them, you will not get them again. Your body has developed antibodies to protect you by making you immune to these same diseases.

Mumps

Mumps is not as highly contagious as measles or chicken pox. In addition, fewer than 10 percent of all cases of mumps occur in people over 15 years of age, thus making it uncommon in pregnant women. However, if a woman does get mumps during the 1st trimester of her pregnancy, it doubles her chance of having a miscarriage. Mumps may also cause preterm labor (see pages 40-41). It is not known whether mumps is linked to birth defects.

Rubella (German measles)

Rubella is caused by a virus that is known to be a teratogen, a compound which can cause structural changes to a fetus during development. Rubella is a very dangerous disease for pregnant women and their babies. If you contract Rubella early in your pregnancy, your fetus can be severely damaged. The first 6 weeks are the most critical time, because the disease can then affect your fetus' heart, eyes, and ears, which develop in the second 6 weeks.

There is less possibility of damage the later in your pregnancy that you contract the disease. If your fetus' organs are already structurally sound, there is generally no damage. Here are some points to remember:

- If you have had German measles before, you will not get it again.
- The expectant mother must have German measles during pregnancy for the fetus to be affected. Exposure alone will not harm the fetus.
- If you have had contact with German measles and have not had the disease or are unsure if you have had the disease, call your clinician. He or she will arrange for you to come to the office in an off-hour so that you will not expose other pregnant patients.
- There are blood tests to determine whether you have had the disease in the past or have it now. Although there was once a time lapse before your clinician got the answer, a test is now available with next-day results.

Vaccines

Safe to take during pregnancy

- *Diphtheria*
- *Tetanus*

Not routinely given but are safe to use if you may come in contact with disease

- *Hepatitis B*
- *Pneumonia*
- *Rabies*
- *Influenza*
- *Polio*

Not to be given during pregnancy

- *Measles*
- *Rubella*
- *Mumps*
- *Varicella-zoster (Chickenpox)*
- *Any vaccine using live viruses*

- Any woman who is given the Rubella vaccine should wait 28 days before becoming pregnant.
- Pregnant women exposed to Rubella should seek counseling regarding the risk to their unborn child.

It is very important therefore, that women in their child-bearing years who are susceptible to rubella, and not pregnant, be identified and immunized. Those women who are so vaccinated, should avoid becoming pregnant for 28 days. This is a recent change by the Center for Disease Control and Prevention (CDC). Those women who are susceptible to rubella, but are already pregnant, should be vaccinated immediately after childbirth, miscarriage or an abortion.

Influenza

A study conducted by a group of physicians at Vanderbilt University School of Medicine in Nashville, Tennessee, recommended that all pregnant women who were beyond the 1st trimester of their pregnancies during the influenza season be given the flu vaccine as recommended by the Advisory Committee of Immunization Practices of the Centers for Disease Control and Prevention.

The CDC recommends that pregnant women who have medical conditions that increase their risk for complications from influenza, be vaccinated before the influenza season, regardless of the stage of pregnancy. Discuss this with your healthcare professional.

Varicella-zoster (Chickenpox)

As mentioned in Chapter 1, chickenpox can be transmitted across the placenta to the fetus. Women who contract chickenpox between the 2nd and 4th months of their pregnancies, have been known to have miscarriages or to deliver babies with congenital malformations. When chickenpox is contracted late in pregnancy, the baby may be born with chickenpox or may be protected by the mother's antibodies. However, if the mother gets the chickenpox within a week of delivery, there is no time for antibodies to develop and cross the placenta to protect the fetus. These babies are more apt to become seriously ill or even die.

There is now a vaccine for chickenpox which the American Academy of Pediatrics recommends be given routinely in early childhood as well as for susceptible older children and adolescents. A single dose should be given between 12 and 18 months of age. You will need to check with your pediatrician or family physician for any contraindications to this vaccine.

The Fifth disease

The Fifth disease, caused by the human parvovirus B19, is so called because it was the fifth to be discovered among a group of diseases characterized by a fever, rash and mild flu-like symptoms in children. Its adverse effect in pregnancy was first recognized in 1984.

Though the infection is mild in children, it is cause for concern if a woman is exposed to the human parvovirus B19 during her 1st or early 2nd trimester of pregnancy.

The Fifth disease has been shown to increase the risk of miscarriage. It is also known to cross the placenta and infect the fetus. When this infection occurs later in pregnancy, it can cause sudden anemia or other problems and may require treatment.

Teachers, health care workers and others who work with children are known to be at higher risk for this disease. If you have been exposed to the human parvovirus B19, be sure to notify your clinician promptly.

Malaria

Malaria is a tropical infection passed on by mosquito bites. Malaria in pregnant women increases the risk of miscarriage and premature birth. You should protect yourself against mosquito bites by wearing long-sleeved clothing and slacks. Check with your clinician if you plan on being in a tropical location. There is a drug effective in preventing and treating malaria, though no drug gives complete protection. Avoid traveling to areas such as East Africa and Thailand because strains of malaria occurring there are resistant to drugs.

Lyme disease

Lyme disease is caused by being bitten by an infected tick. Once the infected tick bites you, a round sore appears with a small center, similar to a bull's eye. This infection can spread to the joints and cause arthritis, even after the round sore has disappeared. Doctors can usually cure Lyme disease with penicillin. But if it is not treated, the infection may spread to your heart and nervous system. Research has also shown that the bacteria can pass from the infected mother to the fetus and cause birth defects or miscarriage. Because of the possible dangers of this disease, clinicians advise pregnant women to avoid heavily wooded areas, or if they have to be there, to wear long-sleeved shirts, slacks, and socks and to keep their hands and face protected.

The FDA has approved a blood test for Lyme disease. The test results are available in 20 minutes. For those who have been vaccinated against Lyme disease, this new test may give a false positive reading because it cannot distinguish between vaccine-induced antibodies and the disease produced antibodies.

Urinary tract infections

Pyelonephritis is a kidney infection. Symptoms include chills, fever, back pain and possibly swelling and pain in your legs. Pyelonephritis is a serious kidney infection which always requires antibiotics, frequently administered intravenously. Occasionaly, kidney stones block the passage of urine and cause pylenephritis

Bladder infections (cystitis) are infections which do not involve the kidneys. Cystitis is common in pregnancy and may cause symptoms such as frequent urination, burning sensation on urination and almost constant urge to urinate but able to urinate only in very small quantities. Sometimes there are no symptoms and bladder infection is diagnosed from testing the urine specimen you brought in. Cystitis is usually treated with oral antibiotics. Not taking antibiotics which have been prescribed for your urinary tract infection (UTI), could increase the health risk to your baby.

Pyelonephritis
(Kidney Infection)

Symptoms
- *Back pain*
- *Chills and fever*
- *Pain with urination or bloody urine*

It is necessary to drink 8 to 10 glasses of water a day in order to flush out the kidneys. Neither condition need be serious, but the infection must be cleared up. If you discover these symptoms, do not wait for your next regular appointment. Call your clinician immediately.

Cytomegalovirus

Modern science has identified this virus which can cross the placenta to the fetus and cause disease or impairment. The symptoms in the mother include fever, infection, sore throat and swollen glands. Sometimes there are no symptoms, and in nonpregnant, healthy adults, the virus may cause no problems even though it exists indefinitely in the body. Since not much is known about the virus or its treatment, it is best to try to prevent getting it.

Researchers suspect that it is spread through personal contact, so personal hygiene is essential. If you work in a day-care center or are around other babies, be careful to wash your hands after handling them or their diapers. The virus can be passed through urine or respiratory secretions.

So far, researchers believe that if a woman is infected with cytomegalovirus for the first time during pregnancy, her baby may be in danger. However, if the woman had been infected before she became pregnant and experiences a flare-up during pregnancy, the risk may not be as great for the fetus. Apparently, the human body produces antibodies during the original infection, and these antibodies protect both the mother and the fetus if there is a reinfection. Breastfeeding is another way that the virus can be passed from mother to baby. However, because the mother has passed antibodies to the virus across the placenta to the fetus, the fetus may not develop the infection. There may be a problem if the nursing mother acquires the virus after the baby is born. There may also be a problem if the baby is given pooled milk from a breast milk bank and one of the bank's donors transmitted the virus in her milk. If you know or suspect that you have been infected with this virus, tell your clinician.

> ***Cytomegalovirus***
> *If symptoms do occur they usually include:*
>
> - *Fever*
> - *Sore throat*
> - *Fatigue*
> - *Enlarged lymph glands*

If the baby has symptoms of this disease at birth it can result in jaundice (yellow pigmentation of the skin and whites of the eyes), microcephaly (a very small head), mental retardation, deafness and eye problems.

Group B Streptococcus

Group B streptococcus (GBS) is a bacteria commonly found in the vagina or rectum of pregnant women. In most women no symptoms or problems occur. A woman with GBS may pass this bacteria on to her baby during labor and delivery. Only a few babies exposed to the group B streptococcus bacteria will become infected. The infection can occur early, within 7 days of birth, with most occurring within the first 6 hours. Early problems in the baby may even result in death.

Risk factors for group B streptococcus are:

- Preterm labor (less than 37 weeks gestation)
- Preterm rupture of the membranes (less than 37 weeks gestation)
- Rupture of membranes 18 hours or longer
- Previous birth of a baby with GBS
- GBS bacteria in the urine during the current pregnancy
- Mother in labor with a fever of 100.4° F (38° C) or higher

The Centers for Disease Control and Prevention (CDC) guidelines now recommend all pregnant women be screened at 35 to 37 weeks gestation, for group B streptococcal (GBS) colonization, not just those pregnant women with risk-based factors, in order to prevent early-onset GBS in newborns. Recent CDC data demonstrated that screening all pregnant women was over 50 percent more effective than screening only those with risk-based factors. The CDC recommends vaginal and rectal GBS cultures at 35 to 37 weeks gestation for all women.

Treatment during pregnancy is indicated when:

- There was a previous infant with invasive GBS
- GBS bacteria is found in urine during the current pregnancy
- A positive GBS screening culture during current pregnancy (unless a C-section is planned)
- The GBS status is unknown and any of the following events occur:
  - Delivery at less than 37 weeks gestation
  - Membranes ruptured for 18 hours or more
  - A fever during pregnancy of 100.4 F (38°C) or higher

The development of a vaccine to prevent group B streptococcal disease in mothers and their infants is now in progress. This vaccine will contain the 5 types of GBS found in 98 percent of GBS infections in the United States.

Listeriosis and Salmonella

Listeriosis and salmonella are two of the most common food-borne illness caused by bacteria. The bacteria responsible for causing listeriosis and salmonella food poisoning are often found in raw poultry, eggs, milk, fish and products containing these ingredients. Salmonella poisoning symptoms occur 24 hours after eating contaminated food. The most common symptoms are diarrhea, fever and abdominal pain that usually lasts from 2 to 4 days but may last longer, or the symptoms may be more severe in pregnant women.

Listeriosis symptoms include the sudden onset of fever, headache, muscle cramps, abdominal pain, nausea, diarrhea, and vomiting. Sometimes there are no symptoms. The listeria bacteria can infect the fetus during pregnancy, causing a spontaneous abortion, stillbirth or an infected newborn. This is why this infection is of particular concern to pregnant women. Epidemic outbreaks of listeriosis have been associated with raw vegetables and dairy products, including pasteurized milk and soft cheeses.

Public health experts warn pregnant women not to eat certain types of cheeses, such as goat cheese, Brie, Camembert, blue-veined or other soft cheeses. Hispanic women are particularly at risk because soft cheeses are used regularly in Latin American kitchens. Do not eat any cheese made from unpasteurized milk since it may contain the listeria bacteria which can cause miscarriage, infection or premature labor.

A pregnant woman with flu-like symptoms, back pain and premature labor should be tested for listeriosis, according to an article in the April 1999 issue of the *Contemporary OB/GYN* Journal. If the infection is diagnosed, the patient should be treated to prevent the infection from spreading to the fetus.

E. Coli

Escherichia coli (E-coli) and other bacteria are commonly found on the surface of meat. When meat is ground as with hamburger, the bacteria is spread throughout the meat during the grinding process. While the cooking of a steak or a chop will kill the surface bacteria, it may not kill all the bacteria in a hamburger cooked to rare or medium doneness because the internal temperature of the hamburger is not high enough to destroy all bacteria. This is why hamburgers and sausages should be cooked thoroughly and eaten well-done. Hamburger should be cooked until it is light gray, not pink or red in the center.

E-coli infections can also occur by drinking contaminated water, unpasturized apple and orange juice, unpasturized milk and alfalfa sprouts. It can also be passed person-to-person in the home, at day care centers, hospitals and nursing homes. It is essential to practice good hygiene including the frequent washing of hands using soap and water to limit the risk of person-to-person transmission. Symptoms can be more severe, and complications more common during pregnancy.

Stomach flu (gastroenteritis)

The viruses that cause gastroenteritis usually have no harmful effect on the fetus. Do not worry if you are unable to eat solid foods for a few days. Continue to drink plenty of liquids so you do not become dehydrated. If your symptoms last more than 72 hours, call your clinician.

What to report to your clinician immediately

Over 90 percent of all pregnancies progress perfectly and are uneventful from a medical viewpoint. The common annoyances mentioned earlier are easily remedied, and their discomfort is only slight.

There are some symptoms which should be reported to your clinician as soon as they occur. Many of these symptoms can be treated before they progress to cause serious problems. Should you develop any of the following symptoms, do not wait until your next appointment to report this, but call your healthcare professional right away.

- Any sign of bloody discharge from the vagina
- Persistent severe headaches
- Severe nausea and vomiting occurring several times within an hour
- Swelling of the face, ankles, feet and hands, particularly if any of these puff up suddenly and your finger rings feel tight. (Slight swelling during last months in hot weather is customary.)
- Chills and fever of over 100° not accompanied by a common cold
- Continued abdominal pains that are not relieved by a bowel movement
- A sudden gush of water from the vagina
- Frequency and burning on urination
- An unusual increase in thirst with reduced amount of urine. If you do not urinate for 12 hours, even though you have had a normal intake of fluids, report the condition
- Blurring of vision or spots before the eyes

We mentioned earlier that your intelligent observations are important. Ask your healthcare provider which of these symptoms, if any, deserve special attention in your case. Some of these may occur during a normal pregnancy. For instance, abdominal pains could be due to something you ate. A sudden gush of water often precedes the beginning of labor. You may become dizzy and nauseated by unpleasant odors. However, sometimes these signs do precede the possibility of a miscarriage, preeclampsia, and/or urinary infection.

In this chapter we have tried to cover most physical situations that may occur during pregnancy. Be assured that no one woman falls heir to every discomfort. The majority rarely experience more than 1 or 2. But being prepared to handle any situation intelligently will safeguard you and your fetus and give you greater peace of mind.

Questions to ask your clinician

Chapter 9 Controlling your weight and diet

OUR SOCIETY PUTS A GOOD DEAL of emphasis on weight control, and most expectant mothers are concerned about how much weight they will gain during pregnancy. The intelligent way to approach the question of gaining weight is to understand how much weight is required to create a new baby. Again, there are guidelines, but since you are a unique individual, there may be variations from those guidelines. The American College of Obstetricians and Gynecologists (ACOG) recommends a weight gain of about 25 to 35 pounds for women of normal weight at the beginning of pregnancy. If you are already underweight, then you should gain near the top of this range. If you are markedly overweight, then you should gain less, about 15 to 20 pounds. Whatever your weight gain, it is important that you eat a nutritious diet to ensure both you and your fetus have an adequate intake of essential nutrients.

As we all know, it is easy for most people to gain weight, but when you are pregnant you have to focus on gaining

Weight Distribution (in pounds)

The average baby weight	7 1/2
The placenta	1 1/2
Increased fluid volume	4
Increased weight of uterus	2
Increased weight of breast tissue	2
Increased blood volume	4
Maternal stores of nutrients	7
Amniotic fluids	2
Total	30

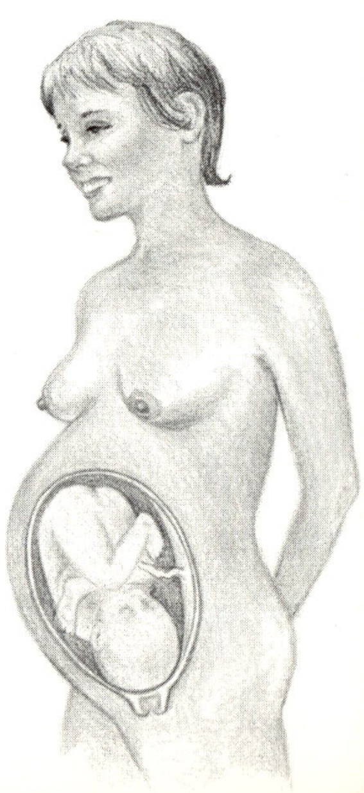

only what you need. There are several problems which come from excessive weight gain during pregnancy. First, the heavy load can cause aches and pains in the legs and back. Second, a rapid and excessive weight gain can cause your blood pressure to rise and strain your heart. Third, if you are excessively heavy, you will have trouble moving and may trip and fall. Finally, your extra weight can make labor and delivery more difficult.

It is a fallacy for pregnant women to think that gaining extra weight will mean creating a larger baby. This is not necessarily true. Gaining extra weight during pregnancy means that after delivery you will be larger.

Controlling your diet

Throughout your pregnancy, you and your baby will need sufficient nourishment to stay healthy. This means that you must maintain a well-rounded diet with a regulated consumption of calories. More than ever before, you will need to control your diet and to exercise discipline over the quality of the foods that you eat.

Unfortunately, too many mothers-to-be have developed poor eating habits. Often these begin during their years in high school and continue into their adult lives. Studies of pregnant women indicate that these "starvation" diets can have serious consequences for the next generation. The fast food craze consisting of hamburgers, french fries, pizza, and soft drinks does not provide adequate nourishment for the pregnant woman and her fetus. If you have fallen into the habit of relying on such a diet, it is essential for you to develop new and healthier eating habits during your pregnancy. Here are three good reasons for you to maintain a healthy diet:

1. Your body will be building new tissues in the fetus, and your body will also be losing some cells to the new life that is growing within you. You need adequate nourishment for both building new tissues and replenishing those lost cells.

2. Both you and your fetus need a supply of vitamins and minerals.

3. Certain foods are necessary to keep your kidneys and intestines functioning properly and to keep you well. Both kidneys and intestines are overworked during pregnancy.

When we talk about controlling your diet, what do we mean? We mean eating a balanced daily diet of foods from each of the basic food groups. We also mean consuming enough calories for you and your fetus but not an abundant quantity of calories.

The new recommendations are best shown with this pyramid structure which indicates the latest daily dietary recommendations.

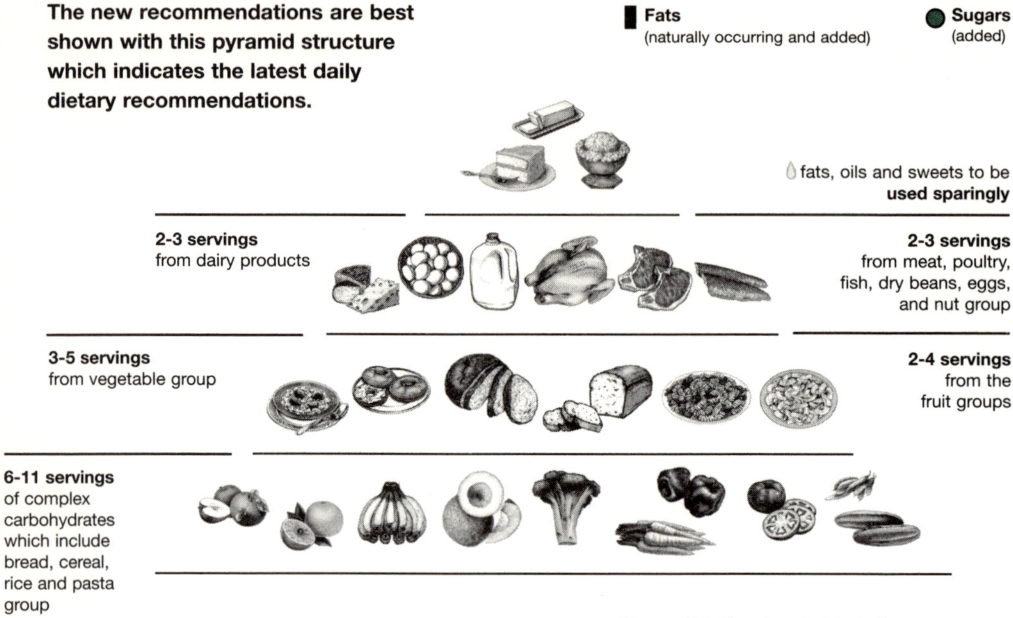

Source: U.S. Department of Agriculture

The American College of Obstetricians and Gynecologists (ACOG) suggests the following food guideline:

	Number of servings
Milk	4
Protein	3-4
Animal	2-3
Legumes/nuts	1-2
Fruits and vegetables	5
Vitamin C	2
Vitamin A	2
Other	1
Whole grain products	4
Others	2

The importance of calories

We hear a lot of talk about calories, but what is a calorie? A calorie is a unit of measurement that expresses how much energy food produces. For example, before women are pregnant, most burn 2000 calories a day. So, if your diet supplies 2000 calories your weight stays the same because you burn off everything you eat. But if you eat more or richer food which contains 3500 calories, then you have 1500 extra calories that are not burned off and these calories become fat. Conversely, if you consume 1500 calories a day but burn off 2000 calories, then you lose weight. Simply stated, then, too few calories mean that you become thin and too many calories means that you gain weight. The only sensible way to control your weight is to know the number of calories that your body needs and to consume that amount.

Recommended Weight Gain in Pregnancy

Condition	*Weight Gain in Pounds*
Underweight	*28-40*
Normal Weight	*25-35*
Overweight	*15-25*
Obese	*15*
Carrying twins	*35-45*

**American College of Obstetrics and Gynecology*

But how many calories do you need when you are pregnant? If you are already at the proper weight for your age and height at the beginning of your pregnancy, then you should consume about 2300 calories each day. Later, near the end of your pregnancy, your fetus will be making greater demands on your consumption of calories and the energy those calories provide. At that time, you may increase your intake of calories to as high as 2600 each day. However, you might also find near the end of your pregnancy that you are not as active as you were earlier. If you are less active, you may not need to increase your caloric intake.

Foods you should eat

The foods you eat contain different amounts of the basic groups of nutrients (protein, carbohydrates, fats, minerals and fluid). Each nutrient has specific functions for you and for your baby. Your body breaks down the foods you eat in the digestive process and the nutrients are absorbed into your blood stream. Some of the nutrients may go directly to the placenta where they are channeled through the umbilical cord into the fetus' circulation. Others may pass in and out of "storage" in your tissues, while still others may be used immediately by your body for its own needs.

Now let's look at your requirements for individual nutrients. Guidelines issued in April 2005, by the U.S. Department of Agriculture (USDA) for the public in general, show a shift in emphasis toward greater intake of vegetables, fruits and grains. See food pyramid chart on page 80.

During pregnancy, special nutritional needs must be met. You will be expending more energy doing the breathing and digesting for the fetus. This will require more calories. But it should be calories that supply the additional nutrients you will need and not just empty calories. For example, you will require more iron, protein and folic acid because your body needs to produce more blood in order to circulate more blood through the placenta. Extra minerals such as calcium and phosphorus are needed for the growing bones of the fetus.

Protein

The protein you eat is digested or broken down by your body into amino acids, sometimes called the "building blocks of life." There are some twenty amino acids known to exist in food, but only eight of them are considered "essential amino acids." This means that these essential amino acids must be supplied from dietary sources; the body itself does not have the machinery to make them. The remaining twelve amino acids, however, can be readily manufactured by your body.

If you think of amino acids as building blocks of varying sizes, and shapes and imagine the body's role in protein synthesis as much the same as that of a carpenter building a house, you can visualize how the growth and maintenance of body tissues might proceed. First, the carpenter needs a supply of materials, in our case the twenty amino acids. Next he needs a plan or blueprint to show the sequence in which the materials (blocks) must be attached. This is supplied in the cells of your body by a substance called DNA (deoxyribonucleic acid). The carpenter then sets to work to building a very specific structure. Obviously, the same materials may be arranged differently, according to a different set of

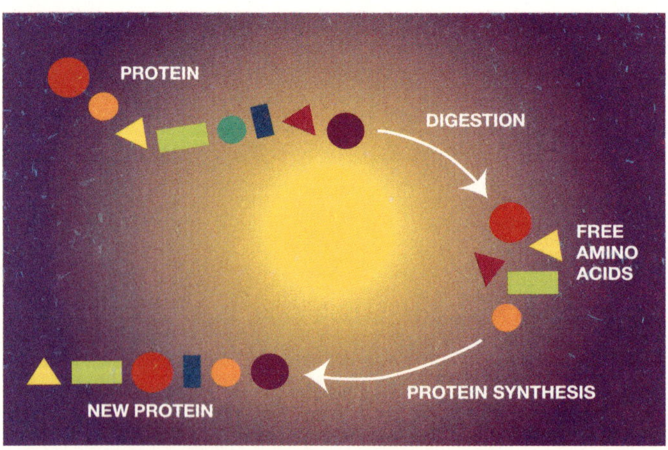

Protein from your diet is broken down into individual amino acids which can then be "reassembled" into new protein for growth and other body functions.

instructions, to build an infinite number of other structures. The carpenter must have a good supply of materials on hand, when he begins work. If he is missing one block and is unable to make it from another which is in abundant supply (and this is the case for the eight essential amino acids), the entire construction project grinds to a halt until that block can be located.

Recommended Daily Dietary Allowances for Adolescent and Adult Pregnant and Lactating Women

	Pregnant 14-18 yrs.	Pregnant 19-30 yrs.	Pregnant 31-50 yrs.	Lactating 14-18 yrs.	Lactating 19-30 yrs.	Lactating 31-50 yrs.
Fat-soluble vitamins						
Vitamin A	750 µg	770 µg	770 µg	1200 µg	1300 µg	1300 µg
Vitamin D*	5 µg	5 µg	5 µg	5 µg	5 µg	5 µg
Vitamin E	15 mg	15 mg	15 mg	19 mg	19 mg	19 mg
Vitamin K	75 µg	90 µg	90 µg	75 µg	90 µg	90 µg
Water-soluble vitamins						
Vitamin C	80 mg	85 mg	85 mg	115 mg	120 mg	120 mg
Thiamin	1.4 mg	1.4 mg	1.4 mg	1.4 mg	1.4 mg	1.4 mg
Riboflavin	1.4 mg	1.4 mg	1.4 mg	1.6 mg	1.6 mg	1.6 mg
Niacin	18 mg	18 mg	18 mg	17 mg	17 mg	17 mg
Vitamin B_6	1.9 mg	1.9 mg	1.9 mg	2 mg	2 mg	2 mg
Folate (folic acid)	600 µg	600 µg	600 µg	500 µg	500 µg	500 µg
Vitamin B_{12}	2.6 µg	2.6 µg	2.6 µg	2.8 µg	2.8 µg	2.8 µg
Minerals						
Calcium*	1300 mg	1000 mg	1000 mg	1300 mg	1000 mg	1000 mg
Phosphorus	1240 mg	700 mg	700 mg	1250 mg	700 mg	700 mg
Iron	27 mg	27 mg	27 mg	10 mg	9 mg	9 mg
Zinc	13 mg	11 mg	11 mg	14 mg	12 mg	12 mg
Iodine	220 µg	220 µg	220 µg	290 µg	290 µg	290 µg
Selenium	60 µg	60 µg	60 µg	70 µg	70 µg	70 µg

Recommendations measured as Adequate Intake (AI) instead of Recommended Daily Dietary Allowance (RDA). An AI is set instead of an RDA if insufficient evidence is available to determine an RDA. The AI is based on observed or experimentally determined estimates of average nutrient intake by a group (or groups) of healthy people.

Data from Institute of Medicine. Dietary reference intakes for calcium, phosphorus, magnesium, vitamin D, and fluoride. Washington, DC: National Academy Press; 1997. Institute of Medicine (US). Dietary reference intakes from thiamin, riboflavin, niacin, vitamin B_6, folate, vitamin B_{12}, pantothenic acid, biotin, and choline. Washington, DC: National Academy Press; 1998. Institute of Medicine (US). Dietary reference intakes for vitamin C, vitamin E, selenium, and carotenoids. Washington, DC: National Academy Press; 2000. Institute of Medicine (US). Dietary reference intakes for vitamin A, vitamin K, arsenic, boron, chromium, copper, iodine, iron, manganese, molybdenum, nickel, silicon, vanadium, and zinc. Washington, DC: National Academy Press; 2002.

Since protein plays such an integral role in the growth and maintenance of your own tissues to support pregnancy, as well as the growth of the fetus, your need for protein is significantly increased. Studies suggest that an increase in protein of about 10 grams per day is desirable in pregnancy. This means that the RDA (recommended daily allowance) for most pregnant women would be about 60 grams per day.

The National Academy of Sciences reported changes in the RDAs for iron, vitamin A and zinc. Protein is available from a variety of ordinary foods, especially from animal sources such as red meats, poultry, fish, eggs, and dairy products.

Complementary Protein Source

Protein Pair	Example
Legumes plus grains	Black beans and rice Kidney bean and tacos Soybean curd, rice, and greens
Legumes plus seeds	Split pea soup with sesame crackers Garbanzo and sesame seed spread Peanut and sunflower seed and tacos
Legumes plus nuts	Dry roasted soybeans and almonds Chili garbanzos and mixed nuts
Grains plus milk	Oatmeal and milk Macaroni and cheese Bulgur wheat and yogurt
Legumes plus seeds plus milk	Garbanzo beans and sesame seeds in cheese sauce
Legumes plus nuts plus milk	Mixed beans and slivered almonds with yogurt dressing
Legumes plus milk*	Lentil soup made with milk Peanuts and cheese cubes
Seeds or nuts plus milk*	Sesame seeds mixed with cottage cheese Chopped walnuts rolled in semi-hard cheese
Legumes plus egg	Cooked black eye peas with egg salad
Grains plus egg	Buckwheat (kasha) made with egg
Grains plus egg plus milk	Potato kugel Rice and raisin custard Cheese muffin
Seeds plus egg plus milk	Cheese omelette with sesame seeds

**Protein quality may not be as good as the other milk "pairs."*

These sources are often called "complete" proteins. That is, they contain the 8 essential amino acids in adequate amounts to support your body's protein synthesis. Protein is also available from vegetable sources, but they often lack one or more of the 8 essential amino acids. Therefore, vegetable proteins are usually designated as "incomplete." Various types of vegetable protein are deficient in different essential amino acids. To overcome this situation and achieve the necessary sources of protein you can combine foods as shown in the chart on page 84. The deficiencies of one food are complemented by the strengths of another.

Avoid foods such as sushi (raw fish) and raw or very rare meat. These uncooked or undercooked protein sources may contain bacteria or parasites. Adequate cooking destroys bacteria and parasites. Cook your food medium-well to well done.

Although the analogy of the carpenter is a simplified view of protein synthesis, remember that he needed to have all of his materials present at one time if his job was to proceed. This holds true for your body's protein production too. This is why you need to be very knowledgeable about the specific amino acid deficits and which food groups are complementary if you are following a strict vegetarian diet. Vegetarian diets which include milk (called lactovegetarian) and those which include milk and eggs (called lacto-ovo-vegetarian) simplify the process of combining vegetable sources. Since both milk and eggs are complete proteins, they will readily complement any "incomplete" protein to make up its amino acid deficit.

Because many families follow vegetarian diets for a variety of reasons, this topic will be treated in more detail in a later chapter. It should be pointed out, however, that if you are following a vegetarian diet, especially while pregnant, you must consider all the nutrients, not just protein composition, when analyzing your diet. Vegetarian diets are particularly prone to deficits of certain other nutrients, noticeably riboflavin, vitamin B_{12} and iron. Careful attention to vitamin and mineral requirements, wise food choices, and use of a vitamin-mineral supplement if necessary, will allow vegetarian women to have successful pregnancies. Your daily diet should include no more than about 15 percent protein.

Fat

Fat is an integral part of all body tissues. It provides energy for body functions and is required as a vehicle for getting the fat-soluble vitamins (A, D, E and K) to the tissues. Although its role is important, no minimum requirements have been established. Many foods, including meats, nuts, eggs, and some dairy products contain significant amounts of fat. Additional fat in the form of oil, margarine, butter, etc., are often added during the preparation and serving of foods. Many people are concerned that the typical diet contains too much fat, especially fat from animal sources, sometimes called "saturated fat," which may play a role in several disease processes. It has been suggested that no more than 30 percent of the calories in your diet come from fat, and that at least two-thirds of those come from unsaturated, polyunsaturated and monounsaturated sources. Soybean, cottonseed, safflower and olive oils are examples of these. Since fat is a very concentrated source of calories, people who are trying to cut down on caloric intake usually eliminate added fat in the form of butter, margarine, and mayonnaise used in seasoning or on sandwiches.

Just as an excess of fat in the diet is unwise, a fat-free diet would not be conducive to good health either. Try to strike a happy medium. Avoid the foods which are obviously high in fat but contain no significant amounts of other nutrients. These foods, such as sauces and pastries are often high in refined sugar too, but contain few vitamins and minerals. We could call them "empty calories". On the other hand, there are many foods such as cheese and eggs which contain relatively high amounts of fat but can also make a significant contribution to your overall nutrition.

Although the fat substitute Olestra has been approved by the FDA for use in snacks, there is evidence that Olestra, as it passes through the gastrointestinal tract, robs the body of the fat soluble vitamins A, D, E, K and beta carotene. It is also known to produce side effects such as diarrhea and cramping. It is best to avoid foods with Olestra during pregnancy and breastfeeding.

Carbohydrates

Like fat, no minimum level of carbohydrate intake has been set. Carbohydrates should make up 55 percent or more of your daily diet, with simple sugars just a small part of your diet. Carbohydrate is widely distributed in foods, particularly those of vegetable origin, therefore, a carbohydrate-free diet would be truly difficult to achieve. If you were successful, the diet would almost certainly lead to malnutrition and shortages of several vitamins, especially B complex and C. Very low carbohydrate diets have been associated with abnormal metabolism and eventually several kinds of diseases. Many people do feel, however, that the average person would benefit from decreasing his or her intake of sucrose or other refined sugars. These include white or brown sugar, molasses, honey and

Food Groups

Milk group: for calcium, protein, Vitamins A and D, riboflavin

1 cup fluid whole, 1%, 2% or skim milk or equivalents
1 cup yogurt
1/2 cup evaporated milk
4 Tbsp. non-fat dry milk
1 cup custard or other milk-based dessert
1 cup cream soup made with milk
1 3/4 cup ice cream
1 1/2 cup cottage cheese
1 1/2 oz. cheddar cheese[1]
1 cup soybean milk[2]
3/4 cup tofu[2] (soybean curd)

Meat group: for protein, iron and Vitamin B

Animal Protein:
3 oz. lean meat (veal, beef, lamb, pork), fish or seafood, poultry or variety meats (kidney, heart, liver)
2 eggs
1/2 cup tuna

Legumes and nuts:
3/4 cup dried beans or peas (cooked)
4 Tbsp. peanut butter
1 oz. nuts or sunflower seeds
3/4 cup tofu
3/4 cup garbanzo, lima, kidney beans, lentils

Fruit and vegetable group: for minerals, vitamins and roughage

Vitamin C:
3/4 cup orange or other citrus juice or enriched fruit drink
1/2 large grapefruit
1/2 cantaloupe, guava, mango or papaya
1 large orange
1 cup strawberries
11/2 cup pineapple juice
3/4 cup chopped green (or chili) peppers
2 tomatoes
1 1/2 cup tomato juice
3/4 cup cooked broccoli, brussels sprouts, raw cabbage, bok choy, cooked collards, kale, mustard greens, spinach, turnip greens

Vitamin A:
3/4 cup asparagus, bok choy, broccoli, brussels sprouts, chard, collards, cress, kale, spinach, turnip greens, or other dark green leaves (cooked)
1 cup of any of the above (raw)
3/4 cup cooked pumpkin, carrots, winter squash, sweet potato or yam
1 cup carrots (raw)
4 fresh apricots
1/2 large cantaloupe

Other fruits and vegetables:
3/4 cup potato or other not listed under vitamin A
3 plums
6 prunes
8 dates
3/4 cup other fruit
1 large apple
11/2 bananas
1 large peach or pear
3/4 cup berries, grapes or raisins

Whole grain products[3]: for carbohydrates, B vitamins, iron and some protein

1 slice bread
1 roll, dumpling, muffin or biscuit
5 saltine crackers
2 graham crackers
3/4 cup ready-to-eat cereal
3/4 cup cooked cereal
3/4 cup cooked corn meal, grits, rice, macaroni, noodles or spaghetti
2 corn tortillas
1 large flour tortilla
1 Tbsp. wheat germ

Others: for additional calories

1 cup non-milk and non-juice beverages
Sweets: pastry, cookies, cakes, pies
1 Tbsp. fats
(margarine, butter, mayonnaise, vegetable oil[4])
Condiments (catsup, mustard, sauces)

[1] Count cheese as a meat or milk, not both simultaneously.
[2] Lacks vitamin B_{12}; if used often, be sure to include other sources of this nutrient.
[3] Whole grain products are richer sources of vitamin E, vitamin B_6, folic acid, phosphorous, magnesium, and zinc than enriched/refined products. At least 75 percent of your daily servings should be met from whole grain sources to help meet your need for these nutrients.
[4] Vegetable oils such as sunflower, cottonseed, etc., and margarines made from them are good sources of vitamin E.

even the so-called "raw" sugars. In place of these refined sugars should be a greater intake of complex carbohydrates (starches) as found in cereals, pasta, grains, breads, vegetables, and fruits. This dietary change is known to result in decreased sucrose intake and consequently reduced incidence of tooth decay. It also provides increased fiber or roughage in the diet, and therefore improved bowel function. There may be other benefits as well. Recent research indicates that fiber may play a significant role in controlling the rate at which foods are digested and absorbed from the intestine. Include about one ounce (20 to 30 gm) of fiber in your diet daily. At the present time there are no known risks to this type of dietary modification.

Currently, there is concern with the now popular low-carbohydrate diet, in women of reproductive age. (See pages 96-97 under subtopic "Folic Acid".)

Craving special foods

It is true that pregnant women do sometimes have desires for unusual foods such as pickles, ice cream, strawberries, or melons out of season. Researchers have found, however, that everyone has food cravings once in a while, not just pregnant women. The cravings of pregnant women are probably intensified because of special emotional or physical circumstances. A pregnant woman may ask for a special food or for greater amounts of a favorite food if she is excited, fearful, or upset about some aspect of her pregnancy. Occasionally, a craving may indicate a nutritional need. For example, a desire for an orange may suggest her body needs vitamin C.

Unusual food and nonfood cravings characterized by compulsive eating habits including eating such substances as dirt, clay and cornstarch, for example, is called pica. Pica does seem to be more common in pregnant women as well as among certain cultural groups. Pica may also occur in patients with an iron or zinc deficiency.

Fluids

You need 2 quarts (8 glasses) of fluids each day. This can include milk and juices. Do not however, include alcohol, coffee or tea as part of your fluid intake. Alcohol should be eliminated entirely during your pregnancy and while breast feeding. Coffee and tea intake should be limited. It is advisable to drink water or juice with your meals, as milk, coffee, tea and soda can interfere with absorption of important nutrients such as iron.

Eating disorders

Two major eating disorders are anorexia nervosa and bulimia. Anorexia is characterized by a loss or lack of appetite, with a refusal to maintain a normal minimal body weight, and with an intense fear of becoming fat, even feeling fat when extremely emaciated (thin). Bulimia is characterized by binge eating followed by self-induced vomiting.

New studies have found that the effects of the mother's eating disorder on the fetus can be devastating. Anorexia has been shown to result in multiple complications in both the mother and the fetus. In bulimic patients, the risk of fetal loss is twice that of normal pregnant women.

Chapter 10 Your need for nutrients – vitamins and minerals

VITAMINS ARE VERY IMPORTANT compounds which cannot be synthesized by your body but are required for its day-to-day function. The major vitamins, their functions, and major food sources are listed on page 91. When your diet is lacking in one or more vitamins, your body operates inefficiently and, in severe cases, your fetus could be affected. Severe vitamin deficiencies are rarely seen today except in cases where people are critically ill and unable to eat for extended periods, or among people who follow unusual or "fad" diets excluding whole groups of foods.

Supplements

A sensible way to maintain your body in good vitamin status is to use common sense in selecting your daily diet. A well-planned diet can, in most cases, provide the vitamins and minerals you and your fetus need. However, a vitamin and/or mineral supplement may be of some benefit. Also, some women may require larger amounts of a given vitamin, particularly vitamin B_6, than can be readily provided by diet alone. If your clinician feels that you are in this category, he or she will probably recommend the use of a supplement containing either this vitamin alone, or a multivitamin/mineral preparation designed for use during pregnancy. Many women, after consulting with their clinicians, decide to take the supplement as insurance against deficiency. No particular problems develop as long as you take only the vitamins prescribed for you. They are designed to contain just the amounts you need each day. In many cases, particularly when tablets containing only one vitamin are taken, the intake may be in excess of what your body can use. You may be tempted to think that if a little bit of a certain vitamin is good, a larger amount would be better. This is not necessarily the case. Some vitamins, particularly those which are readily stored by the body, have been shown to produce structural changes and even deformities in infants when the mother's intake is too high. Self administered supplements, particularly in doses greater than those measured as Adequate Intake (AI) (see page 83),

The Major Vitamins: Their Functions and Food Sources

Name of the Vitamin	Some Reasons Why You Need It	Foods That Supply Important Amounts
Vitamin A	To help keep skin smooth and soft To help keep mucous membranes firm and resistant to infection To protect against night blindness and promote healthy eyes	Yellow fruits, dark green and deep yellow vegetables Butter, whole milk, vitamin A fortified skim milk, cream, Cheddar-type cheese, ice cream, Liver, eggs
The B Vitamins Thiamine, Riboflavin and Niacin	To play a central role in the release of energy from food To help the nervous system function properly To help keep appetite and digestion normal	Meat, fish and poultry, Eggs, dried peas and beans Milk, cheese and ice cream, Whole grain and enriched breads and cereals, White potatoes
Vitamin B_6	To help keep skin healthy To help build tissues To assist in brain function To help prevent anemia	Vitamin B_6—meats, potatoes, dark green leafy vegetables, whole grains, and dry beans Folic Acid—green vegetables, whole grains and dry beans, All three vitamins—organ meats
Vitamin B_{12} and Folic Acid	To help enzyme and other biochemical systems function normally	
Vitamin C (Ascorbic Acid)	To make cementing material that hold body cells together To make walls of blood vessels firm To help resist infection To help prevent fatigue To help in healing wounds and broken bones	Citrus fruits—lemon, orange, grapefruit, lime, Strawberries, cantaloupe, Tomatoes, Green peppers, broccoli raw or lightly cooked, greens, cabbage, White potatoes
Vitamin D ("The Sunshine Vitamin")	To help the body absorb calcium from digestive tract To help build calcium and phosphorus into bones	Vitamin D milk Fish liver oil Sunshine (not a food)
Vitamin E	To protect fatty substances in body tissues from degenerating	Vegetable oils Seeds Leafy, green vegetables Wheat germ

may disturb the delicate balance of the fetus' intrauterine environment. Overall, it is common knowledge that your developing fetus will thrive in a balanced chemical environment.

Vitamin A

Though vitamin A is important in maintaining an adequate diet and is essential to normal reproduction, recent studies have found that too much vitamin A may cause birth defects. Women of childbearing age should be aware of the danger of excessive amounts of vitamin A.

It is far better for women of childbearing age to get their vitamin A from beta-carotene found in fruits and vegetables. The beta carotene is converted by the body into vitamin A. Beta-carotene found in plant food has not been shown to cause vitamin A toxicity. The dietary allowance of vitamin A is not increased during pregnancy (see table on page 83).

Vitamin A deficiency is very rare in the United States. This vitamin is readily stored by the body particularly in the liver. Many dairy products are also fortified with vitamin A.

The B Vitamins

Thiamine (Vitamin B_1)

Your body uses thiamine to release energy from the food you eat and to help maintain normal appetite and digestive functions. The recommended adequate intake amount during pregnancy is 1.4 mg. Thiamine is found in legumes such as dried beans or peas, pork, organ meats such as heart, kidney, liver, and in whole grain or enriched breads and cereals.

The significant contribution of the food sources listed in the chart on page 94, however, can be altered by certain preparation or processing methods. Thiamine is water soluble. This means that as much as one third of the vitamin content of a given food could be lost if you cook the food in water and then discard the liquid. Thiamine is also very unstable in an alkaline medium. The thiamine content of legumes, for example, is largely destroyed if soda is added to the cooking water. Thiamine is present in the outer layer or bran of the seed or grain. Many milling processes destroy this layer. Whole grain or enriched breads and cereals can make significant contributions to your diet. Extreme deficiency of thiamine is recognized clinically as beriberi, a disease characterized by abnormal muscle tone. It is rarely seen in this country except among alcoholics or others on a very inadequate diet for a long time.

Riboflavin (Vitamin B_2)

Riboflavin is found abundantly in liver and leafy vegetables and also in milk products (see chart page 94). The AI for vitamin B_2 during pregnancy has been set at 1.4 mg.

Riboflavin is relatively stable during cooking, but is destroyed by exposure to light. This fact has been a major reason for the use of paper cartons in the packaging of milk. Milk in glass bottles left in direct light exposure (such as on a door step) for 2 hours may lose up to 60 percent of its riboflavin content. Riboflavin plays a major role in the utilization of food energy by your body. Since riboflavin is involved with energy metabolism, the amount required increases as total calorie intake increases. It is widely distributed throughout the body so a deficiency of vitamin B_2 will affect many different tissues. Deficiency symptoms are not frequently seen, probably because this nutrient is widely available in foods and because individual requirements can vary greatly. In the typical diet, 45 percent of the riboflavin intake is furnished by dairy products. If you do not eat these sources, care should be taken to include others from the chart listed on page 91.

Niacin (Vitamin B_3)

Niacin is known as vitamin B_3. Its role in the body is much like that of thiamine and riboflavin. It is a coenzyme, or component, during the chemical reactions which release energy in your body. Lack of niacin, however, produces a specific condition called pellagra. Pellagra is an Italian word meaning "rough skin," and aptly describes the red rash which appears first on the hands, face, and feet when they are exposed to sunlight. Untreated, intestinal problems and mental disturbances may result. Pellagra was widespread, especially among the lower classes, until it was discovered to be cured and prevented by a dietary agent found in liver and lean meats. This substance is now known as niacin. Because niacin can be synthesized by bacteria in the intestines and can also be formed from the amino acid tryptophan, the actual requirement (or AI) is difficult to calculate. Current value of niacin for a pregnant woman is 18 mg. Food sources which make significant dietary contributions are shown on page 95. Niacin content of foods is not significantly affected by most cooking and storage techniques.

You will probably notice that most foods which are good sources of thiamine and riboflavin are also good sources of niacin—namely liver, lean meats, whole grains, seeds, and legumes (dried beans or peas).

Thiamine (Vitamin B_1) Content of Selected Foods

Food	Serving Size	Thiamine (mg)
Legumes		
Soybeans, cooked	3/4 cup	.37
Navy beans, cooked	3/4 cup	.24
Split peas, cooked	3/4 cup	.27
Green peas, fresh or frozen,	3/4 cup	.33
cooked green peas, canned	3/4 cup	.13
Meats		
Pork, lean, roasted	3 1/2 oz	.53
Beef liver, fried	2 1/2 oz	.20
Beef, lean, broiled	3 1/2 oz	.08
Oysters, raw	5-8 medium	.14
Fish, fried	3 1/2 oz	.06
Cereals		
Oatmeal, cooked	3/4 cup	.10
Whole wheat, cooked	3/4 cup	.08
Wheat flakes	3/4 cup	.20
Nuts (except peanuts)	1 oz	.18
Vegetables		
Asparagus, cooked	3 1/2 oz	.16
Cauliflower, cooked	3/4 cup	.09
Broccoli, cooked	3/4 cup	.09
Potato, boiled	1 medium	.09
Milk, whole, fresh	1 pint	.14

Riboflavin (Vitamin B_2)Content of Selected Foods

Food	Serving Size	Riboflavin (mg)
Meats		
Beef liver, cooked	3 oz	3.14
Beef, lean, cooked	3 1/2 oz	.20
Dairy products		
Milk, whole, fresh	1 cup	.39
Milk, skim, fresh	1 cup	.41
Cheese, cheddar	1 1/2 oz	.21
Egg, boiled	1	.15
Leafy vegetables, cooked	3/4 cup	.39
Legumes		
Green peas, fresh	3/4 cup	.13
Baked beans, canned	3/4 cup	.39

Vitamin B_6

The recommended amount (AI) of vitamin B_6, also called pyridoxine, for the pregnant woman is currently 1.9 mg or about 0.6 more than recommended for the nonpregnant woman. Just how much you and your fetus actually need is not exactly known. There is evidence that some pregnant women on normal diets show chemical changes commonly associated with vitamin B_6 deficiency. In these women, administration of additional vitamin B_6 as a dietary supplement corrects the chemical abnormality. Some researchers have recommended that the requirement may be as high as 10 mg per day. Whether this is sound advice remains to be demonstrated by additional observation in pregnant women. It is interesting to note that some women with depression and/or nausea seem to note improvement of these conditions when vitamin B_6 supplements are begun. Again, you should discuss this or any other vitamin supplement with your clinician before you begin taking the tablets.

The best sources of this vitamin are liver, muscle meats, some vegetables, and whole wheat products. During the milling of white flour, more than 75 percent of the vitamin B_6 is destroyed. Since this vitamin is not added to flour products as part of an enrichment program, processed or refined products contain significantly less vitamin B_6 than their whole grain counterparts.

Niacin (Vitamin B_3) Content of Selected Foods

Food	Serving Size	Niacin (mg)
Peanut Butter	4 Tbsp	9.5
Beef liver	3 oz	11.7
Meat, lean	3 oz	3.9
Bread, whole wheat	1 slice	.8

Vitamin B_{12}

This vitamin has been isolated as the “anti-pernicious anemia” factor. That is, it is essential for the production and development of red blood cells; without vitamin B_{12}, anemia will eventually develop. All of the vitamin B_{12} available to animals and man originally come from bacteria or fungi. Intestinal bacteria in man is a significant contributor in this respect. Dietary sources are exclusively animal products such as liver and other organ meats, fish, eggs, shellfish, and some dairy products. The possible exception to this is seaweed and some ground nuts. This can be a significant problem for people on strict vegetarian diets.

Vitamin B_{12} deficiency is seen chiefly among people on these diets and where special absorptive problems exist.

The requirement for vitamin B_{12} during pregnancy has been set at 2.6 µg (micrograms). This is quite easily met by the typical moderate budget diet. Restricting intake of animal products, whether because of cost or because of religious or ethical reasons, can pose a significant threat of deficiency during pregnancy and breastfeeding. In such cases, a dietary supplement or periodic intramuscular injection of vitamin B_{12} is indicated. Insufficient vitamin B_{12}, caused by strict vegetarian diets during pregnancy and breastfeeding, has sometimes resulted in a failure to thrive, and developmental delay in infants and young children.

Folic acid

Chances are, if your clinician has mentioned the need for a supplement of a single vitamin, it has been folic acid. Some rather serious complications of pregnancy have been associated with, but not necessarily proved to be caused by, folic acid deficiency. Because of folic acid's role in the synthesis of maternal blood cells and also in fetal tissues, the requirement of 400 µg for a pregnant woman may be quite high. These high levels may be difficult to obtain from dietary sources unless the diet is very carefully planned. Under these circumstances, recommendation of a folic acid supplement is clearly justified if dietary intake is suspected to be low or requirements to be exceptionally high—as in the case of multiple pregnancies, or during or following certain types of drug therapy. Recently, the Recommended Daily Dietary Allowance (RDA) has increased folic acid to 600 µg for all women of reproductive age. See page 83.

In an article appearing in the August 2004 issue of *OB/Gyn News*, a University of Toronto professor of pediatrics, pharmacology and medical genetics, noted that diabetic women and women who drink large amounts of alcohol, require a higher amount of folic acid than other women to help prevent neural tube defects. There is also concern that popular low-carbohydrate diets will result in women of childbearing age not getting enough folic acid. An estimated 10 to 15 percent of women in the United States and Canada are on low-carbohydrate diets. Those women of reproductive age on this type of diet should supplement their diets with a prenatal vitamin.

Dietary sources which furnish significant amounts of folic acid are liver, yeast, asparagus, broccoli, leafy green vegetables, legumes, nuts, and whole wheat products. The folic acid content of foods is partially destroyed by processing at high temperatures. Storage of foods such as leafy green vegetables for 3 days at room temperature will reduce folic acid activity by up to 70 percent.

An airtight container and refrigeration will reduce these losses for leafy greens. Remember, too, that most B vitamins, as well as vitamin C, are partially destroyed by long cooking periods and/or poor storage conditions. Quick cooking methods, especially for vegetables, and careful storage according to guidelines in your cookbook or on the package label will help preserve the quality of the food.

Vitamin C

Although the acute lack of vitamin C, called scurvy, is one of the oldest diseases known to man, there is still considerable controversy about the precise role of this vitamin in metabolism and about the optimal dietary intake. Many of the symptoms seen in scurvy are directly related to the role this nutrient plays in the formation of collagen, a protein found in skin, tendons, and bones. In vitamin C deficiency, collagen is poorly formed and abnormalities of bone, teeth, and gums are common. Wounds, surgical incisions, and burns heal more slowly. More recently, an increased demand for this vitamin has been demonstrated by animals forced to live in stressful environments. It appears also that vitamin C may play a role in helping the body to fight infection.

Significant Dietary Sources of Vitamin C

Food	Serving Size	Vitamin C (mg)
Fruit		
Strawberries	3/4 cup	63
Orange juice	3/4 cup	93
Grapefruit	1/2 medium	38
Grapefruit juice	3/4 cup	61
Cantalope	1/2 medium	50
Watermelon	1/16 of a 10" x 16" melon	67
Vegetables		
Broccoli, cooked	3/4 cup	98
Peppers, green, cooked	1 medium shell	83
Brussels sprouts, cooked	6 average	61
Kale (leaves), cooked	3/4 cup	75
Cauliflower, cooked	3/4 cup	55
Tomato, raw	1 medium	35
Tomato juice, canned	3/4 cup	30

Ideally, the optimal intake should assure that tissues remain saturated since excess amounts are excreted in the urine. Although the amount required to achieve this level of saturation varies considerably from one woman to another, the requirement for this vitamin has been set at 85 mg during pregnancy. Fruits and vegetables are the primary dietary sources of vitamin C. Since this nutrient is not stable in the presence of heat, foods containing vitamin C which may be eaten uncooked furnish the most significant amounts. Vitamin C is also destroyed by exposure to air. This makes it important to purchase only quantities which will be used promptly. Avoid long standing times between preparation and serving, and store vitamin C-rich foods in airtight containers to preserve their nutrient content.

Vitamin D

Vitamin D is involved in the processes by which your body makes use of calcium. It is sometimes called "the sunshine vitamin" because in the presence of sunlight, your body is able to make its own vitamin D from a substance already present in your skin. There are few sources of preformed vitamin D, but fortified milks (which contain 400 IU per quart) are the most reliable sources. Poor intake of the preformed vitamin, coupled with low sunlight exposure may cause problems, particularly with the enamel development of baby's teeth. If you do not use commercial milk or milk products and are only infrequently exposed to sunlight, you should discuss the use of a vitamin D supplement with your clinician.

Vitamin E

A recommended daily allowance of 15 mg has been established for vitamin E during pregnancy. This nutrient is widely available in our natural food supply. It is generally associated with fats and oils in seeds or grains, and in milk, eggs, liver, and leafy green vegetables. The chief function of vitamin E is as an antioxidant, helping to prevent fats and oils from becoming rancid.

Since its discovery, various reports have linked vitamin E with improved reproductive performance in humans. It should be pointed out that these claims, based on experimentally induced deficiency in rats, have been extended to normally nourished humans, with no additional scientific support. It is known, however, that neither sterility nor abortion can be prevented by this or any other vitamin supplement. When high dosage supplements are taken, symptoms of toxicity (fatigue, nausea, headaches, etc.) occasionally develop. The risks in taking vitamin E supplements when pregnant are unknown.

Vitamin K

Vitamin K is a necessary ingredient for your body's blood clotting mechanism. An injection of this vitamin may be given to you late in your pregnancy so that both you and the fetus will be well prepared for delivery. Normally, the intestinal bacteria synthesize enough of this vitamin for our bodies. However, since the newborn baby's intestines will not have much bacteria for several days after birth, he/she may receive an injection of vitamin K to decrease the likelihood of bleeding problems.

Minerals

Selected Minerals: Functions and Food Sources

Mineral	Function	Food Sources
Calcium	To help build bones, teeth To help blood clot To help make muscles react normally To delay fatigue and help tired muscles recover	Milk Cheese, especially cheddar type Ice cream Turnip and mustard greens Collard, kale, broccoli Canned sardines, salmon
Iodine	To make thyroxine, an essential hormone that regulates metabolic rate To prevent (simple) goiter	Seafoods Iodized salt
Iron	To combine with protein to make hemoglobin, the red substance in the blood that carries oxygen to the cells	Liver Meat and eggs Green leafy vegetables Raisins, dried apricots
Phosphorus	To help build bones and teeth To help balance the body's acid/base environment	Widespread in the food supply Milk Cheese Lean meats
Zinc	To help many body reactions function normally To help maintain skin integrity To support growth and sexual maturation	Seafood Meats Nuts Whole grains Legumes

Minerals are needed by your body as part of structural compounds, for example, calcium in bone, or as helpers in a variety of chemical reactions. Minerals are just as important as vitamins in assuring the maintenance of a healthy body. The important minerals are listed on page 99, along with their significant functions and major food sources. You will notice that some, such as sodium, potassium and phosphorus, are readily available through common food sources. Others are more difficult to obtain in the needed amounts, for example, iron, calcium and zinc.

As a general rule, if you make reasonably good food choices and eat a wide variety of foods, you will usually meet most mineral requirements before, during and after pregnancy. The one major exception to this statement is iron. Iron is needed to help produce red blood cells. These blood cells help to transport oxygen throughout your body and to your fetus. Iron is required in greater amounts by women in general because of the losses incurred during menstruation, but the requirements are further increased to meet maternal and fetal needs during pregnancy. Iron is found in relatively limited amounts in the typical diet.

Iron and anemia

The increased amount of iron required to support pregnancy has been estimated to be 5 to 6 mg per day. This would make the required intake (RI) for pregnant women 27 mg per day. This extra iron is needed to support a 20 to 30 percent increase in maternal blood supply, the requirements of the placenta, and the needs of the fetus. Many people would find it difficult to meet this requirement from dietary sources alone. The chart on page 101 lists iron content of several foods to aid your menu planning. Much of the iron content of the foods listed on page 101, however, is not easily used by your body. Ascorbic acid (vitamin C), when eaten during the same meal as a food containing iron, can significantly increase the amount of usable iron from the food. For example, a citrus fruit salad served with a pork chop will allow your body to make better use of the iron content of the meat.

Because of the difficulty of meeting your additional need for iron during pregnancy, the use of an iron supplement is generally recognized as reasonable and effective. The preparations commonly used contain ferrous gluconate, ferrous sulfate, or ferrous fumarate (simple iron salts) in amounts from 30 to 60 mg daily. These amounts are considerably greater than your actual requirements to compensate for the fact that such supplements are less efficiently absorbed than is iron from food sources. Larger doses, however, are usually not advised except

Iron Contents of Representative Foods

Food	Serving Size	Iron Contents (mg)
Liver, lamb	2 slices	13.4
Liver, beef	2 slices	6.6
Liver, chicken	1/4 cup	4.3
Hamburger	1 large	3.0
Roast beef	2 slices	2.6
Pork chop	1 medium	2.5
Baked beans, canned with pork and molasses	1/2 cup	3.0
Apricots	4 halves	1.7
Prunes	4-5 medium	1.2
Figs	2 small	0.9
Raisins	2 Tbsp	0.6
Soybeans	1/2 cup, scant, cooked	2.5
Lima beans	1/2 cup, cooked	2.0
Peanut butter	2 Tbsp	0.6
Leafy green vegetables	1/2 cup, cooked	1.0-2.0
Potatoes	1 medium	1.0
Bread	1 slice	0.6

for the treatment of established iron deficiency. You can also raise the iron content in foods by cooking in iron pots and skillets.

Maternal anemia, a condition in which the blood is deficient in red cells, hemoglobin, or total volume, is the major consequence of iron deficiencies but its effects on the outcome of pregnancy are poorly understood. Anemia is usually determined by measurements made from a sample of your blood. About one-third to one-half of the pregnant women who do not take iron supplements develop anemia. Maternal risks associated with anemia involve reduced tolerance to possible hemorrhage at delivery and increased risk of postpartum infection. The risks to the baby are not well defined. About one fourth of the pregnant women who are iron deficient exhibit pica, a term used to denote an appetite for strange, usually non-food items. In the past, consumption of dirt, starch, clay, etc., was cited as a cause of iron deficiency. Recently, the opposite view has been proposed—that iron deficiency causes pica. Whatever the case, if you feel that you may be affected by pica, or if you have unusual food cravings, you should discuss it with your healthcare provider. Usually it is of no concern, but in rare cases it may compromise your own and your fetus' health.

Calcium and phosphorous

Since calcium functions as an essential part of bone and tooth structure, your need for this mineral is obviously great. Your body compensates for this additional need by increased absorption and retention of calcium long before your fetal skeletal mineralization begins. Approximately 30 gm of calcium are accumulated during pregnancy, almost all of it by the fetal skeleton. About 300 mg of calcium per day is deposited during the last three months of pregnancy. Observations have led researchers to suspect that maternal tissues retain calcium as well, possibly in preparation for meeting the extensive calcium requirements of breastfeeding.

The current RI for calcium is approximately 1000 to 1300 mg per day. Some scientists feel that this recommendation is too high since successful pregnancies are sustained on much lower calcium intakes by many cultures. But it is likely that the difference between intake and requirement would be met by the body removing calcium from maternal stores such as bones and teeth. After several pregnancies, the harmful effects of this practice may show up in your body as decreased amounts of calcium in your bones. Babies born to women under these conditions show poor bone formation as well. Also, it is known that the calcium requirement is linked to protein and phosphorus intake, and that diets high in one or both of these nutrients cause higher calcium losses in the urine. This loss presumably increases the dietary requirement for calcium.

While calcium is found in a number of foods, it is present in highest quantities in milk and other dairy products. If you are intolerant to milk, you will need to find an alternative calcium source. Soybean products and leafy green vegetables are among the better nondairy sources. Other substitutes are listed in the chart on page 103.

Calcium-phosphorus balance is frequently discussed in relation to nerve and muscle function. Some pregnant women seem to be particularly prone to cramping of the muscles of the lower leg, especially at night. 20 years ago, several doctors suggested that this condition might be caused by the presence in the blood of too little calcium for the amount of phosphorus (or phosphate) present. In order to treat this problem, they prescribed reduction in milk intake (a food high in phosphorus and calcium), supplementation of the diet with non-phosphate calcium salts, and aluminum hydroxide (to reduce absorption of phosphorus from the intestine). These measures were shown to increase the blood levels of

Calcium Content of Foods

Food	Serving Size	Calcium (mg)
Milk	8 oz	285
Cheese	1 oz	225
Leafy vegetables, cooked (excluding spinach, beets, greens, chard)	3/4 cup	210
Broccoli	3/4 cup	95
Peanut butter	2 Tbsp	22

calcium in these women. However, not all of the studies demonstrated a beneficial effect on leg cramps.

Thus, there is still controversy regarding the cause of leg cramps. Improvement of calcium-phosphorus balance by the use of calcium gluconate and aluminum hydroxide may be helpful if you are severely affected by leg cramps. But, as with all other diet supplements, consult your clinician before beginning treatment. Avoiding milk products as a portion of the treatment seems appropriate only if all other measures have failed. The high nutritional value of milk products, particularly in pregnancy, certainly justifies its presence in the diet if at all possible. Reduction of low-calcium, high-phosphorus dietary agents such as carbonated beverages, and foods which are processed with phosphate salts, as found in refrigerated doughs, may be useful alternatives.

Recent evidence indicates that women with a history of high blood pressure prior to becoming pregnant, as well as women with poor nutritional status, should receive calcium carbonate supplements before and during pregnancy. Discuss this with your clinician before taking this supplement.

Avoid calcium supplements based on bone meal, dolomite or oyster shell because of the risk of lead contamination.

Sodium and fluid balance

Throughout the course of your pregnancy, significant hormonal changes are taking place. One change which may occur is some accumulation of fluid in your body. This may cause some swelling of your hands and feet, particularly in hot weather.

This condition should generally not cause you or your clinician any alarm since it occurs to some degree in all women during pregnancy. The accumulation of fluid is not associated with an increase in maternal or fetal problems. It is, however, inappropriate to treat this condition with diuretics (water-losing pills) or by restricting salt or sodium intake. The need for sodium in fact, is increased during pregnancy. Studies with animals suggest that rigorous sodium restriction may make your body less able to maintain its normal fluid balance. Ultimately, this could cause damage to the kidneys and adrenal glands. While moderation, particularly in the use of added salt and the intake of excessively salty foods (see chart on page 106), is appropriate for everyone, severe restriction of salt is not advisable since your body and your fetus have increased needs for sodium.

Trace minerals

Trace minerals are those minerals the body requires only in small amounts. The requirements during pregnancy for many trace minerals have not been established because of the obvious problems involved in experimentally producing diet deficiencies or excesses. Some observations have been recorded, however. When maternal diets are deficient in iodine, abnormalities of growth are seen. Iodized salt as well as some seafoods, particularly shellfish, and commercial dough products in which iodine is used as a dough conditioner are important dietary sources.

Maternal chromium deficiency has been suggested as a cause of gestational diabetes, an abnormality of blood sugar metabolism which is sometimes seen during pregnancy. Chromium was once plentiful in our diets when whole-grain breads were a staple item. However, because of increased processing of our food supply, a potential for deficiency does exist. Thus, the simple solution of including whole-grain products such as breads and cereals and/or brewer's yeast provides significant sources of this nutrient and should relieve any fear of deficiency.

Zinc is another trace element which has received much attention recently. The current recommended daily allowance for pregnant women is 11 to 13 mg per day. Dietary deficiencies are known to produce abnormalities in the skeletal and/or central nervous systems of some animal species. Also, a few cases of similar abnormalities have been reported among humans in the geographic areas where zinc deficiency is common. Since zinc content of many foods is reduced by commercial refining, an unprocessed or "natural" food source would be advisable. Animal sources can also contribute significant zinc to the average diet. The relative zinc content of several food sources is listed on page 105.

Snacks

If snacks supply a significant amount of your daily calorie intake, they should also make a contribution in terms of nutrients. Very few of us can afford the additional "empty calories" found in many snack foods. Filling-up on these won't leave enough available calories to meet our daily nutritional requirements. Pregnant and lactating women, growing children, and teenagers usually need some food between meals to meet energy and nutrient requirements. Snacks should be selections from the Food Groups (see pages 83 and 86) and should be planned as part of your daily menu. Foods which are concentrated sources of sugar or fat are more likely to dull appetites for mealtime, furnish few nutrients, and contribute to excess weight gain. Snack foods which are high in sugar also increase the risk of tooth decay if prompt and thorough cleaning of teeth is not possible.

Zinc Content of Some Foods

Low (less than 5 mg/kg)		
Apples	Bananas	Oranges
Cabbage	Cauliflower	String beans
Cucumbers	Lettuce	Tomatoes
Butter	White bread	White sugar
Medium (5-20 mg/kg)		
Carrots	Potatoes	Turnips
Haddock	Sardines	Whole wheat
Bread		
High (20-50 mg/kg)		
Almonds	Peanuts	Walnuts
Eggs	Beef	Liver
Very High (over 1000 mg/kg)		
Herrings	Oysters	

Foods Especially High in Sodium (Salt)

Seasonings	
Salt	Worcestershire sauce
Garlic salt	Salt brine
Onion salt	Baking soda
Celery salt	Baking powder
Catsup	Monosodium glutamate
Prepared mustard	Meat tenderizers
Chili sauce	Soy sauce

Meats and Fish (smoked, cured or dried)	
Ham	Canned corned beef hash
Canadian bacon	Dried beef (chipped)
Regular bacon	Frankfurters
Sausage	Caviar
Cold cuts (luncheon meats)	Sardines
Corned beef	Tuna (packed in oil)
Pastrami	Anchovies
Salt pork	TV dinners

Cheese	
American, cheddar	Cheese spreads
American, processed	Parmesan

Snack Foods (all those with obvious salt on them)	
Potato chips	Party mixes
Pretzels	Salted nuts
Crackers	Salted popcorn
Corn chips and corn curls	

Miscellaneous	
Bouillon	Salad dressings
Sauerkraut	Relishes
Soup—all canned, frozen, dried	Ethnic foods: Chinese,
Olives	Italian, and kosher,
Pickles	for example

Chapter 11 Foods to limit or avoid during pregnancy

VERY LITTLE IS KNOWN about specific chemicals in foods and the environment and their effect on fetal development. In the early 1900's, concern for the safety of our food supply prompted the federal government to prohibit the addition of "poisonous or other deleterious (harmful) ingredients" to foods. As our scientific knowledge expands, along with more sophisticated testing procedures, we continue to update our guidelines for protecting the health of pregnant women and their fetuses.

Providing accurate information for these women regarding what substances should be restricted or avoided is an important goal. In this chapter we'll look at certain substances and recommend ways to avoid or minimize their effect during your pregnancy. There are three categories of compounds every pregnant woman should be aware of. First are mutagens, which change the genetic material in body cells. Second are teratogens, which can cause structural change during fetal development. Third are carcinogens, substances known to cause cancer.

Consumer interest in these substances was heightened by the thalidomide tragedy of the 1960's and the diethylstilbestrol (DES) findings in the 1970's. Thalidomide was prescribed for pregnant women to aid in relaxation and prevent nausea. Many of the babies were born with shortened limbs and other abnormalities of muscle and bone. In a similar manner, DES was given to women in the 1950's to prevent miscarriage. In the 1970's, an increased incidence of vaginal cancer was found among adolescent girls whose mothers took DES during their pregnancies. The widespread press coverage of these events also caused the public to question the hazards posed by chemicals added to our environment. As a result, the government has been pressured to investigate any substances in our foods which may be harmful to developing fetuses.

Although it would be very difficult to avoid every potentially harmful factor, there are several significant substances which can be eliminated to greatly reduce the risk to your fetus. Even foods such as eggs and fish have new limitations.

Eggs

It has long been known that cracked eggs could be contaminated with the Salmonella organism which is known to cause food poisoning.

In the October 1988 publication of *Nutrition Action Healthletter*, there appeared an article reporting on the suspicion of researchers that Salmonella can be found in uncracked eggs as well. It is believed that the organism responsible has contaminated the hen's ovaries which contained the yolks before the shells of the eggs were formed.

Salmonella is destroyed by thorough cooking. The Centers for Disease Control (CDC) in Atlanta, Georgia, recommends the following:

- Avoid foods made with raw or undercooked egg such as Caesar's salad dressing, hollandaise sauce, eggnog and homemade ice cream. Some restaurants, in response to concerns about Salmonella, have eliminated the coddled egg (1 minute egg) from their Caesar's salad dressing. Ask your server or the chef before ordering.
- Boil eggs for 7 minutes, poach for 5 minutes or fry for 3 minutes on each side.
- Do not eat eggs "sunny side up" (not turned). Tests have shown the Salmonella bacteria often survive even if the eggs are overcooked on only one side.

Fish

Also in the October 1988 issue of the *Nutrition Action Healthletter*, was a recommendation that pregnant women and women who are breastfeeding limit the fish they eat to offshore ocean fish because of the amount of lake pollution (even the Great Lakes) and ocean pollution near the shoreline. In an article published September 15, 2004, a study by the Environmental Protection Agency (EPA), found mercury levels in fish from these areas higher than the limit considered safe in women of childbearing age. This study was of fish from 260 to 500 lakes in the United States. The highest levels of mercury were found in predator fish such as small mouth bass, walleye, large mouth bass, lake trout and northern pike.

Nearly half of all mercury emissions in the United States originate from coal fired plants, as well as other industrial sources. Reducing the emissions from these facilities will help to reduce the presence of mercury in the environment.

Fish is an excellent source of protein. It is high in the B vitamins, low in saturated fat, but high in omega-3 fatty acids which are believed to reduce the risk of heart disease. Fish is also lower in calories when baked or broiled rather than fried.

A recent report from the Centers for Disease Control and Prevention (CDC) states that 10 percent of American women may have amounts of mercury in their blood that are approaching dangerous levels. The Food and Drug Administration (FDA) recommends that women of childbearing age, nursing moms and children under the age of 5 avoid eating fish known to contain high levels of methyl mercury, including shark, swordfish, king mackerel and tilefish. Smaller fish are considered safe to eat. To date, the recommendation is that up to 12 ounces of fish (not specifically excluded) is safe to eat.

Canned white albacore tuna has more mercury than canned light tuna. Light tuna has one-third the level of mercury than albacore tuna. If you eat albacore tuna, limit the amount you eat to one 6-ounce can per week.

- Avoid eating fish caught close to a major city or industrial area. Ask where the fish was caught before purchasing it.
- Be aware of any health advisories issued in your area, particularly regarding fishing in local waters if family and friends enjoy the sport and share their catch with you.
- Smaller fish tend to have fewer contaminants (they have had less time to become tainted).
- Avoid parts of the fish with the highest amount of contamination. These include the skin, fatty belly side and the dark meat. Remove these parts before cooking.
- Broil or bake fish on an elevated rack so fatty drippings can fall into pan below. Do not use fish drippings to make a sauce. Avoid fish recipes which call for whole fish including sushi, sashimi and shell fish. It is wise to vary the kinds offish you eat within the guidelines just mentioned, rather than eat large amounts of any one kind of fish.
- Contaminants are known to concentrate in the “mustard” in blue crabs and the “tamale” in lobsters. Avoid eating these parts. The best fish to select are those that are low in fat and found offshore.

- Women of childbearing age, nursing moms and children under 5 should avoid eating shark, swordfish, king mackerel and tile fish.
- For specific recommendations on which fish to avoid, contact your local, state, or county health department.

Alcohol

Alcohol is a drug. And although it was once thought that moderate drinking did not threaten the fetus, it is now acknowledged that alcohol can have devastating effects on the fetus. Recent studies also indicate that even moderate drinking increases the risk of miscarriage.

The Surgeon General advises pregnant women, or women considering pregnancy, not to drink alcohol. The Food and Drug Administration recommends that alcoholic beverages carry warning labels to inform pregnant women of the hazards of drinking. Many doctors agree that there is no minimum level of alcohol a pregnant woman can drink and be certain the fetus is not harmed.

Binge drinking, rather than just the total amount of alcohol consumed during pregnancy, doubles the risk of mental retardation and behavior related problems in children.

Scientists are searching for the reason why alcohol is so damaging to the unborn. So far the studies are inconclusive except for the fact that alcohol affects the brain of the fetus. The effects of alcohol on the fetus remain after birth even though the alcohol has been removed.

For most pregnant women the question of alcohol revolves around social drinking. The best answer, of course, is to treat alcohol as you would any other drug and not use it. When attending social gatherings drink non-alcoholic beverages. You wouldn't give a gin and tonic to your newborn, don't offer it to your fetus.

The evidence that alcohol may play a role in the birth of abnormal babies was known to the early Greeks. They prohibited drinking of alcohol on the wedding night for fear a damaged child would be produced. In the 1700's a report to the British parliament described the offspring of alcoholic mothers as having a "starved, shriveled and imperfect look." This information, however, was not pursued by medical researchers of the time. Instead, they concentrated on investigations of the possible genetic damage in alcoholism. In 1968 in France and again in 1972 in the United States, doctors noted a similar pattern of features in children born to alcoholic women. These children were characterized by poor growth both before and after birth, abnormalities of the face, ears, joints, limbs, and heart, and mental retardation. The term "Fetal Alcohol Syndrome" (FAS) was given to these children whose mothers consumed high levels of alcohol during pregnancy.

Babies born to alcoholics are also addicted to alcohol.

The presence of specific structural changes in these infants is important since it clearly shows that the damage occurs while embryonic and fetal tissues are developing. Follow-up studies of these babies have not been encouraging. Physical and mental handicaps persist even when the infant has been raised in a superior environment. This indicates that the damage induced by excessive alcohol consumption is permanent.

In addition to FAS, an increase in the number of stillbirths and low birth weight infants has been found among women who consume alcohol. It has also been noted that mild characteristics of FAS may appear among women who drink socially, but not to the same extent seen in the typical alcoholic. This leads us to wonder "how much alcohol can safely be consumed by the pregnant woman?"

Unfortunately, definitive answers are not available. The impact of alcohol on the child clearly increases with the level of exposure. Some mothers may be more susceptible than others to the adverse effects of alcohol or its breakdown products. Smoking, drug abuse, and malnutrition undoubtedly complicate the picture further.

The problem of alcohol can also be related to the father. Published results from a recent 12-year study indicate that if a man consumes alcohol prior to mating, there may be fetal abnormalities even if the woman does not drink any alcohol. These studies suggest that alcohol can have a mutagenic (an abnormal change in the genes) effect on the sperm.[1] One of the interesting findings was that these damaging effects are primarily on moderate drinkers rather than very heavy drinkers as a large intake of alcohol frequently causes infertility.

Caffeine

If you stop drinking alcohol and switch to coffee or tea, you should know that both are stimulants for you and your fetus. Exposing the developing fetus to high amounts of caffeine may have harmful effects. Caffeine is thought to have strong chemical effects on the human body and is known to cross the placenta. In addition, tea interferes with iron absorption. However, there is no proof that one or two cups of coffee a day will cause a problem during pregnancy. Because little is known about the effect of herbal teas on pregnancy, it is best to avoid them. The herb comfrey is known to cause serious liver disease.

During pregnancy you should switch to decaffeinated coffee which has the flavor of regular coffee but is not as powerful. If you must have coffee or tea, limit your intake to minimal amounts.

Remember, too, that cola, many other soft drinks, and cocoa contain caffeine. So do many over-the-counter medications. Take the time to check product labels carefully for items containing caffeine.

Caffeine and its close relatives theobromine and theophylline are consumed by many on a daily basis. Coffee is by far the most popular, but tea, cocoa, and colas are also consumed in large amounts. The caffeine content of many beverages is shown in the chart on page 113. A number of factors can affect the caffeine content of these products including plant variety, geographic location, climate in which it was grown and preparation method. Particularly with coffee and tea, the strength of the brew and the type of brewing method are major factors affecting caffeine content. Cola beverages get about half of their caffeine from the kola nut itself and half from added caffeine.

[1] Rush-Presbyterian-St. Luke's Medical Center, Insights into clinical and scientific progress in medicine.1991. Vol. 14, No. 2, page 34

In 1977 the American Academy of Science estimated that 74 percent of the pregnant women in the United States consume caffeine and that the average intake for these women was 144 mg per day. Newer data suggest that caffeine consumption is increasing.

The common effects of caffeine on the central nervous system and other organs have been well documented. Caffeine is a potent stimulant. Its use is associated with wakefulness, increased and sometimes erratic heart rates, and increased urinary output.

In 1980, the FDA recommended that pregnant women eliminate or use sparingly all foods containing caffeine. This advice came as a result of animal studies indicating a decrease in the intrauterine growth rate, lowered birth weight, and skeletal abnormalities in the offspring. Harvard Medical School conducted the first study on humans in January, 1982. Of the 12,400 women in the study, over 5200 drank 1 to 4, or more, cups of coffee per day. The evidence suggested that coffee consumption had a minimal effect, if any, on the outcome of the pregnancy. These studies are by no means conclusive because of the limited nature of the evidence. Nevertheless, the Food and Drug Administration is taking action to

Caffeine Content of Common Beverages

Beverage	Caffeine (in mg) per 5 oz Serving
Coffee	
Dripolated	146
Percolated	110
Instant	66
Decaffeinated	4
Bagged tea	
Black—5 min. brew*	46
Black—1 min. brew*	28
Loose tea	
Black—5 min. brew	40
Green—5min. brew	28
Cola beverages	47
Cocoa	13**

* 1 tea bag per 5 oz. cup water
** Also contains about 250 mg theobromine

ensure that studies to determine the risk of caffeine during pregnancy are initiated and carried out. As a first step, the FDA is proposing to remove caffeine from its list of substances Generally Recognized as Safe (GRAS) and to place it on an interim list. This means that the FDA will allow continued use of caffeine while further studies of its risk are considered.

An article which appeared in the June 1, 1998 issue of *OB-GYN News*, reported an association between sudden infant death syndrome (SIDS) and caffeine in women who consumed large amounts of caffeine—the equivalent of 14 cups of tea, 7 cups of coffee or 12 to 15 glasses of cola per day.

Since the human risk factors are not conclusively known, moderate use or elimination of caffeine during pregnancy would be prudent advice. Decaffeinated coffee, fruit juices and non-cola drinks can be substituted. Cutting back on tea is also beneficial because tea interferes with iron absorption.

Natural toxins and related compounds

Very little is known about the effects of food toxins on developing fetus. Among the compounds occasionally found in food which have been investigated are nitrosamines and aflatoxins. Both of these compounds have received considerable news coverage since they are known to produce cancer in laboratory animals.

Nitrosamines

Nitrosamines are potent carcinogens (cancer-causing agents) in animals. Since humans are often affected similarly, concern about nitrosamines in our food supply is great. Recently it was demonstrated that nitrosamines cross the placenta and therefore a fetus would be exposed to the compound. In animals, this has been shown to induce tumor growth. Humans probably respond in a similar way.

While nitrosamines are rarely found in food, nitrites in common food constituents are (see chart on page 115). Nitrites are compounds which can be readily converted to nitrosamine when combined with other chemicals. Sodium nitrite and sodium nitrate are added to most cured and smoked meats and fish. Nitrate, which may be broken down to nitrite, is found in leafy vegetables, particularly when nitrate fertilizers have been used. The relatively acid environment in the stomach and upper intestine would favor the development of nitrosamines from these compounds. In fact, nitrosamines have been found in the feces of people on typical American diets.

Natural and Artificial Dietary Sources of Nitrosamines*

Meats	Fish	Other Foods
Nitrate/nitrite cured or preserved Meats: Ham Bacon Sausage, including salami and frankfurters Luncheon meats Corned beef	Chinese salt dried fish Raw and smoked sable Raw and smoked salmon Raw and smoked shad	Beets, broccoli, carrots, cabbage, celery, spinach—nitrates derived from both commercial and natural fertilizers Cheese Soy bean oil Drinking water in areas experiencing fertilizer runoff Improperly distilled spirits Milk Flour

**Nitrosamines are both naturally occurring and artificially added as antioxidants, mainly in preserved meats.*

Government regulations have been proposed which would limit the use of these products in food processing. Several new compounds which appear to be non-carcinogenic are being studied as alternatives for sodium nitrite and sodium nitrate. It also appears that vitamin C may retard the process of nitrosamine formation and its use in preserved meats has been suggested as a safety measure.

Aflatoxin

Aflatoxin is produced by a fungus which contaminates some foods. It is generally found in vegetable materials which have been stored with excessive moisture. Peanuts are particularly susceptible, but rice, wheat, barley, corn, millet, and sorghum are occasionally affected. Fungal toxins have also been isolated from soy beans, peas, cottonseed, cocoa, cassava, sesame, sweet potatoes, dairy products (from animals given contaminated feed), and improperly fermented foods and alcoholic beverages.

The presence of aflatoxins causes serious illness in humans and is suspected of causing cancer when ingested over a period of time. Animal studies have also shown that aflatoxin is a teratogen, an agent which can cause structural or growth changes in the fetus and may induce miscarriages. Its precise effects on humans are not known.

Aflatoxin is not destroyed by ordinary cooking and freezing techniques. Milling of cereal grains is an effective method of control since the outer layer, which may have been affected by the fungus, is removed. Most infected nuts have broken shells or are discolored, rancid, or shriveled. Commercially processed peanuts and peanut products intended for human consumption are routinely subjected to testing for aflatoxin contamination. The consumer is further protected by high standards for harvesting, storage, and marketing of peanuts and susceptible grains.

Food additives and contaminants

Check with your doctor before using any sugar substitutes. Cyclamates have been banned in the United States. and Canada. The sweetener aspartame, commercially known as Equal or Nutrasweet, is composed of two amino acids, phenylalanine and aspartic acid, that appear naturally in many foods. Although most people can eat these amino acids without any problems, high levels of phenylalanine in the blood of women with phenylketonuria (PKU) may harm the nervous systems of these women and/or their unborn babies. PKU is an inborn condition in which the body is unable to use phenylalanine properly, thus allowing accumulation of the amino acid in body fluid. The results may be mental retardation and other nervous system disorders.

All of this can be prevented by a diet low in phenylalanine. Thus, women with PKU should not use the sweetener aspartame. As a general precaution, all pregnant women should consider limiting or eliminating this sweetener until more is known about the effects of it on a pregnant woman and her fetus. As a precaution, government warning labels have been added to artificially sweetened products limiting their use to diabetics and others who must curtail their use of sugars. During pregnancy and breastfeeding the use of artificial sweeteners for the purpose of calorie reduction is a questionable practice. Pregnant women obviously should avoid any unnecessary exposure to materials which might harm the fetus.

A sweetener called Sucralose has recently been approved by the Food and Drug Administration (FDA). It is about 600 times sweeter than sugar. So far the FDA has not found any evidence that it has any toxic side effects. Sucralose does not break down when heated. According to the manufacturer, Johnson & Johnson, no warning labels are required and no segment of the population is excluded from using this sugar substitute.

Miscellaneous substances

Many pregnant women often develop strange ideas about the virtues or dangers of specific foods. The origin of many of these ideas is unknown. Most are based on nothing more than traditional myths and folklore lacking in factual support. There is no reason to avoid any nourishing food which you enjoy and tolerate. Likewise, there is no single food item which must be consumed if you and your baby are to thrive. Eating moderate amounts of a wide variety of foods is the best way to ensure a healthy baby.

Chapter 12 Maintaining a healthy lifestyle

TO COMPETE SUCCESSFULLY in any sport, an athlete must prepare his or her body to accomplish the goal. In many ways you are similar to an athlete. Like the athlete, you must go through a training period in which you exercise, get sufficient rest, and modify your normal lifestyle.

Instead of an athletic competition, you will be preparing to create a new human being. The success of your training period should make your delivery easier and your baby healthier. You'll be giving your child a solid start in life, and you will look and feel better yourself. Let's look at the guidelines you need to follow during this period and see how following them can make you and your baby both winners.

Resting

During the first few months of your pregnancy you may feel constantly fatigued, as if you can't seem to get enough sleep. If possible, try to organize your time so that you can rest or take a nap during the middle of the day. Or, if possible take a nap in the morning and another in the afternoon.

By the end of your pregnancy, however, it may be the inability to fall asleep (insomnia) that is most troubling. With the uterus growing and pressing on the rib cage, it is not uncommon to experience shortness of breath. Try using an extra pillow or two to prop yourself up in bed. Slow down, avoid rushing when doing chores, climbing stairs or carrying out various tasks.

Your increased size and weight may require a change in sleep positions. If you have difficulty falling asleep, try taking a walk before bedtime. Other relaxing techniques include taking a warm bath or shower before retiring. Drinking a glass of warm milk before bedtime can also help you relax. But under no circumstances should you take any sedatives (sleeping pills) or tranquilizers.

Your job

If you are working, you may have some concerns regarding how it will affect your pregnancy.

The first question may be whether or not you should continue working? Generally speaking, most women can continue to work during their 9 months of pregnancy until the onset of labor. The American College of Obstetricians and Gynecologists agrees that a woman can work if she is healthy, her pregnancy is normal and uncomplicated, and her job is no more hazardous than daily living. The final decision regarding work during pregnancy is up to you, but you should also consult with your clinician.

When should you tell your boss that you are pregnant? Many women wait until the third or fourth month of their pregnancies before telling their co-workers. This allows time for thinking over the situation and planning for the changes both at home and at work. Once you are ready to discuss this at work, it is best to tell your boss first, rather than letting the gossip of co-workers carry the message in a way which could undermine your working situation. If you are your own boss, be sure to allow yourself a reasonable amount of time to find a replacement to manage your business while you are absent.

Should you tell your boss and co-workers whether you will return to work after the baby is born? Since they will certainly ask, it is probably best to put off making that decision until you have time to make long-range plans. If staying at home with your child is an option, do not make a commitment to others until you have decided for yourself.

Law Regarding Work and Pregnancy

The 1978 Pregnancy Act is an amendment to the Civil Rights Acts of 1964 requiring all employers to offer the same medical disability compensation for pregnancy-related disabilities as is offered for other disabilities.

There are three major federal laws protecting the health, safety and employment rights of a pregnant employee:

- **The Pregnancy Discrimination Act** requires employers to offer the same disability leave and pay to pregnant employees as they do for other employees who miss work for other health-related problems. This Act makes it illegal to fire or refuse to promote a woman because she is pregnant. Should you feel your are being discriminated against because of your pregnancy, call 1-800-669-3362.

- **The Occupational Safety and Health Act (OSHA)** requires employers to reveal to their workers information regarding harmful agents in the workplace. This Act requires employers to provide a hazard-free work place. If you think your workplace is exposing you to hazardous agents and think it should be checked, contact 1-800-356-4674.

- **Family and Medical Leave Act.** This Act requires employers with 50 or more employees to allow pregnant employees up to 12 weeks of unpaid leave during any 12 month period for:

  - The birth, adoption or foster care of a child
  - A serious health problem interfering with her ability to do her job due to a pregnancy, or birth-related disability
  - The employee's need to take care of a spouse, a child, or a parent with a serious health problem

For additional information about family and medical leave, contact the Department of Labor at 1-800-959-3652.

Safety

Will you and your fetus be safe if you work? This is certainly the most important consideration concerning your job, and you will need to consider many factors concerning how safe your working conditions are for the health of you and your fetus. Ultimately, you will have to discuss this problem with your clinician, who needs to know all of the details about your job. For example, if you work in a hospital or teach small children, are you exposed to infectious diseases? If you operate machinery, will your enlarged abdomen become dangerous, especially as your pregnancy progresses? Is there physical labor such as lifting, pushing, pulling, or constant sitting or standing which could be hazardous or uncomfortable for a pregnant woman? Standing all day can lead to varicose veins, hemorrhoids, and fatigue. Do some of the machines that you work with in your office use toxic substances?

One important safety factor is contact with certain chemicals. According to the American College of Obstetricians and Gynecologists, the following chemicals have been found to be dangerous to the fetus or the reproductive systems of animals:

- Heavy metals: cadmium, lead, mercury
- X-ray exposure
- Hypoxic agents: carbon monoxide
- Anesthetic gases: halogenated gases
- Pesticides: carbaryl, chlorinated hydrocarbons, chlordecone (kepone)
- Miscellaneous: carbon disulfide, ethylene oxide

If you and your clinician determine that your job is potentially dangerous to you during pregnancy, perhaps you can work out an acceptable alternative position with your employer so that you will not have to quit your job, be transferred, or lose seniority, pay, or benefits. If this isn't feasible, then perhaps a temporary position in another company is a possiblity. Even if you do not work outside the home, you should still take safety precautions and stay in training. That means you should not overwork yourself, and you should still allow yourself adequate rest when you are tired. Any job, whether in the workplace or at home, requires setting priorities and providing time for the relaxation you need.

Discuss your situation with your clinician and your employer. Your health, and that of your baby, must come first. If your job involves exposure to certain chemicals, radiation, strenuous work, heavy lifting, long periods of time on your feet and/or unusually stressful conditions, you should request a transfer to less stressful or hazardous work.

The Occupational Safety and Health Administration (OSHA)

sets and enforces standards which require employers to provide a workplace free from recognized hazards likely to cause death or serious physical harm. State municipal statutes also give employees and unions the right to request the names of chemicals or other substances used in the workplace.

Radiation

Radiation used in X-ray of the internal organs is called ionizing radiation. Pregnant women who work around ionizing radiation should wear protective clothing or

You don't deserve to be hurt by your partner

If you are being hit, slapped, beaten, punched, kicked, or in any way hurt or threatened by your partner, you are not alone. Sadly, many women are abused by a husband, boyfriend, or ex-partner. Abusive partners are usually very jealous. They may try to control what you wear, what you buy, where you go, and whom you visit. Although they may apologize after fits of rage, abusers are likely to hurt you again and again. Over time, the abuse gets worse.

Financial concerns, religious beliefs, children and both love and fear of the partner are just some of the many things that make it hard to leave an abusive relationship. Even If you are not ready to leave the relationship, start thinking about your safety and what to do in case of an emergency. The following safety tips can help you.

- Let someone know what is happening to you. Abuse is NOT entitled to privacy.
- Teach your children to dial 911 during an emergency.
- Remove weapons from your home. If a gun must remain in the home, make sure it has a safety lock on it.
- Keep a copy of important papers such as rent receipts, birth certificates, insurance policies, and important phone numbers with a friendor family member.
- Keep extra items, such as clothes for you and your children, car keys and house keys, with a friend or family member.
- Memorize or keep available the numbers of a local emergency shelter as well as domestic violence and child abuse hotlines.
- Notify your children's school about the problem to protect your children's safety.
- Hide some money. A woman, for example, can hide money in a tampon container and keep it in her purse.
- If possible, open your own bank account. If you need to leave immediately, do whatever you can to take your children with you.
- If you cannot remember the phone number of the domestic violence hotline or the nearest shelter, dial 411 for that information.
- Avoid drugs and alcohol, which may slow your reflexes and impair your judgment.
- If you have visible injuries, show them to a doctor or nurse. He or she can photograph the injuries to provide documentation.
- Even if you do not have visible injuries, describe incidents of abuse to your doctor or nurse. A statement in the medical chart will be helpful in the event of a custody battle.
- If you have a restraining order, keep it with you at all times.

National Domestic Violence Hotline
(800) 799-SAFE
(800) 787-3224 (TTY)

National Child Abuse Hotline
(800) 422-4453

Source: Janice Asher, MD, Director, Women's Health and Student Health Service Department and Assistant Professor of Obstetrics and Gynecology, Hospital of the University of Pennsylvania, Philadelphia; Founder and Director, Physicians' and Nurses' Domestic Abuse program; and Clinical Director, Philadelphia Physicians for Social Responsibility.

September 2001 *Contemporary OB Gyn Journal*

shields against exposure to this radiation. Much larger doses of ionizing radiation used in treatment, for example, of cancer, can harm the fetus.

The radiation from color television sets, video display screens and microwave ovens known as nonionizing radiation, is not thought to be at dangerous levels. According to the Oregon Occupational Safety and Health Division of OSHA, there is not enough evidence available to support the position that exposure to video display terminals (VDT) electromagnetic fields may cause birth defects and miscarriages. A study by the National Institute for Occupational Safety and Health and the American Cancer Society found no increase in the risk of miscarriage associated with occupational use of VDTs. Their conclusion was that "VDT use alone is not a hazard to the pregnant worker, but that poor work postures and job stresses often associated with prolonged or intense work are hazards." Other studies have shown that the bulk of the evidence "thus far indicates that VDTs in themselves do not increase the risk for adverse pregnancy outcome." This finding was reported by the U.S. Department of Health and Human Services in September 1999.

The Abused Woman

Physical, sexual or emotional abuse is one of the most common health problems in America. It frequently begins or gets worse during pregnancy, putting both the mother and fetus at risk.

Exercise

An important part of training for the athlete is exercise, and the pregnant mother should exercise as well. There are exercises you can do, exercises you should not do, and special circumstances for women with particular conditions. After your 1st trimester you should avoid exercises requiring you to lie flat on your back. A consultation with your clinician regarding your unique situation is important before undertking any exercise program.

Researchers report that vigorous exercise during pregnancy helps to shift delivery beyond the preterm period and to trigger a timely delivery.

If you are healthy and your pregnancy is proceeding normally, there are a number of exercises you can do. You need controlled exercises which strengthen the muscles used in childbirth. You also need to use common sense when you begin. Start by doing 1 or 2 exercises the 1st day and then build up gradually until you can do 3 to 5 exercises per day. Always begin with a warm-up period before and a cool-down period after exercising.

Most forms of yoga during pregnancy are fine, but avoid those exercises requiring you to lie flat on your back or over-stretching. Some yoga teachers offer special classes for pregnant women.

The backward stretch exercise helps strengthen the muscles of your back, pelvis and thighs. Begin by kneeling on your hands and knees keeping knees about 8 to10 inches apart and your arms straight. Slowly curl backward, tucking your head toward your knees and keeping your arms extended as shown. Hold this position for a count of 5. Slowly come back up to original position on your hands and knees. Repeat this this routine 5 times

---

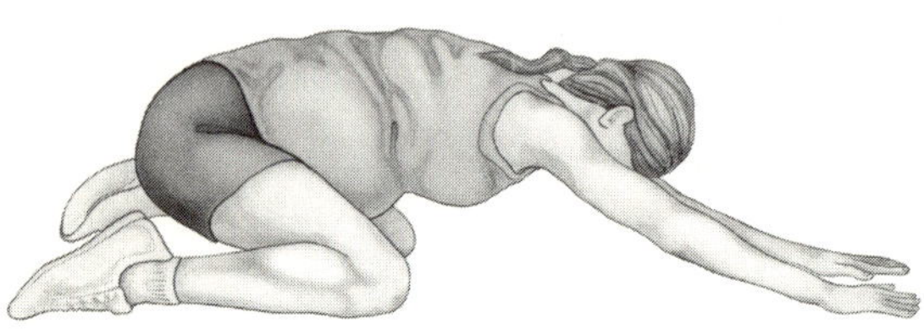

Tailor sitting strengthens groin and leg area used during childbirth. Sit on the floor and bring your left foot toward you so it touches your body. Bring the right foot toward your left foot but do not cross your ankles. Lean forward slowly until your knees touch the floor. Sit this way, back straight, knees almost touching the floor, for a few minutes several times a day.

This exercise helps strengthen the muscles of your back and abdomen. Begin by kneeling on your hands and knees — your arms straight. Lift your left knee bringing it toward your elbow (straighten your leg without locking your knee). Now extend your leg up and back as shown. Move slowly — do not swing your leg back or arch your back. Follow the same movements with your right leg. Repeat 5 to 10 times with each leg.

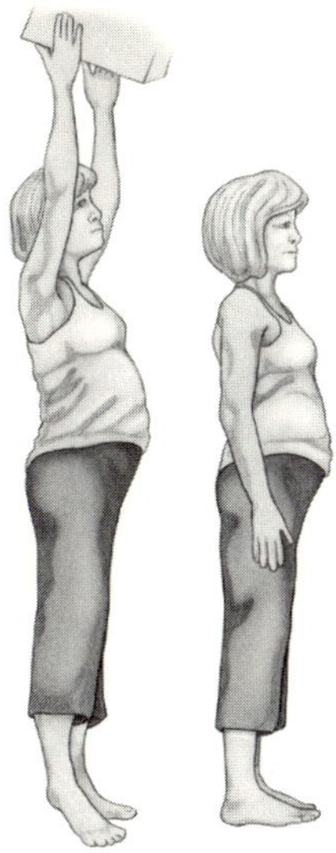

Reaching and stretching for items on high shelves should be considered an exercise in controlled breathing. Before you stretch (not beyond your comfortable reach, of course) inhale, raise up on your toes and bring both arms upward at the same time. Then drop back on your heels and exhale slowly while returning your arms to your sides.

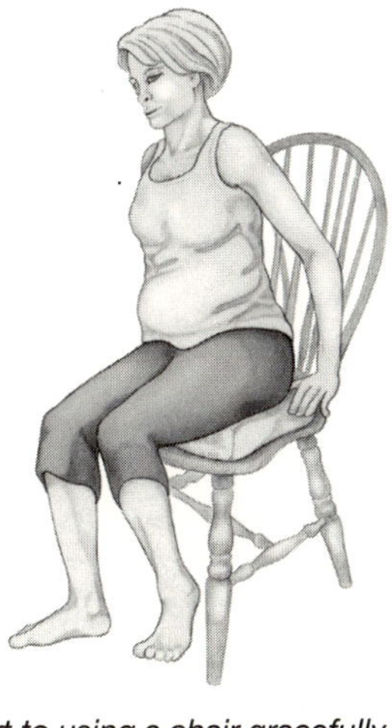

There's an art to using a chair gracefully when you are pregnant. Use your leg muscles to lower yourself rather than "dropping" into the chair. To get up, slide to the front edge of the chair then push yourself up with your legs.

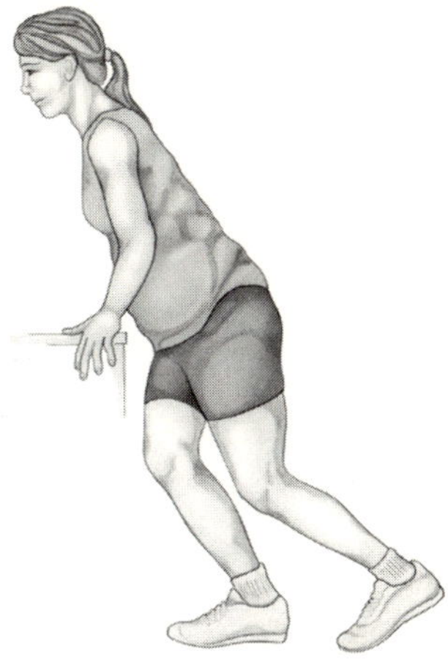

When you are working at a counter for a long period of time, bend your knees every little while and lean forward at the hips for a few minutes. This simple exercise is excellent for relieving backaches.

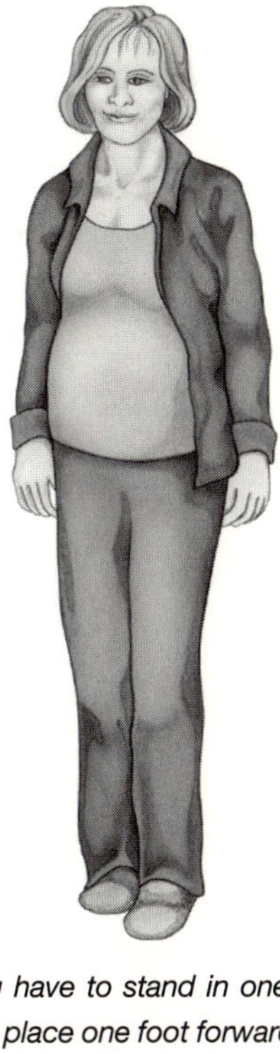

When you have to stand in one spot for a long time, place one foot forward and place all your weight on that foot for a few minutes. Then do the same with the other foot.

The exercises recommended on the following pages are from the Maternity Center Association. If your clinician approves, you can continue swimming, golf, or other sports which you do regularly. Walking outdoors is good exercise for anyone, and you should make an effort to walk each day as part of your daily routine.
Some hospitals offer a series of prenatal exercise classes to help make your labor easier and more efficient. All of this exercise will help you to relax, tone your muscles, and condition your body for the delivery of your baby.

There are also some exercises which you should avoid. For example, avoid activities that could cause an accidental fall. Do not exercise so hard that you become exhausted and do not continue any exercise that hurts. The following are some guidelines from the American College of Obstetricians and Gynecologists:

- Do not exercise in hot, humid weather, or if you are ill with a fever.
- Do not allow your heart rate to exceed 140 beats per minute.
- Discontinue strenuous exercise after 15 minutes.
- Avoid jerky, bouncy, or jumping movements.
- Drink plenty of fluids to prevent dehydration.
- Do not stretch to the limit since hormone changes in pregnancy increase the looseness of the joints, so stretching to the limit may lead to injury.
- Avoid deep knee bends, sit-ups, raising both legs at once and straight-leg-toe touches.
- Stretch your muscles as you warm up or cool down, to help avoid soreness and stiffness.
- Discontinue exercising and call your clinician if any of the following symptoms occur: pain, vaginal bleeding, shortness of breath, irregular or rapid heart rate, or feeling faint or dizzy.

Some women have special circumstances which require caution in regards to exercise. If you have heart disease or other chronic ailments, including high blood pressure, diabetes, anemia, or thyroid disease, you must modify your activity. Some women may not be able to exercise at all—for example, those who have a history of 3 or more miscarriages, multiple births, bleeding, placenta previa, or an incompetent cervix. Any woman with 1 of these conditions should consult her clinician before considering the exercise portion of her training program.

Stress urinary incontinence, the loss of urine when you cough, sneeze or laugh, is not unusual during pregnancy. As your uterus grows it may put pressure on your bladder.

One of the most important groups of muscles which you should exercise are the pelvic floor muscles. It is not uncommon for these muscles to relax late in the 2nd or 3rd trimester of pregnancy. The pelvic floor muscles form a figure 8 around the urethra, vagina and anus, and will be very important when you deliver your baby.

In Kegel exercises, you tighten the pelvic floor muscles the way you would to stop the flow of urine in midstream. The muscles will pull in together in the form of a figure-8, and the pelvic floor will lift slightly. You should hold these muscles tightly for 2 or 3 seconds, then release them. Kegel exercises should be repeated 3 to 5 times a day, or as often as possible throughout the day.

Travel

Seventy years ago, travel was a problem because cars and roads were less efficient and the bumps and jolts could cause problems. It was essential then to avoid long trips by car. Today, technology has made travel in cars, boats, planes, or trains fairly smooth and rapid so that there is little need to worry. Still, you should use common sense, and there are still a number of precautions you should take. There are 7 basic guidelines you should follow when planning to travel:

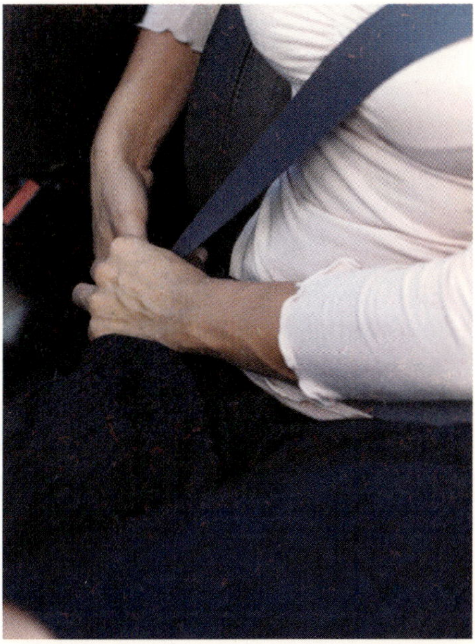

1. When you take a trip some distance away, be sure to ask your clinician for the names of a reputable health care provider in the area in case of premature labor or miscarriage. Either problem can happen at home as well as away.

2. If you are taking a long trip by car, be sure to allow time for frequent stops so that you can drink a glass of water or juice, eat some nourishing food, stretch and urinate.

3. Whether you are a passenger or a driver, always wear the lap-shoulder belt throughout your pregnancy.

Here are some important guidelines for using seat belts while you are pregnant. Place the upper part of the belt between your breasts. Place the lower part of the lap-shoulder belt under your abdomen as low as possible. Never place the lap belt above or across your abdomen. Keep the lower and upper belts snugly against you. If your car only has a lap belt, you should still use it—under your abdomen. Seat belts of any kind prevent damage and are much safer than no seat belt at all, so you should always use them.

4. Unless you can fit comfortably behind the wheel, it is best not to drive.

5. The current position of the American College of Obstetricians and Gynecologists (ACOG) on air travel is as follows: Any woman with an uncomplicated pregnancy can safely travel by air until 36 weeks gestation. Pregnant women at risk for preterm labor, pregnancy-induced high blood pressure, abnormalities of the placenta, uncontrolled diabetes or any other condition that could result in an unexpected emergency, should avoid air travel altogether. In-flight environmental conditions such as low humidity and changes in cabin pressure, combined with the body's hormone changes, can affect the fetus.

   ACOG also recommends checking with the individual carrier to see if there are any specific requirements a pregnant woman should be aware of. International flights allow a pregnant woman to fly only until the 35th week of gestation.

   It is very important, particularly for a pregnant woman, to move about and stretch during the flight to help prevent blood clots.

6. You should consult with your clinician if you are planning to travel to a foreign country because of possible health risks. Some countries may have diseases which are not common in the United States. In some areas the food or drinking water may have contaminents against which you have no built up resistance. Diarrhea, for example, is a common problem for a pregnant woman. Tell your clinician what country you are going to visit and discuss any possible health hazards that might arise. Also, do not worry about the metal detectors used for airport security because these detectors will not harm your fetus.

Be sure to notify your dentist of your pregnancy so that special precautions can be taken.

7. When you reach your 9th month of pregnancy, it is usually best to stay at home. It is not unusual for your baby to be born 2 weeks before or after your due date. Since that due date is uncertain, you will be most comfortable if you know you can quickly contact your own clinician and easily get to your local hospital.

Maintaining good health

The common cold is a problem for everyone, but it is especially harmful to a pregnant woman. Colds seem to last longer for the expectant mother and are difficult to fight. It is a good idea to avoid those situations where you can get a cold. Stay away from crowds during the cold and influenza season and be careful not to get chilled. If you do get a cold, call your clinician before taking any medication. Remember that any drugs that you take can pass from you to the placenta and into the fetal system. All drugs must be used with caution and only under the direction of your physician.

Going to the dentist

Scientific studies have shown that there is a relationship between pregnancy and dental decay, also called "caries." Pregnancy can affect the condition of the teeth and gums. Any untreated dental problem is more likely to get worse. Bleeding gums, possibly leading to an infection, can also occur during pregnancy. Using a softer toothbrush may help control or minimize the bleeding.

It is a good idea to visit your dentist early in your pregnancy and follow his or her recommendations. A complete dental checkup early on in your pregnancy can save you toothaches later. If you need an extraction, the dentist can use a local anesthetic. Be sure to tell your dentist you are pregnant so special precautions can be taken if your teeth need to be X-rayed.

Following your dentist's recommendations is essential, and the American Dental Association even issues special brochures about the importance of dental care during pregnancy. Your teeth and gums can be strengthened by improving your eating habits, getting sufficient vitamins and calcium and, if necessary, other supplements. It is your responsibility to conscientiously brush your teeth each morning, each night, and if at all possible, after each meal. Rinsing your mouth once or twice a day, and the proper use of dental floss, will help eliminate decay-causing bacteria.

Chapter 13 Drugs and other substances

DRUGS OF ALL TYPES are available today as effective remedies for a variety of ailments. Anyone suffereing from the endless list of minor health problems such as diarrhea, constipation, headache, backache, nervous tension, insomnia, and so on can easily visit the local pharmacy and obtain the appropriate pill, potion, ointment, or lotion. Both prescription and over-the-counter drugs are so prevalent in our modern society that we often look to them as if they were the answer to all of our problems.

However, when you are pregnant, no drug can be considered safe and harmless. In this chapter, we will examine chemicals and hazards that might seem ordinary, but can actually be very threatening to the pregnant woman.

It is very important to discuss any and all medications you have been taking with your clinician. Do not stop taking medication for preexisting medical problems such a diabetes, hypertension, epilepsy or heart disease, without first discussing it with your clinician who is aware of your pregnancy. He/she may want to adjust the dosage or change your medication now that you are pregnant.

The FDA has issued a warning to all patients not to consume any product which contains phenylpropanolamine (PPA) and has asked manufacturers to discontinue marketing products that contain PPA. Many cold and cough medications and appetite suppressants contained PPA. Some pharmacies have already removed all product that contain PPA from their shelves. Be sure to read the labels of any prescription or over-the-counter medication to be sure it does not contain PPA. Check your medicine cabinet to be sure you have no over-the-counter or prescription medication containing PPA.

Agents which can cause birth defects when a woman is exposed to them during her pregnancy are called teratogens. These agents can be drugs or chemicals in the environment, at home, or in the work place.

Common drugs

If you are pregnant and your clinician is aware of your pregnancy, you should not take any pill, capsule, powder or liquid medicine unless your clinician prescribes it. A common drug or household remedy which may be safe in normal situations can be dangerous to an embryo/fetus or pregnant woman. These common drugs include over-the-counter remedies such as aspirin, laxatives, cough and cold medicines, nose drops, external ointments, vitamins, antacids, tranquilizers and sedatives. Before you take any medicine, you should consult with your clinician because he or she knows about your body and your pregnancy.

There are a number of drugs commonly used today which should be discussed. One of these common drugs is aspirin. The American College of Obstetricians and Gynecologists (ACOG) notes there are conflicting conclusions regarding aspirin's role in causing birth defects. It has not been proven that aspirin does not cause birth defects. Some evidence from the research suggests that aspirin taken during pregnancy can change blood clotting factors in the mother and the baby, thus ACOG recommends that pregnant mothers do not take aspirin except under the supervision of their clinicians because aspirin may be potentially dangerous during pregnancy.

The research into the effect of aspirin on a pregnant woman and her fetus is continuing. As an alternative for relieving a headache, try taking a nap with a cold cloth covering your eyes, or go for a walk. If these aren't helpful ask your clinician for other recommendations.

Even if you put aside your aspirin bottle during your pregnancy, you must still be cautious, because aspirin is a common component of other medications. You'll need to read the labels of over-the-counter drugs such as pain relievers, cold remedies, sinus medicine and sedatives, most of which contain aspirin. Look for the words "acetylsalicylic acid" or "acetylsalicylate". These are scientific terms for aspirin, and they often appear on labels of other medications. Two other ingredients which are related to aspirin and should also be avoided are salicylates and salicylamides. The safest way to deal with aspirin derivatives is not to use any of these medicines at all. If you have a cold and need relief from the symptoms call your clinician. Do not take any over-the-counter medication without his/her advice.

The Harvard Health Letter published by the Harvard Medical School reported recent studies which indicated that if a pregnant woman took a low dose of aspirin (one baby aspirin) a day, she would decrease her risk of developing a complication of pregnancy called preeclampsia or toxemia. Preeclampsia is characterized by an increase in blood pressure, swelling of hands and feet, albumen in the urine, and/or headaches (see pages 42-43). Aspirin alone is not effective in relieving the symptoms once preeclampsia develops.

Unless specifically ordered by your physician

All pregnant woman are not advised to take low-dose aspirin daily. There is no evidence at this time that low-dose aspirin is even effective when taken during the early months of pregnancy. Do not take aspirin without first discussing this with your clinician.

There are many other nonprescription medications which have not been studied extensively, and thus it is not known if they can damage a fetus. It is wise to refrain from using any drug when little or no information about that drug's effect is known.

The drug **Accutane® (isotretinoin)**, used to treat severe acne, may cause birth defects and should not be used during pregnancy or for the month prior to becoming pregnant. Retin A, which is molecularly similar to Accutane, may also present a risk of birth defects and should not be used in pregnancy.

The Food and Drug Administration (FDA) and the manufacturer of the drug Accutane developed a system to manage Accutane-related teratogenicity (abnormal changes during the development of a fetus), known as SMART, which is designed to strengthen the existing pregnancy prevention program. The FDA recommends the pregnancy prevention program be required, including documentation of a negative pregnancy test to the pharmacy before a prescription for Accutane can be filled. An FDA advisory panel is now recommending even more restrictions to help reduce exposure of the fetus to this drug.

Two studies recently reported in the British medical journal, *Lancet*, indicated that males who were exposed to the drug phenobarbital before birth had long-term lower intelligence test scores. Exposure to this drug in late pregnancy had

Accutane® is a registered trademark of Roche Pharmaceuticals.

an even more profound effect. However, it is unclear if the effect is due solely to phenobarbital. Do not discontinue seizure medication without consulting with your physician.

If you use any mind altering drugs such as marijuana, cocaine or LSD, stop immeniately. There are important reasons why doctors insist that pregnant women avoid mind-altering drugs.

1. Recent studies have shown that women who use cocaine may have a higher rate of spontaneous abortion than women who do not use cocaine. In addition, if a fetus is exposed to cocaine, it may have a greater risk of birth defects and even death at or near the time of birth.

2. According to the American Academy of Pediatrics in a news release on September 8, 1993, researchers at the National Association for Perinatal Addiction Research and Education (NAPARE) tested 3-year-olds whose mothers used cocaine with alcohol, marijuana, and tobacco during pregnancy. Their findings showed there was a direct effect on the child's intelligence. The study indicates that children exposed to cocaine and other drugs prior to birth scored lower on intelligence tests. The level of development also depends on other factors such as individual behavioral characteristics and quality of home environment.

3. Because these are mind-altering drugs, some clinicians feel that a pregnant woman who is under their influence might not be fully in control of her situation during her pregnancy and, once the baby is born, might not provide the careful attention the child needs.

4. Research has shown that if a mother is addicted to a narcotic, her baby may be addicted at birth, and the baby could suffer from unrecognized symptoms of withdrawal.

5. Infants born to mothers who used cocaine during their pregnancies are more likely to have neurological and behavior problems, seizures and sudden infant death syndrome (SIDS) than are babies born to mothers who did not use cocaine during their pregnancies.

Smoking

There is no reason for you to smoke even if you were not pregnant. Your pregnancy is an excellent reason for you to quit. Smoking is not only a known health risk for you, but it can affect your fetus in a number of ways. Tobacco smoke is a major source of carbon monoxide which can interfere with the amount of oxygen your fetus receives. Carbon monoxide is also found in the exhaust fumes from automobiles. Consequently, if you are pregnant, you should avoid waiting in long gas lines or in traffic jams where cars are idling their engines.

Studies have shown that newborns whose mothers smoked have an increased incidence of birth defects and a higher risk of sudden infant death syndrome (SIDS). A study in Sweden found that mothers who smoked during pregnancy were more likely to give birth to babies with limb-reduction malformations. These risks increase in proportion to the number of cigarettes you smoke each day.

Researchers have also discovered that smoking can result in miscarriage, smaller babies, and premature births. A pregnant woman who smokes heavily may increase the chances of premature birth as much as 2 1/2 times the rate for non-smokers. Your smoking could make the difference if you have had repeated miscarriages or premature labor. A low birth weight can threaten the health of a baby—maybe even threaten its life—and smokers tend to have smaller babies.

Smoking during pregnancy can be an additional risk factor for very low birth weight (VLBW). According to studies, VLBW children whose mothers smoked

during pregnancy, were more likely to have an IQ score below 85. This is another good reason to give up smoking.

Passive smoke is also implicated in small-for-gestation babies and genetic mutations. Not only are pregnant women advised not to smoke, but they should also avoid spending time in places where other people smoke. A group of researchers at the University of Minnesota found evidence of nicotine in the urine of newborn babies whose mothers smoked. Researchers believe this proves nicotine, a known cancer-causing substance, crosses the placenta.

Should you have any questions regarding your pregnancy or the information found in this book, ask your clinician or other health professional.

Morning sickness can be complicated by smoking, and pregnant women often find smoking irritating. The American Cancer Society has designed programs to help pregnant women "kick" the smoking habit. For more information, call your local American Cancer Society office. For more information on how smoking affects your baby, see page 193-194.

Drugs that may be necessary

Our emphasis in this chapter has been on the dangers of drugs and the reasons why you should avoid them. However, in certain situations, drugs are necessary and sometimes vital for the health of both the mother and the fetus.

If a pregnant woman requires surgery, develops a severe infection, or suffers an injury, she would need some drugs for her treatment. In fact, not using drugs in those situations might be disastrous. Similarly, women with chronic diseases such as high blood pressure, diabetes or epilepsy may have to use drugs on a routine basis. If a woman finds herself in a life-threatening situation, drug therapy may be the only answer.

The key to using necessary drugs wisely is to remember the risk but consider the alternative. Often a drug that is equally effective but less powerful can be substituted or dosages changed. The clinician will evaluate the pregnant woman who needs drugs and monitor her usage. This close relationship with the clinician is the best way for a pregnant woman to minimize the risks while at the same time regaining or maintaining her own health.

Another example of necessary drug usage for the expectant mother might be vaccinations. Some vaccines, such as immunizations against diphtheria, tetanus and hepatitis, are permissible if the mother has not already been vaccinated or is in some risk of contagion. These vaccines should not be administered, though, until the 2nd or 3rd trimester of pregnancy. In contrast, live vaccines, such as those for rubella, measles or mumps, should not be given at all. (See pages 68-70) Statistics show that your chances for having a healthy baby are good, and you can handle most problems without endangering your baby's health. If you are taking any medication prescribed by your clinician, be sure he or she knows if you are trying to conceive. If you become pregnant, your clinician should be notified promptly.

Herbal supplements

Some products claim to treat pregnancy-related discomforts. Since herbs come from plants and are all-natural, many people believe they must be safe. This is not necessarily true. Some herbal preparations are known to be toxic, and on rare occasions fatal. Herbal medications can pose special risks to pregnant women and their fetuses.

There are about 400 herbs in common use today. Many sold as capsules, extracts, tablets and teas, for a variety of ailments. Unlike conventional drugs, herbal preparations are not regulated by the FDA. Manufacturers of herbal preparations are not required by law to submit studies demonstrating their safety and effectiveness. There are no standard quality controls over these preparations. As a result, the composition of an herbal supplement can vary from one batch to the next. Herbal products, on occasion, have been known to be contaminated with lead or other ingredients which could pose a threat to a pregnant patient.

An article appearing in the April 2003 issue of *OB-Gyn News*, specifically cited goldenseal, black cohosh and ephedra as herbal supplements which should not be used during pregnancy. An article appearing in the August 2004 issue of *Ob-Gyn News*, indicated that blue cohosh should be avoided entirely in pregnancy. Blue cohosh is often used in combination with black cohosh as a uterine tonic. Both have been known to cause complications in the fetus.

Dr. Ruth Lawrence, a pediatrician and lactation specialist warned that some herbals taken by breastfeeding mothers can cause problems. There are no scientific studies to back up the claims some herbs make, touting the improvements in the milk supply when taken by lactating women. Some herbs are known to interact with certain drugs.

Herbal teas such as chicory, orange spice, peppermint, raspberry, redbush and rose hips are considered safe for lactating mothers according to Dr. Lawrence. There are other herbals popular with breastfeeding mothers, which Dr. Lawrence states have no scientific studies backing up their claims and are known to have toxic side effects. These include:

- Fenugreek. At toxic levels this herb can induce labor and hypoglycemia (low blood sugar). Due to possible cross-allergic reactions, it should not be used in patients with a known allergy to peanuts.
- Comfrey. This herb can cause liver, failure particularly in infants, and should not be used by lactating mothers.* Comfrey is illegal in Canada.
- Ginkgo. Neither the American or Chinese variations have proven their claim that this herb increases the milk supply. The toxic effects of ginkgo are not known.
- Fennel. This folk remedy is for increasing milk supply. The amount used in tea is said to be harmless, however it is considered to be a volatile oil that can cause allergic rash and pulmonary edema (an accumulation of fluid in the lung tissue).
- Ginseng. This herb is purported to improve mental sharpness and stamina, though no such effects were shown in several scientific studies of this herb. Ginseng can cause withdrawal symptoms and apparent toxicity.

Studies are currently under way at the National Center for Complimentary and Alternative Medicine to clarify who can benefit from supplements. Until more is known, pregnant women and those who could become pregnant should be very cautious about using any herbal preparations. Always discuss this with your clinician before taking any herbal supplements. If you have any questions about specific herbal supplements call Motherisk at 416-813-6780 or go to the website www.motherisk.org.

Substances in the household

Just as there has been an increase in drugs in today's world, so too has there been an increase in the chemicals that we use in our homes. There are parts of our environment that we cannot control, but we should try to be aware of these chemicals in our own homes and avoid unnecessary exposure.

**The Food and Drug Administration recently sent out a warning letter to supplement manufacturers stating comfrey poses a serious health threat and should not be used as a dietary supplement.*

Paints and paint fumes should be avoided by the pregnant woman, especially oil-based paint and turpentine. There is no proof that these petroleum products cause harm, but there is also no proof that they do not. So it is best to let someone else paint the nursery. If you must help, stay off the ladder and keep the room well ventilated. The fumes could lead to dizziness and a fall.

Another household job that you should avoid is spraying the house or garden with insecticides or herbicides. These chemicals are potentially dangerous, and some can be absorbed through the skin. Give another family member the task of spraying insects and weeds.

A third category of household chemicals which you should handle with care are cleaning products. Many cleaning products have strong chemicals that can be absorbed through the skin. You can use these products safely if you take the proper precautions.

It is also a good idea to find substitutes whenever possible for aerosol sprays. The reason is that their mist can enter your lungs. So far, not much is known about the danger of these chemicals, but there is no point in taking a chance. Fortunately, mechanical pump containers have replaced many aerosol cans making it easier to find a suitable product for you needs.

Substances in the environment

Our environment contains a variety of chemicals and you can take some precautions against them. Air pollution caused by auto exhaust fumes should be avoided (see “Smoking” on page 133-135). The sanitation systems of some communities may not treat agricultural chemicals in the water. You can compensate by installing a filter on the tap that you use for drinking water, or you can buy bottled water. Some building materials contain formaldehyde or asbestos and should be avoided. When you buy produce, it is best to select products which have not been sprayed with agricultural insecticide or fertilizer. Since you may not know what chemicals were sprayed on them, it is best to wash all fruits and vegetables thoroughly.

Toxoplasmosis

Toxoplasmosis is caused by a one-celled organism called Toxoplasma, which often exists in cats and some food animals such as pigs, sheep and cattle. The organism causes a minor infection of the blood and other organs in human beings. Because it is such a mild disease, its victim usually does not notice it.

Toxoplasmosis can seriously damage a fetus. About one third of the babies born to mothers infected during their pregnancies are also infected at birth. These babies may be born prematurely, have a low birth weight, be jaundiced, have eye problems, and suffer from other long-range complications.

Therefore, precautions must be taken if you are a cat owner. Cats acquire the parasite by eating rats or mice which carry the parasite eggs. The parasite lodges in the cat's intestinal tract and completes a full life cycle, making new larvae. You may feel safe because you think that your cat does not eat rodents, but it is difficult to be sure if your cat spends any time outdoors.

Consequently, it is always best to be on the safe side to protect yourself and your baby. You do not have to get rid of the cat. You just need to take the following precautions:

- Do not empty or clean the cat's litterbox. Let someone else handle that chore. The reason is that the parasite's eggs are passed from the cat's intestinal tract into its feces.
- Changing the litter every day will prevent the parasite eggs from becoming infective during the first 24 hours after they are passed.
- Whenever you handle the cat or any of its belongings, wash your hands thoroughly.
- Wear gloves when gardening.
- Avoid stray cats.

If you own a dog, you do not need to worry about toxoplasmosis. This parasite does not use dogs as a host. In fact, we do not know of any other disease carried by dogs that is dangerous to pregnant women. If you do not own a cat, there are still some precautions you should take because toxoplasma eggs are carried by some food animals which pick up the eggs from the soil and grasses that they eat. The most common offenders are lamb and pork, but beef cattle can be infected as well. In order to be completely free of toxoplasmosis, all of your meat should be well cooked. Heat kills this organism. You should also wash your hands thoroughly after handling raw meat.

In summary

Some people think that a fetus is safely sheltered inside its mother, away from the toxic environment outside, but this is not entirely true. This chapter examined how drugs and other substances can pass from the outside environment to the mother and subsequently to the fetus. This information is not meant to frighten you. It is provided to make you aware of what can help as well as harm your fetus as it develops. The rule of moderation operates in regard to drugs. If you combine common sense with the information in this chapter about drugs, your fetus will grow and develop properly. Be assured that statistics continue to show most babies will be born normal and healthy. See chart on page 230, "Agents Known to be Harmful to Fetus."

Chapter 14 Personal hygiene and appearance

NOW THAT YOU ARE PREGNANT you will likely be even more aware and conscientious about your personal appearance. For both reasons of comfort and hygiene, changes in your bathing routine, hair style, cosmetics, and wardrobe can help improve your overall sense of well-being during pregnancy.

Bathing

You can assure a feeling of freshness by taking a daily shower or bath, whichever you prefer. Bathing can have many benefits. A daily bath will wash away accumulated wastes that may lodge in the enlarged pores of your skin. And, a warm bath can be very relaxing, though there are a few precautions you should take. As your abdomen gets larger and heavier, you may need assistance getting into and out of the tub. To prevent falls use a non-slip mat on the floor. Tub baths are not harmful even at the end of your pregnancy, but you do need to limit the temperature of your bath water.

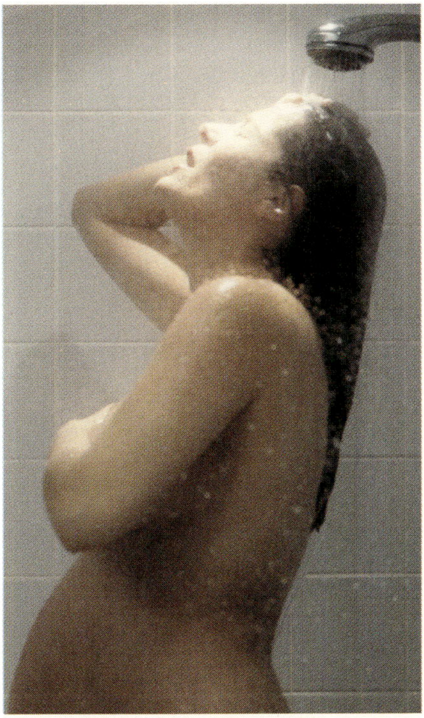

There have been several studies indicating that hot baths, saunas, hot tubs, and sitz baths during the first 3 months of a pregnancy may increase the risk of birth defects. Lukewarm baths are permissible. A recent study of 23,000 women who had heat expo-

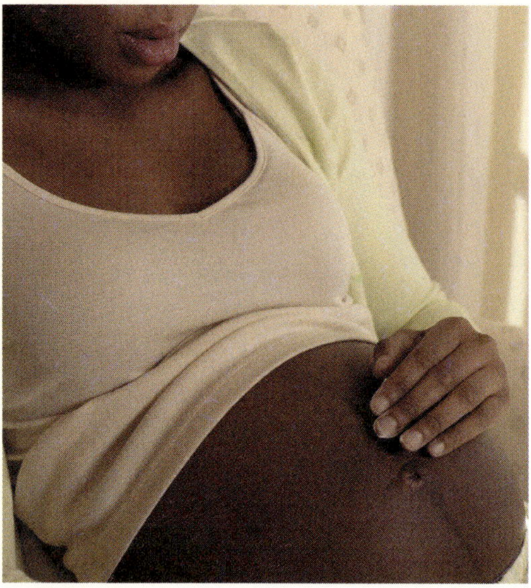

sure from a sauna, hot tub or a fever during the first three months of their pregnancies supports the theory that heat is a teratogen, an agent that can cause birth defects when a woman is exposed to it during her pregnancy.

Personal Hygeine

In an earlier chapter, we discussed the fact that your body is excreting waste material for the fetus as well as for yourself. As a result, your pregnancy has increased both the frequency of urination and amount of urine you are excreting. Trips to the bathroom will be more frequent, and the pressure of the fetus on your bladder may cause some occasional leakage when laughing or moving around.

If you have a vaginal discharge, mild soap and water is all you need to cleanse yourself. Douching, vaginal deodorants and sprays should be avoided during pregnancy.

Be aware also that during pregnancy your nipples may become caked from a discharge of colostrum. They should be washed gently with soft cotton and warm water without using soap. Avoid stimulating the nipples by gently patting, not rubbing them dry.

Your skin

During pregnancy, your skin may undergo a variety of changes. You may notice you are perspiring more. Your skin may be drier or more oily than usual. Also, your skin tone may be more florid. All this is normal.

You can easily adapt your grooming routine to accommodate the changes you are experiencing to maintain your appearance and comfort throughout your pregnancy. If your skin becomes drier it may need lubrication to smooth and soften it. For this, use a liquid moisturizer. Always applying it before your make-up. Dark circles may occur around your eyes, especially if you are a brunette. These circles will eventually disappear. In the meantime, you can cover them with foundation. If your skin color becomes too rosy due to the increased circulation of blood, you can tone it down by using a soft, translucent shade of powder.

Chloasma is the name for brownish blotches that appear around the eyes and nose. These will disappear or fade after delivery when hormone levels return to normal. Skin changes seem to increase with sunlight.

You may notice red spots on your body called angiomas. Some women also notice a reddish color on the palms of their hands. This is palmer erythema. Both of these conditions are caused by the high level of estrogen in the body and will disappear after delivery.

Hair removal from your legs can also irritate dry skin, but you can compensate by shaving with a lotion instead of soap lather, and moisturizing the area afterwards. Depilatories contain strong substances that may increase dryness and irritation should be avoided.

Sometimes your glands will be overly active and may cause a skin condition that resembles acne. The best solution is to treat it like acne with extra washings of warm, sudsy water. However, do not use the drug Accutane, which is used to treat severe acne, because it has been linked to birth defects. Do not use wrinkle creams containing Retin A or Renova, since both products contain vitamin A derivatives. As discussed in Chapter 10, vitamin A is important to good health, but may be responsible for birth defects when taken in large amounts during pregnancy.

There is one type of rash which only occurs in pregnant women called pruritic urticarial papules or PUPP. This rash can cause severe itching. It is characterized by hives or red patches which appear first in the stretch marks on the abdomen. The rash can then spread to the arms, legs and back. Fortunately, it almost never spreads to the face.

PUPP is more common during a first pregnancy and in women having twins. This condition usually occurs late in the pregnancy and poses no risk to the fetus. The only sure way to make it disappear is to deliver your baby. If you are still weeks away from your due date, ask your healthcare professional to recommend something to relieve the itching.

Many women notice another change in their skin called the linea nigra. This is a darkening of a line running from the top of the abdomen to the bottom. As your pregnancy progresses, other streaks or stretch marks may appear on your abdomen or breasts. You cannot prevent these stretch marks, but they will slowly fade after your delivery.

Your hair

There are several possible changes that may occur to your hair during pregnancy. Hormone changes and glandular secretions may cause your hair to become oilier or drier. You may need to wash your hair more often than before you became pregnant. Changing shampoos or hair dressing to recondition your hair may help.

You may also want to try different hairstyles. For example, if you have long hair that becomes thin and scraggly, you might try a shorter hairstyle that is higher on the head. If your face becomes fuller, perhaps you can change your hair to a style which better complements your new appearance.

One problem that some women have is loss of hair. If your hair does start to thin out, you should avoid processes such as permanents, straightening, or coloring. All of these use chemicals which can damage thin or dry hair. The safety of hair dyes on the fetus has not yet been determined conclusively. For this reason many women postpone coloring their hair until after their pregnancies. Should you decide to permanent your hair, keep in mind the solution used contains ammonia. To ensure your own safety, be certain you are in a well ventilated area when applying the solution to your hair.

Avoid hair removal creams (depilatories) containing chemicals that have not been extensively studied. Waxing or shaving unwanted hair is safe.

Your clothes

Today's mother-to-be is fortunate to have a wide variety of fashions available to choose from. You can find clothes that will allow you to dress for every occasion in comfort and style. Designers have become more and more aware that they need to offer women maternity fashions which are attractive and inexpensive. You will probably feel the need for larger clothes about the middle of the 4th month of pregnancy.

Department stores offer a wide variety of maternity clothes. You can also find many styles in mail order catalogs and online. There are many selections of sports outfits, bathing suits, and lounging apparel available. If you enjoy styling and sewing your own clothes, and have the time, there are patterns available which can be assembled quickly and inexpensively. Or you could take some of your existing clothes and tailor them.

In selecting clothes, it's wise to choose those that don't bind and are attractive and serviceable. Look for clothes with details near the shoulders, and a neckline that takes attention away from your middle.

For the clothes you will wear every day, look for durable, easily washable fabrics. There are fashionable clothes available in styles for everything from cocktail parties to wedding receptions.

Avoid wearing high-heeled shoes.

Your choice of clothes really depends on your life style, whether you stay at home or work elsewhere, whether you socialize or entertain, or whether you like to sit by the fire in slacks. Generally you will need only a few new outfits, and you can accent these with the accessories you already own. Any new accessories that you buy can become a part of your regular wardrobe in the future.

Another sensible alternative for your wardrobe is the inclusion of separates. By mixing and matching a variety of colorful blouses, you can recycle a pair of slacks and a skirt many times.

As your breasts enlarge, you can either buy a maternity bra or a regular bra in a larger size. Maternity bras are specially designed to give more support than ordinary bras, and most women find them more comfortable. You will have to decide what type you prefer and decide when you feel you need one, based on the size, heaviness and discomfort of your breasts. When you get to the later stages of your pregnancy, you may want to select a nursing bra which has panels on the cup that unhook for easy breastfeeding. Some clinicians recommend that you wear a bra at all times.

Most women now prefer to wear pantihose. There are two styles of maternity pantihose available, support maternity pantihose and regular sheer maternity pantihose. Regular queen-size pantihose (for larger, not taller figures) are less expensive than maternity pantihose.

Underpants should be larger than your normal size so that they don't bind or cause irritation. A cotton crotch is preferred because it is more absorbent and also because it allows air to flow to the genital area. You will have to wash these garments numerous times, so unless your finances are well above the average, you should choose less glamorous designs rather than frilly, fragile lingerie.

Flat-heeled or low, broad-heeled shoes are the most sensible for the pregnant woman. As your abdomen becomes larger, your center of equilibrium changes. There should be no major problems adjusting to this change, but you may not be able to move as gracefully, quickly or with the same surefootedness as before. You'll find high heels are impractical from the point of view of both safety and comfort. They tend to thrust the abdomen forward and create a swayback posture, possibly resulting in backaches and leg cramps. Clinicians recommend avoiding footwear that lifts your heels 3 to 4 inches off the ground and pushes your weight forward, so that it has to be supported by the balls of your feet and your toes.

Chapter 15 The father's role

FOR A LONG TIME, CHILDBIRTH had been viewed from a narrow perspective in which everyone involved was thought to be excited and happy. Recently, however, a study by two prominent sociologists discovered that having a child can be a serious crisis in a marriage. The question is why this occurs?

The reason is that having a child can threaten the balance of responsibility and compatibility in a marriage. For example, if both young parents have been working, the new child can mean additional expenses for only one income. Also, a woman who enjoys her work and the time spent with adults may now find that her new responsibilities are stifling and boring. The woman may understand that she has to give up many aspects of her former lifestyle, but she may be resentful. Even though she may be interested in everything associated with childbirth, she can still become temperamental and irritable.

In such situations, the woman can make the mistake of shutting the husband out because she feels that she is the only one involved in the childbirth. One husband who faced such a situation spoke for many husbands when he said, "Karen has been so wrapped up in having a baby for so long that sometimes I feel as though she has forgotten about me." Such an example can help the woman to remember that childbirth is a family affair, and that the father should not be left out. What can be done to make sure that the father is involved and feels important?

Sharing with the father

One of the changes that takes place in the pregnant woman is the increased production of great quantities of certain hormones which are needed for motherhood. These hormone changes affect your brain as well as your body, and they help to prepare you psychologically for an innate maternal feeling. While these changes are occurring in your delicate system, no such changes are taking place inside the father. In fact, the father often does not grasp the feeling of fatherhood until he finally holds the new child in his arms.

It is important to help the father gradually share the experience of pregnancy. You can do this in several ways. First, have the father talk with your clinician as soon as you find out that you are pregnant, and tell the father about each step you are going through and what the clinician is advising. Clinicians much prefer to have both of the prospective parents involved and informed. Second, give your partner this book so that he will be able to understand all of the changes, both physical and emotional, that are occurring within you. After reading this book, the father will be more understanding when you complain about a backache, stomach upset, or leg pains, and he will also know that these conditions are normal. Instead of worrying over each of your minor physical changes, he can be solicitous and helpful. Third, as your pregnancy develops, encourage the partner to put his hand on your abdomen so that he can feel the baby's movement and share the experience. Consult with him when you select the baby's furnishings and planning the routine for your new baby. Finally, you need to remember that while so much of your time and energy is being spent planning for the baby, that you can't forget to make time for each other. You are both under more than the usual amount of stress at this time, so it is especially important that both of you are more understanding and thoughtful of each other, and that you set aside quality time to spend together.

Sexual relations

There is so much misinformation about sexual intercourse during pregnancy that clinicians often marvel at the highly imaginative questions which their patients ask. Because sex is an important part of your life, an objective look at the facts will help.

During a normal pregnancy, sexual relations are not harmful. If there is no bleeding and your membranes have not ruptured, intercourse anytime during your pregnancy is desirable, permissible and safe. The rule of moderation should also be followed.

Of course, the woman's body is changing shape, so some adjustments may be required from your normal habits. Pregnancy can even be a good time to experiment with new sexual positions. The changes in the woman's shape during pregnancy can make the position in which the male is above the female awkward or uncomfortable. If so, you may find it more comfortable for the female to assume the position above the male. Other positions can be tried to satisfy individual needs. If vaginal discomfort occurs due to lack of lubrication, try applying a lotion, jelly or cream to the genital area, but be sure to check with your clinician first.

Sex play during pregnancy is alright as long as you observe certain restrictions. The most important is that air should not be forced into the vagina at anytime. Although it is rare, an air embolism can occur. During pregnancy there is an increase in blood flow, and air passing into the uterus can enter the blood stream and cause serious problems.

There are no rules concerning frequency of sexual intercourse. Simply consider your own physical desires and use mature judgement. Interestingly, it has been recognized that some women experience heightened sexual desire during pregnancy because of the increase in their female hormones. Having an orgasm is not harmful in any way, and in fact, knowing that you do not have to fear becoming pregnant tends to increase the sexual enjoyment.

More than ever before, it is important for both parents to remain faithful to each other in a monogamous relationship. During pregnancy there are greater risks involved with sexually transmitted diseases. Such diseases can be dangerous to both the mother and the fetus (see pages 10-12). Beyond these simple guidelines, any further questions about the practice of sexual activities should be discussed with your clinician. Have an open, candid discussion with him or her. In the last four weeks of pregnancy, it may be desirable to limit some sexual relations, but only rarely is it necessary to completely abstain from sex at any time during the pregnancy.

Fathers in the labor and delivery rooms

There are arguments for each side on whether the prospective father should accompany his partner throughout labor and delivery. While some hospitals permit it, others do not. Your clinician will be able to tell you whether this is possible, practical and, depending on your personal situation, recommended. Usually if a hospital allows the father into the delivery room, he may be required to attend classes for new parents.

Classes for the father

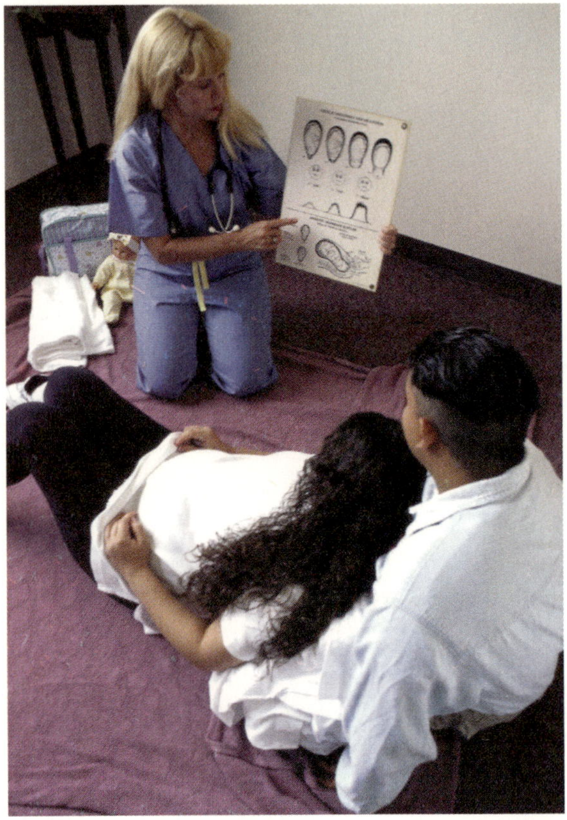

Classes for first-time fathers are sponsored by many civic organizations including your hospital, the local Red Cross, the YMCA or Maternal Health Centers. To find such programs, you should ask your clinician, call your hospital, or look in the phone book for the appropriate organization. The classes usually focus on giving practical advice concerning the father's role during pregnancy. They also show the father how to help with the new baby.

Men are also able to reassure one another during these classes, and most sessions include both the prospective father and the mother. If you take the classes together, you can not only have fun as a couple, but also build a solid basis of shared companionship for your adventure ahead.

Chapter 16 Making plans

PLANNING FOR YOUR NEW BABY'S FUTURE is a fun and exciting part of of the new adventure ahead of you. Preparing yourself for your baby's birth, and understandiing how to care for and nourish your child before his or her arrival, will give you confidence as your new life as a family begins.

Prepared childbirth

For the general public, this has become one of the most interesting aspects of childbirth. Still, there are many people who are confused by the term prepared childbirth and have misconceptions regarding exactly what it means.

In prepared childbirth, the pregnant woman strives to deliver her baby using the natural function of labor. She can and does take advantage of modern facilities, and there is complete medical supervision. Whether medication and instruments are used depends on the mother's progress during delivery. If a woman would like to have her baby naturally and without anesthesia, she needs to take childbirth classes which prepare her both psychologically and physically. In prepared childbirth, the clinician is at the woman's side to supervise and guide, direct the progress of labor, and manage any situation that may arise. Prepared childbirth stresses that the team around the woman— the father or attending coach, the clinician, and the nurse— assist and encourage her.

Practicing relaxation techniques before the delivery helps relieve tension and stress. Not only is this important during labor and birthing, it also helps you cope with anxiety and stress in everyday life. Choose a quiet environment and a comfortable position when practicing. For some, sitting in a tailor position (see page 124) or lying on your side with pillows under your knees or supporting your back and/or your abdomen, may be most relaxing. Breathing exercises such as inhaling slowly through your nose, holding for 4-5 seconds, then slowly and deeply exhaling, repeated 3 or 4 times, will help you relax. Listening to soft music, looking at a picture that has a pleasant meaning for you, or writing your feelings in a journal, are relaxation techniques that may work as well. A gentle massage may also be relaxing. Childbirth classes will help you learn additional breathing and relaxation techniques. Training yourself to relax can help decrease:

- Pain perception
- Lessen muscle resistance to the dilation of the cervix
- Reduce fatigue during childbirth.

The idea behind natural childbirth and the appeal it has for mothers are the same— safety for the baby and satisfaction for the mother. The main advantage for the clinician is also increased safety because fewer drugs are needed. Safety for the baby is always the prime consideration for the mother. Another important consideration for her is that she will enjoy the experience more if she has learned and practiced the routine and knows what she is doing.

Lamaze is one of the best known techniques of prepared childbirth. It focuses on shallow rapid breathing to make the pain more bearable. Other techniques include the Bradley method and the Dick-Read techniques.

You do not have to decide right away whether you prefer this type of delivery, but you should consider it. You can even get a better idea of what it is all about by attending some prepared childbirth classes. Your pregnancy will be unique to you, so your needs and reactions may change as your pregnancy progresses. You can discuss the types of delivery with your clinician sometime during the second trimester. Regardless of your decision, in the delivery room you must be prepared to let your clinician decide on the proper procedures. He or she will determine the best and most appropriate course of action for you and your baby.

Doula

Doula is a Greek word meaning "mothering the mother." There are courses available that are designed to train individuals to become doulas. Some doulas stay with the woman during labor, providing emotional support, comforting measures and a listening ear in order to help promote positive birth experiences. An article appearing in the June 15, 1998 issue of *OB-GYN News*, explained that doulas gave the mother an emotional support that could not be provided by family members and medical personnel in the delivery room. By focusing entirely on the emotional needs of the woman, the cesarean rate was purported to be reduced. Doulas do not replace a woman's partner or any of the healthcare providers. Some doulas are trained to provide in-home postpartum care for the new mother and her family.

Breastfeeding

Breastfeeding offers many benefits not only for the baby but also for the mother. Your decision whether or not to breastfeed should be based on a knowledge of these benefits as well as your own feelings about breastfeeding and those of your partner. Your clinician, nurse or childcare educator can answer any questions you may have about this.

Some advantages of breastfeeding for the mother are:

- Breastfeeding aids in restoring your figure more quickly to its normal, non-pregnant state. As the baby sucks on the nipple, contractions of the uterus are stimulated which help to expel any remaining bits of tissue lining the uterus. These contractions during nursing also help "firm" the uterus, which helps control bleeding. This is effective only if your clinician's examination reveals no other cause for the heavy bleeding.

- Breastfeeding is safer, easier, faster, more economical and more convenient. There's no formula to buy, mix, refrigerate and reheat, and no bottles and nipples to sterilize.

- Surveys by the American Cancer Society and other researchers in the field found women who breastfeed have a lower incidence of breast cancer.

- Breastfeeding may temporarily eliminate, delay or reduce the menstrual flow. This helps to prevent a drain on the mother's iron reserves when she needs every bit of energy. As menstruation resumes, the mother may continue to nurse without any harmful effect.

- A first-time mother will gain confidence sooner in her ability to take care of her baby. You get a chance to observe your baby more often and more closely. This constant contact makes you more aware of your baby's needs, reactions and development.

If breasts become too full or mother has to be away for a feeding or two, the breast milk may be easily expressed by hand or with the aid of a device called a breast pump. Breast milk can be stored for brief periods and used by caregivers to feed the baby while you are away. You should discuss this with your clinician.

Breastfeeding and contraception

Although there is frequently a delay in the return of menstruation in women who breastfeed, this does not mean you cannot become pregnant. Breastfeeding should not be relied upon as a means of contraception. To avoid pregnancy while breastfeeding, it is essential that you use some medically approved method of contraception, provided you have no religious or moral objections to this.

> *Oral contraceptives are not contraindicated in breastfeeding women as long as they are initiated after the milk supply is fully established.*

The American College of Obstetricians and Gynecologists (ACOG) issued a directive published in their May 1989 newsletter to alert members to its current opinion "...that oral contraceptives are not contraindicated in breast feeding women." Birth control pills that contain estrogen and progesterone may decrease your milk supply. Alternative pills with just progesterone do not have this effect. Discuss this with your clinician. Remember, there are also alternative contraceptive measures such as the diaphragm or a condom.

Some advantages of breastfeeding for baby

Breast milk is a perfect baby food because it has all the necessary food elements in just the right proportions necessary for healthy development.

Among its other advantages:

- Breast milk offers immunological protection. The substance found in colostrum, the milky or yellowish fluid secreted by the mammary glands a few days before and after birth, as well as in the mature milk, protects your baby against a number of infections. The colostrum also acts as a laxative, helping clear the baby's body of mucus and meconium, a black stool which builds up during the last months of pregnancy. Colostrum also contains growth factors and hormones which can stimulate cell growth. It is therefore beneficial to your baby to breastfeed if even for only a short period of time.
- Recent studies indicate breastfed infants may be less likely to fall victim to sudden infant death syndrome (SIDS) than those fed cow's milk or formula.
- Breast milk is more easily digestible. Breastfed babies have fewer feeding problems and intestinal disorders.
- Breast milk is sterile and always fresh.

- Breastfed babies have fewer skin disorders and allergies.
- Breastfeeding is reported to have the potential to prevent obesity in children.
- Breastfeeding develops a close mother-baby attachment that extends far beyond infancy.

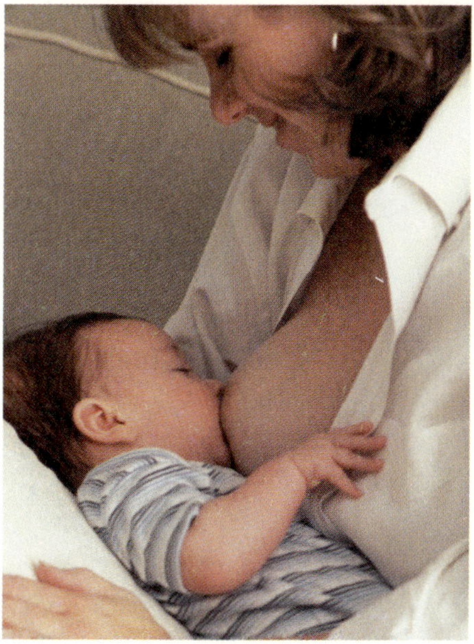

Preparing your breasts

Preparation of the breasts for breastfeeding should begin during your pregnancy. Avoid using soaps, creams, lotions, and ointments on your nipples unless you have a problem and your clinician advises or prescribes something specifically for you. Dr. Ruth Lawrence, Professor of Pediatrics and Obstetrics and Gynecology at the University of Rochester School of Medicine in Rochester, New York, stated in her book *Breastfeeding* (1994),"...aggressive and abrasive treatment of the nipples does not prevent nipple pain postpartum and may actually enhance it." She does suggest that the most effective preparation is usually gentle love-making involving the breasts.

Formula feeding

Doctors enthusiastically advocate breastfeeding and encourage their patients to consider it and at least give it a fair trial. Formula feeding is an option which has been successful with millions of babies who have grown and developed normally. Bottle feeding has both advantages and disadvantages. With bottle feeding,

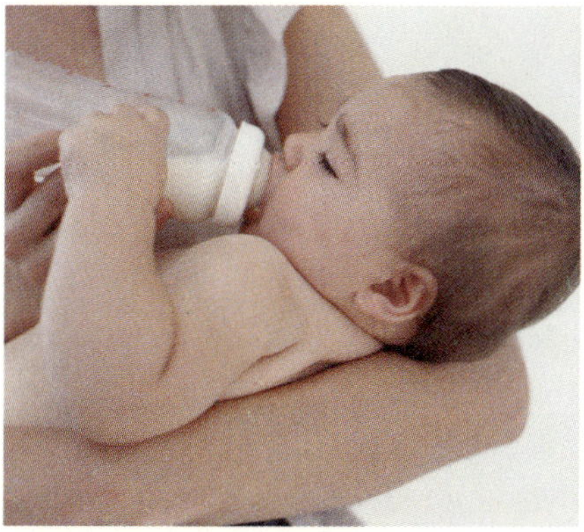

you can more easily determine whether the child is sufficiently satisfied because you have control over and knowledge of the amount of formula your baby drinks. For example, you can easily increase the amount of formula per feeding if you find that your baby still seems hungry after an initial feeding. Bottlefed babies tend to require fewer feedings fairly soon, although you still need to plan time each day for preparing the formula. Bottle feeding enables your partner or someone else to take over some of the night feedings. And when feeding from a bottle, your baby will still be held in your arms and feel your love and affection from the experience.

One disadvantage is that colic and other intestinal disorders are not uncommon among babies fed from a bottle. This may be cause for some anxiety and frustration until the best and most satisfactory formula is developed.

Certainly it is true that the advantages of breastfeeding far outweigh those of bottle feeding, but with either option, think over the various advantages and disadvantages discussed here. The final decision can really wait until after your baby is born. Consult with your healthcare provider to determine which method of feeding will work best for you and your baby. Your final decision should not be based on the advice of friends. If you are a healthy mother, and most are, you should try breastfeeding and then decide whether you want to continue with it. **If, for some reason, you cannot breastfeed, you should not feel guilty. Your baby can still grow up healthy and well adjusted if it is fed from a bottle.**

If you will be bottle feeding your child, the following supply of bottles and other equipment are recommended:

- 8 bottles with nipples and caps, 8-ounce size. These are available in boilable plastic as well as glass. You may also want to buy a few 4-ounce bottles for water, but the 8-ounce bottles are sufficient.
- A 32-ounce measuring pitcher
- Funnel
- Tongs for taking bottles out of boiling water
- Extra nipples
- Bottle sterilizer or large pot
- If you breastfeed, you will want a few bottles for water, supplemental feedings, or expressed-milk feedings.

It is a good idea to investigate the selection of disposable bottles available and discuss them with your clinician.

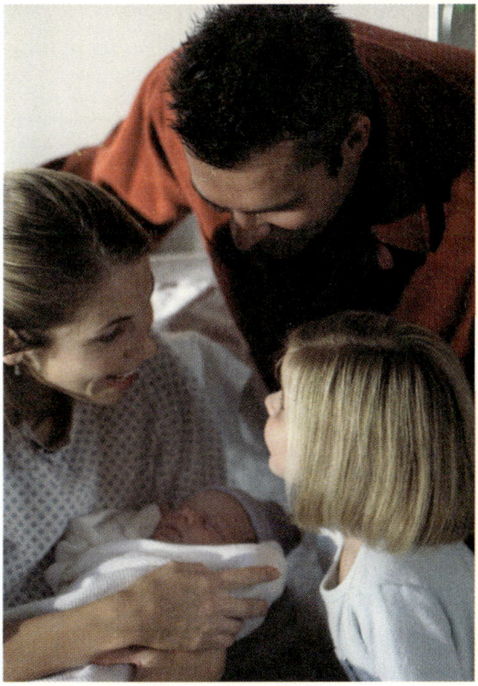

As for baby formula, your clinician will advise you before you take your baby home about the formula preparation. These things can be purchased at the drugstore.

Telling other children about the baby

When is the best time to tell your other children about the new brother or sister who will be joining the family? It really depends upon the ages of the older children. But regardless of their age, it is always best to inform them before going to the hospital and the baby is born. An older child should not be suddenly surprised with a newborn baby as though the baby were a new toy. Let your common sense and intelligence guide you when deciding the appropriate time to convey the news. In the following paragraphs, are some suggestions that may help you with possible approaches to the issue.

Because your 2-, 3-, or 4-year-old children have little concept of time, it is unnecessary to tell them from the moment you are pregnant. Children have difficulty distinguishing between tomorrow and 8 months from now, so there is no need to burden them with the suspense. A good time to tell them is about the 4th or 5th month, when your abdomen is obviously growing larger. By then your child will probably recognize that something important is about to happen. Since the lives of the other children will certainly be affected, they will want to know what is going on and should be told.

A natural and intelligent method of breaking the news is for the mother to casually and simply take the child aside and say, “In a little while, there will be a new baby in the house.” You could then explain what babies look like and what will happen to the family when the baby arrives. Some questions should be avoided. For example, do not ask your child: “How would you like to share your room?” or “How would you like to sleep in a big bed so that the new baby can have your crib?” Both questions are likely to elicit a negative response from the child.

Your attitude needs to be positive and firm as you plan for the new addition to your household. Try to help the older children of school age see the newcomer as an event that is exciting and one in which they will continue to be important and necessary. For example, you could take them to a maternity hospital or show them pictures in a book to help eliminate their apprehensions. Include them when you begin planning the baby's room. One good way to make older children feel involved is to give them additional small responsibilities as though they are helping you. Depending on their ages and capabilities, small chores like making beds or cleaning tables can give them the sense that they are being helpful. They will then enjoy their new importance and independence and understand the reasons behind it.

There are also some attitudes you should avoid. Do not give the older child the impression that the new baby is taking his or her place, and do not tell older children that the attention which they formerly received must now be shared. In fact, it is important to give the older children even more attention when you bring the new baby home. Another good idea is to keep a few items on hand to give to the other children when friends send gifts to the baby. Whenever you think that the older children need it, you should bestow your attention on them because young children need constant reassurance that they are loved. Occasionally you may even want to express some slight annoyance toward the new baby so that the older children will be reassured that the baby is not the center of the universe. Keeping your other children feeling important, loved, and involved can be a delicate balancing act, but it will pay dividends in avoiding unnecessary problems later.

Information on complex topics like jealousy and rivalry can be found in other books which your pediatrician can recommend. One book, by the same publisher as the one you are now reading, entitled, *A Doctor Discusses Your Life After the Baby is Born*, devotes a special chapter to these issues. Books can be helpful as guidelines, but do not substitute them for your own thinking when problems arise. The best decisions you make concerning the raising of your children will come from your intelligence, your practical experience, and your common sense.

Preparations for your return home

During the latter part of your pregnancy, you should make plans to have someone at home to help you when you return from the hospital. This can be a family member or close friend. Earlier we mentioned the role of the Doula, a woman trained in the postpartum care of new mothers and their families. (See pages

152-153) For some mothers, such a person may provide the care needed.

To request the form needed to apply for a social security number for your baby call: 800-772-1213

Your brief stay in the hospital after hours of labor and delivery may leave you exhausted. Do not expect to return home from the hospital with your baby and immediately step back in to your previous household routine as well as caring for a new baby. If you are unable to have a doula, try to arrange for a mother's helper or housekeeper to be at your home when you arrive from the hospital. It will be worth the cost. If, however, you can't do this, arrange to have a member of the family or a close friend come in during the day to give you a hand. If you can't arrange help with the baby, at least have someone there to help you with housework and preparing meals. Your partner and older children, if you have any, can assume a few more chores until you get your strength back.

Fatigue is to be expected during those first few weeks postpartum. You should arrange to take naps while your baby is sleeping. Let someone else clean the house or prepare a meal. The additional rest you get during those first weeks home will allow you to regain your strength and emotional well-being more rapidly.

Baby's doctor

Planning ahead should not only include your needs, it is also the time to select a doctor for your baby. Your baby's doctor could be your family physician or a pediatrician. He or she should check your baby before you are discharged from the hospital. If the doctor you have selected is not on staff at the hospital where your baby is, ask your clinician to arrange for a hospital resident or staff member to examine your baby before you bring him/her home.

During your baby's first year, he or she will need to be checked once a month, unless there is a problem requiring more frequent visits. As a rule, visits to the baby's doctor during his or her second year of life are once every three months. At these visits, the baby's weight and development will be checked. If necessary, changes may be made in the feeding schedule, and required inoculations will be administered. Should any problems arise such as colic, rashes or digestive disorders, the doctor you selected will be familiar with your baby and better able to make recommendations.

Packing a bag for the hospital

If your hospital requires a reservation, you or your healthcare provider can make one at the appropriate time prior to your due date. The hospital will take care of many of your needs, so there won't be a great many items you'll need to bring. For example, nightgowns and basic sanitary items are provided.

For style and comfort, you can certainly improve on some of what is provided in the hospital. Which is why it is a good idea to have an overnight bag packed and ready in case you have to leave for the hospital in a hurry. The following is a list of basic items you will need, but if you happen to forget a few, do not worry. The hospital gift shop stocks some items, or your partner can bring any others when coming to visit you.

Bring with you:

- Bathrobe, flat slippers
- Two or three nightgowns (perhaps with a front opening for breast feeding)
- Toothbrush and toothpaste, deodorant
- Hair brush, comb, compact, and other cosmetics
- One or two bras the same size as you wore when pregnant, or nursing bras if you plan to nurse
- Your address book for making phone calls and sending out birth announcements
- Birth announcement cards, stamps, stationery, pen, pencils
- A book or some magazines
- Small change
- Loose fitting clothes to wear home
- Camera with film and batteries
- Insurance card and identification

What to pack for the baby

While the baby is in the nursery, the hospital will provide diapers and shirts, but when you take your baby home, you will need the following items:

- Two or three diapers
- Waterproof panties
- Cotton shirt
- Diaper safety pins if using cloth diapers
- Wrapper
- Knit Cap
- Blankets or bunting

Depending on the weather, the nurse will advise you on what you need and will help you dress the baby for going home. Also, before bringing the baby home, remember to install the infant car carrier (see pages 162-164).

Homecoming plans

It is a good idea to get things ready before the baby is born because you will have more time to make careful selections. On a practical level, a sturdy, well made, full-size crib is your best investment because your baby can use it until the age of 2 or 3. You might think this crib looks gigantic, but remember that time passes quickly. Money spent on fancy furniture is really fulfilling your desires, not the baby's. For example, there are beautifully decorated bassinets available, but they are not practical because the baby outgrows them in a month or two. You can also buy a small-size crib, but again, the baby will outgrow it by the 4th month.

The American Academy of Pediatrics has issued the following crib safety recommendations:

- Crib slats must not be more than 2 3/8 inches apart to prevent the baby from catching his or her head between the slats.
- When lowered, the crib sides should be 4 inches above the top of the mattress or 9 inches above the mattress support.
- When the mattress is placed in its lowest position and the crib side is up, there should be 22 to 26 inches from the top of the side rail to the mattress support.
- The sides must be operated with a locking latch that cannot be accidentally released.
- The mattress must be the same size as the crib so that it fits snugly into the crib frame. This is to prevent the baby from wedging his/her body between the mattress and crib side, and suffocating. For the same reason, a bumper guard should be used until the child is able to stand alone. The mattress cover should be moisture-proof and easy to clean.
- The surfaces of the crib should be free of splinters and cracks, and painted with nontoxic, lead-free paint. The latches and hardware should not have rough edges.

New Federal Recommendations

No child aged 12 years or younger should ride in the front seat of a car with a passenger-side air bag.

It is a good idea to buy sturdy furniture that is well made because it will get a great deal of wear and tear. You can purchase a dresser which matches the crib, and there are furniture sets available which can grow with your baby. In other words, as time passes, you can add a toy chest, desk or other dressers, all of which match the crib.

What else will you need? A night light is essential. Many mothers recommend a dressing or changing table with drawers for diapers and clothing. This eliminates the strain caused by bending over to change and bathe the baby. Washable throw rugs are preferable to wall-to-wall carpeting because the latter retains too much dust. Be sure to have a non-slip pad under the rug to prevent slipping or falling while carrying the baby. Eventually you will need a high chair and a stroller.

Car Carrier

You must have a car carrier for the baby. The recommended car safety seat is a high-backed, molded bucket seat which faces the rear of the car, never the front.The carrier is designed to be strapped to the car seat with the lap belt and should have a harness to restrain the baby.

For more information on car seats send a self-addressed stamped envelope to:

SAFE RIDE PROGRAM

American Academy of Pediatrics

141 Northwest Point Blvd.
P.O. Box 927
Elk Village, IL
60009-0927

The advantage of the infant car seat is that it is small, portable, and best fits small newborns. The disadvantage is that it must be replaced by a convertible seat when baby reaches about 20 pounds. Infant seats come with a 3-point harness or a 5-point harness.

Several infant-only seat models come with detachable bases. The base attaches to the car and the car seat snaps into the base. The base must fit tightly into the car. In some cases the seat may fit better without the base.

The advantage of the convertible car seat is that it fits a child from 7 to 8 pounds to about 40 pounds. The disadvantage is that it is bulky and less portable than an infant car seat.

According to an article in the August 2002 issue of the *American Academy of Pediatrics News*, about 80 percent of car seats are installed incorrectly. To locate a free seat-inspection-facility, contact 866-732-8243 or www.seatcheck.org.

See pages 208-209 for guidelines in transporting premature and low birth weight infants.

Remember these important points:

- The rear seat is generally the safest position for any child.
- Always put your baby in the back seat of your car, facing the rear.
- Use a rear-facing car seat for babies weighing up to 20 pounds and as close to 1-year-old as possible. There are some infant carriers for use up to 35 pounds.

- Car seats come with a 3-point harness or a 5-point harness. The harness holds the baby in the car seat. The vehicle's seat belt holds the seat in the car. Both the seat belt and harness must be snugly attached to prevent injury.

- Secure the baby in the car carrier every time you take the baby in the car, even for a 2-minute trip to the corner drugstore.

- Be certain that an inherited, borrowed or used carrier meets the current recommended safety requirements. If you are unsure about how a previously owned carrier should be used, contact the manufacturer for an instruction manual.

- Do not substitute a household infant seat used for feeding or carrying the baby for a safe car carrier. Regular infant seats are not designed to withstand a collision.

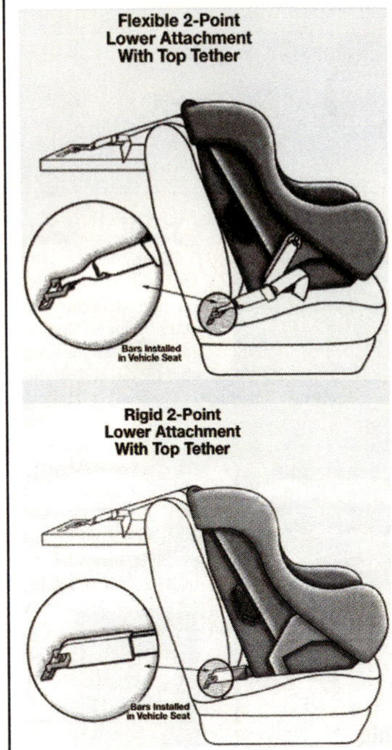

- Use the recommended carrier until the child outgrows the toddler model. And if you obtain a convertible carrier, which can go from infant o toddler use, be sure that you top-anchor the seat according to its instructions for toddler use.

- Universal use of safe infant car carriers would eliminate most of the almost 70,000 injuries each year to babies and toddlers in automobile accidents, injuries which are the leading cause of death among young children.

- Follow the manufacturer's instructions on how to use your car seat; always keep these instructions with the car seat.

Latch Program

LATCH stands for Lower Anchors and Tethers for Children. It is a system mandated by the federal government in an effort to standardize and simplify the installation of child restraints. Nearly all new vehicles and child safety seats manufactured on and after September 1, 2002 will be equipped with the LATCH system. Cars, minivans and light trucks will be required to have anchor points between the vehicle's seat cushion and the seat back in at least 2 rear seating positions. Child safety seats will have tether straps or rigid connectors that hook into these anchors, thereby eliminating the need to secure the safety seat to the vehicle using the vehicle's seat belt system.

Baby's clothes

Shopping for the baby's needs can be fun, but it is also easy to overdo it. Remember that your baby will outgrow small clothes quickly, so you do not really need to buy more than is necessary. The time of the year when your baby will be born should be considered. The following list is a good foundation, and as you get to know your baby, you can add those items which work best for you.

- 2 to 4 dozen diapers (1 dozen is enough if you plan to use diaper services or disposable diapers)
- A package of diaper pins if using cloth diapers
- 6 undershirts (sleeve length depends on the weather)
- 6 nightgowns or 1-piece pajamas
- 6 pairs waterproof pants if using cloth diapers
- 2 sweaters, 1 wool or synthetic and 1 cotton
- 4 flannel receiving blankets
- 3 contour sheets for crib, and flannel-covered rubber sheeting to place beneath the sheet to protect the mattress
- Quilted mattress pad—to be placed between sheet and rubber sheeting so the baby won't perspire excessively
- A baby bunting or snow suit for cool weather
- Woolen blanket
- A washable cotton blanket

Diapers are available in different types with varying amounts of absorbency and softness. Some are sewn with extra layers of absorbency in the center where it is needed. Other types are pre-shaped. Disposable diapers are also an option if your budget can afford the expense. You should be careful that they do not cause irritation or diaper rash on your baby. Look over the whole range of products before you make a selection. Trial and error in selecting your baby's clothes will ultimately result in what works best for you.

Baby's bath needs

You will need the following items for the baby's bath:

- Changing table-optional but convenient for changing, bathing and dressing the baby
- Plastic infant bathtub to fit over the sink or on countertop for bathing. A large plastic dishpan may be used instead, or you can line your kitchen sink with a large towel and bathe the baby there if it is warm enough
- Large plastic diaper pail with lid
- 2 to 4 soft towels and 3 soft washcloths (you don't need to buy new ones, use clean soft bath towels you already have on-hand)
- 2 large, soft towels, 1 to cover the changing table
- Mild soap
- Sterile cotton
- Cotton-tipped applicators
- Baby shampoo
- Rectal thermometer
- Supplies for feeding

Repairing used equipment

The Consumer Product Safety Commission makes the following recommendations concerning the use of used equipment which you buy or inherit:

- Check and repair latches and harnesses.
- Scrape or sand off all old paint.
- Refinish with lead-free household enamel (check the label).

Chapter 17 Going to the hospital

DELIVERING A BABY is the first hospital experience for many women. Even if you have been treated previously in a hospital, you'll see that the maternity process is different from any other. Most times, no one is really sick on a maternity floor. Women arriving there are looking forward to a positive experience. Consequently, the maternity sections of hospitals tend to be cheerful, friendly places.

Let's look step-by-step at the process of an expectant mother's delivery in the hospital, beginning with her time at home just prior to leaving. Knowing what to expect will reduce your anxiety and help you feel more relaxed.

Notify your healthcare provider at the first sign of labor. Chapter 18 has detailed information describing each of the 3 stages of labor. He or she can discuss the timing of your contractions and instruct you when to leave for the hospital. Typically this will be when your contractions are rythmic and maybe 8 minutes or less apart. During this time, your abdomen hardens for the duration of the contraction. By now, you or your partner should have already arranged for the care of your other children. Your partner should be dressed and ready to leave-with you. Don't forget your pre-packed suitcase, and remember, don't rush.

Being admitted

You will arrive at the hospital where your clinician is a staff member. Registration at the hospital can be accomplished in one of 3 ways:

1. You can pre-register before arrival, in which case some hospitals may take you directly to your room.
2. Someone may register for you upon arrival.
3. You will register at the admitting office when you arrive. The admitting secretary will ask you for some necessary information. This will include:

- name
- address
- next of kin
- phone number
- insurance plan
- the type of room you prefer— private or semi-private

It is also important for you to have your hospital plan card and number with you if you have one, as well as any personal identification the hospital may require.

Though it may seem longer, this only takes a few minutes. As the secretary proceeds to gather information, your contractions will continue. When the secretary is finished, a nurse will arrive, probably place you in a wheelchair, and take you and your partner to the maternity unit.

Preparing for delivery

Depending on the facility, your partner will probably be allowed to accompany you, but may be directed to a special waiting area. A nurse will help you undress and you will be given a hospital gown. Your clothes will be tagged and placed with your suitcase. A word of caution: although hospitals are conscientious about identifying your belongings, it is wise to leave jewelry and any other valuables at home.

The hospital staff will then help you into bed and begin the steps in your preparation for delivering your baby. Hospitals follow different procedures, so ask your clinician or childbirth educator about the preparation process at your hospital so there will be no surprises. The "prep" will include an assessment of your blood pressure, pulse, respirations, fetal heartbeat and contractions. The nurse or other health care provider may do a vaginal examination to check cervical changes. Occasionally, a cleansing or shaving of the pubic area, or an enema may be ordered. Each step of the preparation has a purpose. The information that you have given will be recorded for the clinician to study when he or she sees you. You should also not be surprised if your doctor does not appear immediately.

The hospital staff you meet during this 1st stage in your labor, the nurses, interns, and resident physicians, are thoroughly trained to carefully observe your progress and respond to your needs.

The labor, delivery, recovery and postpartum room (LDRP)

More and more hospitals, and all birthing centers, now have single-room maternity care centers. Everything takes place here — the labor, delivery, recovery and postpartum period— so that you spend your entire stay in the hospital in the same room. This room has several chairs or couches as well as a bed for family members or support persons who are with you. There is also a private bath with a shower and/or a bathtub. The necessary equipment for the birth and care of the baby will be located either in this room or in an accessible location nearby.

Other hospitals may have the labor, delivery and recovery rooms (LDR) combined but transfer you after delivery to a postpartum unit where you continue to rest until you go home.

Traditional labor and delivery suites

Other hospitals continue to have traditional labor and delivery suites where you are evaluated for labor in one room, transferred to a labor room for the duration of the labor, to the delivery room for the birth, then to a recovery room to recover prior to being transferred to the postpartum unit. The delivery room is similar to an operating room. You would move to a delivery table and your legs would be lifted into supports. Ask your clinician which type of facility is available where you will be giving birth.

Unless an emergency arises, the baby's father should be able to remain with you for the birth.

Birthing room

An alternative to the "labor-delivery-recovery rooms" procedure that is now being offered by many hospitals is the birthing room. This alternative has been designed for couples who want a family-oriented experience, or who might have wanted to deliver their child at home but were concerned about medical safety. Designed to resemble a home-like sitting room and bedroom, the birthing room in a hospital offers an atmosphere of privacy in order to provide a family-centered birth experience. In the atmosphere of surroundings that are similar to home, the mother labors, delivers and recovers. Accompanying the mother in the birthing room are the partner, perhaps other family members and friends, and depending on the hospital, even older children. Because the birthing room is inside a hospital, the mother can be easily moved into the conventional facilities if problems develop during any stage of labor or delivery. The home-like birthing room allows

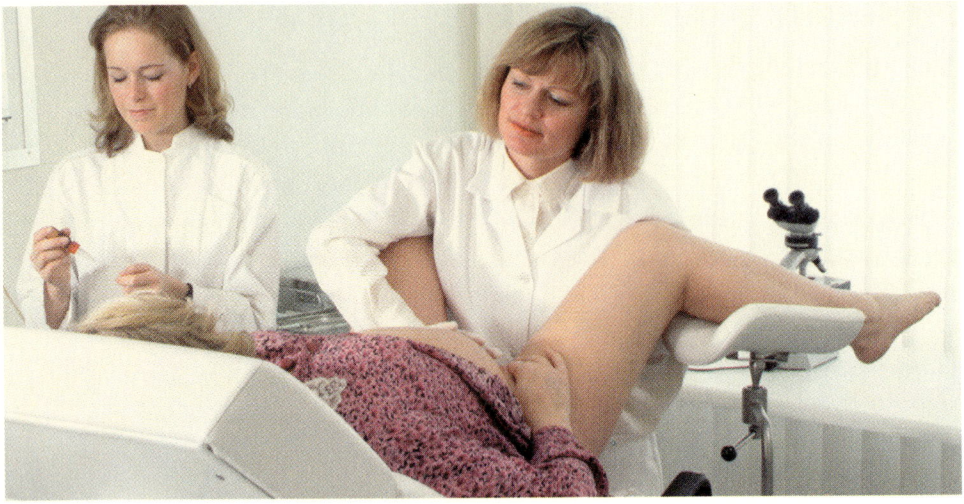

For delivery, your legs may be lifted into stirrups position.

for a "bonding period" in which the new parents have immediate physical contact and can cuddle their new baby. In addition, the mother can even begin breast feeding within 10 or 15 minutes of birth. Along with rooming-in later, the experience of the birthing room is intended to help the family establish their new relationships before they return home.

These facilities are not available for high-risk expectant mothers. The health and safety of mother and child remain the most important priorities of childbirth. Consequently, high-risk mothers and babies may be required to have a more conventional delivery to take advantage of sophisticated equipment and techniques.

Discuss the type of facilities your hospital has, and whether the baby's father can be present during the entire delivery.

The hospital nursery

You and your partner will have time to become acquainted with your newborn either in the delivery room or the birthing room. Following this, your baby will be identified, weighed, measured, bathed and examined. A complete physical examination of the baby will follow within a few hours, with all the findings reported to you.

Your baby will remain in the hospital nursery, except for feedings, unless you have a rooming-in or LDRP plan. The nursery provides an unobstructed view of the babies being diapered, dressed and fed. Most of the time, they will be sleeping.

Sometimes, particularly before feeding times, they may be crying. Nurses are in constant attendance, closely observing all babies. You will be constantly encouraged to visit and hold your baby, or the nurses will bring the baby to your room.

Rooming-in

Nursery facilities in hospitals take care of the needs of many newborn babies as we described above. Another alternative available at many hospitals is a service called "rooming-in." Rather than keeping the baby in a large nursery, the mother keeps her baby with her in the same room or in a small area nearby.

The rooming-in arrangement has primarily 3 benefits.

1. As soon as the mother has rested sufficiently, she can tend to her baby herself. Depending on the hospital, there are several modifications to this plan.
2. Rooming-in permits immediate parent-child contact called bonding, which parents and babies thrive on.
3. If a woman is having her first child, rooming-in is helpful because she can learn to care for her baby under the hospital's supervision.

A special premature nursery is reserved for those babies born ahead of schedule, and in need of extra attention and closer supervision.

There is one drawback, however. New mothers need all the rest they can get. A conventional hospital nursery provides more rest time for the mother than does rooming-in. If your hospital has a rooming-in plan, weigh the benefits of having your baby with you as opposed to being in the nursery.

Bonding

Two Cleveland physicians have defined bonding as "a unique relationship between two persons that endures through time." Early bonding consists of close physical and emotional attachment. Cuddling, kissing, holding and breast feeding are important in bonding. Eye contact is also important, and it has been shown that a baby can often follow the parent's eyes immediately after birth.

The topic of bonding has been widely discussed, and researchers have noted that early parent-child bonding (from birth to 3 years) is important in the development of the child and in the development of parent-child relationships. Some of the evidence available also suggests that bonding strengthens the family group and causes a decrease in child abuse.

Bonding is most easily accomplished in the birthing room or rooming-in facilities, but if you cannot take advantage of these options, you can still establish close contact with your baby in the delivery room, during feeding and later at home.

The appearance of a healthy newborn baby

Many mothers honestly admitted that they were surprised by the appearance of their babies after birth. It is not unusual for the newborn to appear swollen and the eyes puffy. The skull bones are not fused and baby's head may appear elongated and large in proportion to the rest of the body. The greasy whitish coating covering the baby upon delivery is called vernix. Most of the photographs you see which are supposedly of newborns are really pictures of infants 1 or 2 months old. Be assured your baby will look differently 1 month and even 1 week after delivery. A picture and description of a 1-week-old baby appears on page 228.

About 2 to 5 days after birth, the baby's skin takes on a yellow-orange tinge. This is called physiologic jaundice of the newborn and occurs in about 1/3 of all babies. The jaundice is caused by an increase in the concentration of bilirubin in the baby's blood. Bilirubin is made up of by-products of hemoglobin from the baby's red blood cells. Normally these by-products are disposed of through the liver and kidneys. Sometimes, especially in preterm babies, the baby's liver is not yet fully mature. Feeding the newborn soon after birth may help to decrease the risk of jaundice. The feeding ensures the baby is well hydrated and stimulates the baby's digestive tract.

If the bilirubin is high enough, or the jaundice lasts longer than usual or occurs very early, the baby's doctor may want to start therapy. This involves placing the baby under special phototherapy lights. The lighting helps breakup the bilirubin so that it can be excreted more quickly.

You may notice a dark greenish tarry substance in your baby's bowel movement within 24 hours of birth. This substance, called meconium, is a mixture of secretions from the intestinal glands and some amniotic fluid. It is found normally in the intestines of a full-term fetus and excreted in the stool of the newborn.

Chapter 18 Giving birth

NOW THAT THE STAGE HAS BEEN SET for you to give birth and become a mother, you may have a number of questions about what is going to happen: How will I really know when I am in labor? What if I am out when it happens? Will I reach the hospital in time? What if my clinician is not home when I need him/her?

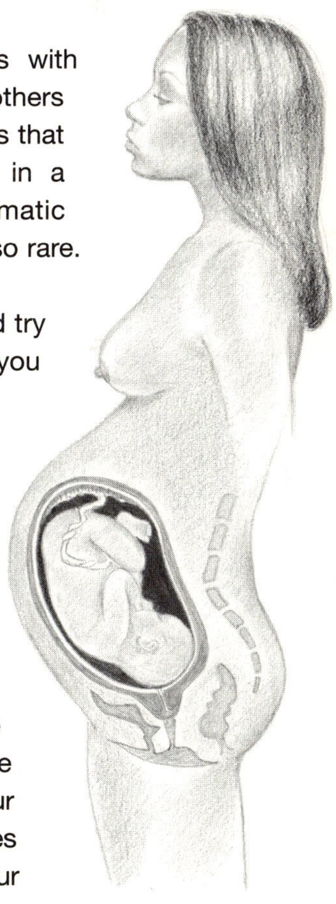

You may also have heard stories about ambulances with screeching sirens roaring through the streets or mothers giving birth in the back seats of taxi cabs. But the truth is that most deliveries are normal, uneventful and proceed in a routine fashion. The reason you hear about dramatic deliveries in the news media is that those deliveries are so rare.

Let's look at the process of giving birth step by step, and try to set the stage for your upcoming performance so that you will have as little apprehension as possible.

The beginning of labor

As we have said before, your delivery will probably occur somewhere between 2 weeks before and 2 weeks after your due date. Only a few women deliver on their due date, or within a day or two. Your natural apprehension and impatience during this time can be eased if you understand the process of labor and recognize what is happening to you. As your baby prepares to emerge into the outside world, it will change its position and your uterus will sink forward and downward. When these changes occur, observant, experienced friends may say to you, "Your baby has dropped. It looks like you're ready to go."

Some other changes may take place as well. There may be an increase in vaginal discharge. As the baby shifts position, you may notice that former backaches and abdominal pressure have now become leg pains. This is because different muscles are now supporting the load. You might also notice that your clothes fit differently.

All of these changes indicate that the baby is assuming its birth position, and its head will be pushing against the cervix, as shown on page 173. "Lightening" is the term used to describe this new positioning, and there may be some intermittent pain and discomfort at this time. If you are having your first baby and do not know what real contractions feel like, you may mistakenly think that this "lightening" is the start of labor. Very often such mothers call their clinician or even go to the hospital, but then nothing else happens. During these false alarms, the contractions are far apart and irregular. After checking you over, you will be sent home to wait for the beginning of real labor. It is frustrating for a woman to continue to wait patiently, but clinicians know that such "false alarms" occur frequently.

How then will you know when real labor begins? There are 3 main signs that you will recognize:

1. Contractions will occur with timed regularity. At the beginning, your contractions may last 45 seconds to a minute, and occur every 10, 15 or 20 minutes. An hour or two later, they will be more frequent. A contraction begins lightly across the back and then slowly builds in intensity like a wave as it travels across the abdomen. The reason for these contractions is that the muscles of the uterus are preparing to push the baby from the uterus.

2. Bright red bleeding must be reported immediately. However, blood tinged mucus called "show" may occur before real labor, or even several days or weeks before labor begins.

3. Your membranes rupture. There may be a gush of watery liquid or a slow leak from the vagina. You may have heard this referred to as "your bag of water breaking."

This liquid is called amniotic fluid, and its job was to cushion the baby. The liquid is discharged as the uterus contracts and the birth passage opens. The membranes usually rupture toward the end of labor, but sometimes it can rupture earlier. You should contact your clinician if they rupture, even if you are away from

Contractions

	True Labor	False Labor
Frequency of	Regular with contractions getting closer and closer	Irregular
Intensity of	Progressively more painful	No increase–not that painful
Length of	40 to 60 seconds	Irregular
Site of	Upper abdomen or lower back - radiates to lower abdomen	Lower abdomen

home. The gush of water means that your real labor may be starting, and you should be ready to go to the hospital. If you are unable to reach your clinician, go directly to the hospital.

Remember that real labor can occur on the night of a "false alarm" or a week or two later. The actual date when your baby will be born varies from woman to woman, and no one can determine the exact time.

There is an additional "change" your clinician will look for; it is called effacement. Effacement is the thinning out and softening of the cervix. In most cases, labor will not progress until the cervical canal softens and begins to thin even if the membranes have ruptured. This softening and thinning of the cervix is also known as cervical ripening.

A final word of advice: when real labor begins, refrain from eating or drinking—ice chips, however, are permissible. Should you need an anesthetic, a full stomach could cause nausea and vomiting, and result in aspirating food or fluid into the lungs.

Calling your clinician

The 3 signs of real labor may occur all at the same time, or they may occur in any order at different times. When then should you call your clinician? If your membranes rupture, you should call whether you experience any discomfort or not. If "show" (the mucus-like, bloody discharge that is one sign of labor) appears, you know that real labor is commencing. By itself, "show" does not warrant calling the clinician, though you may want to alert him or her. It is also important to understand that first-time babies take their time being born. The reason is that the

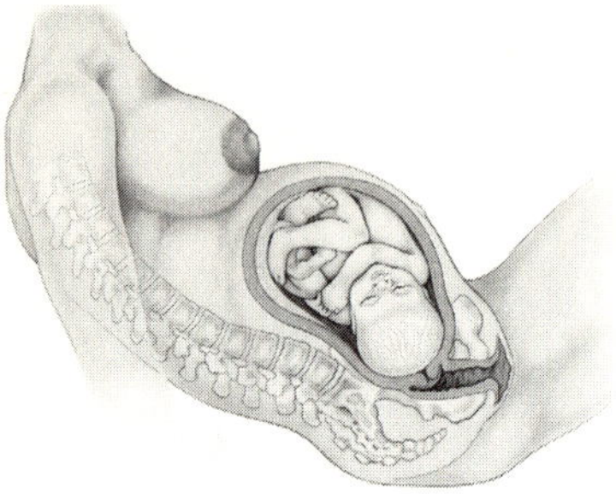

Fig. 1—*As labor progresses, the cervix becomes thinner and more dilated.*

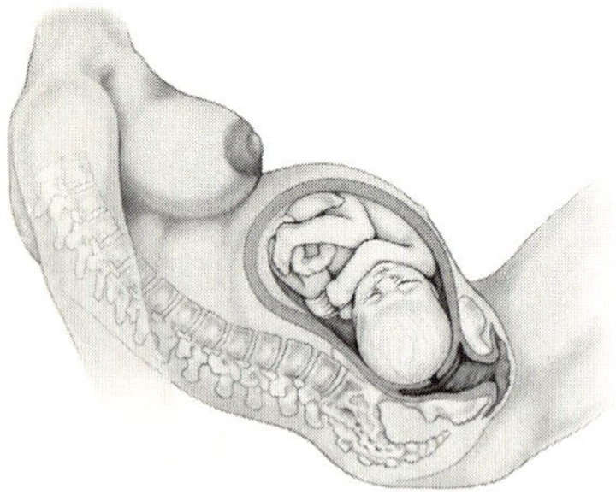

Fig. 2—*The membranes forming the bag of water rupture.**

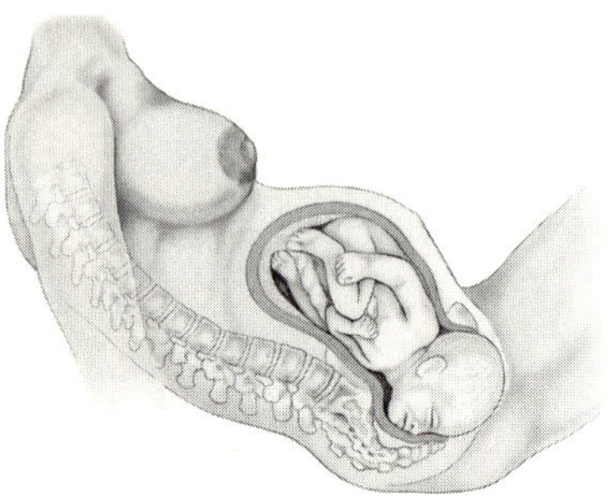

Fig. 3—*The head molds to the shape of the pelvis as the baby gradually descends in the birth canal.*

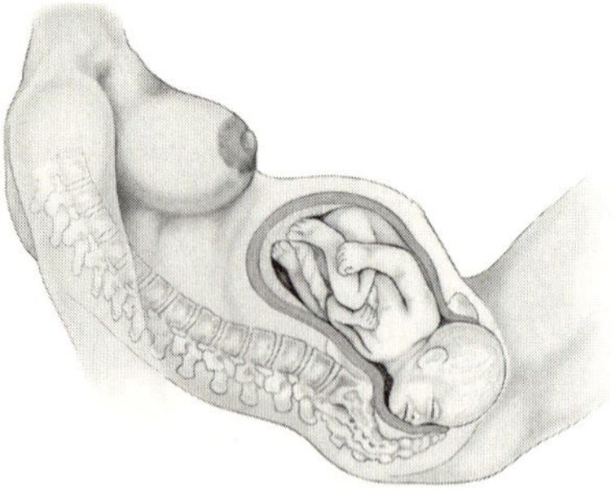

Fig. 4—*Baby slowly rotates as descent continues.*

birth passage is tense and unyielding because it has not been used before. Many healthcare providers request they be notified when contractions are 5 to 8 minutes apart. This may vary, so be sure to ask your clinician when (s)he wants to be notified. (However, you will have to factor in the amount of time it takes to get to the hospital.) If you live a distance away, it is a good idea to take a practice "run" to the hospital to determine how long it takes you to get there, and then allow for that extra travel time when you call your clinician. Remember, it is better to arrive at the hospital too soon rather than too late. A previous delivery often affects (shortens) the timing of the next delivery.

Despite what you might hear, most babies are not born at night; those births just seem more vivid and memorable. No matter what time of the day or night it is, notify your clinician when your membranes rupture or when Stage 1 of labor begins.

Labor is divided into 3 stages. The entire labor process lasts an average of 12 to 14 hours for a first birth. Generally, subsequent labors are shorter. Most of your work will occur during the 1st and 2nd stages. Learning muscle relaxation and breathing techniques better prepares you for these stages of labor. It is important to try and relax, even read a magazine during contractions if possible.

First stage: The 1st stage of labor, what is referred to as the cervical dilation stage, begins with the onset of real labor until the cervix is fully dilated. Regular contractions are a sign of labor. In most cases, the baby's head is down, pressing against the cervix (see Fig. 1). Your clinician will note how low the baby's head is.

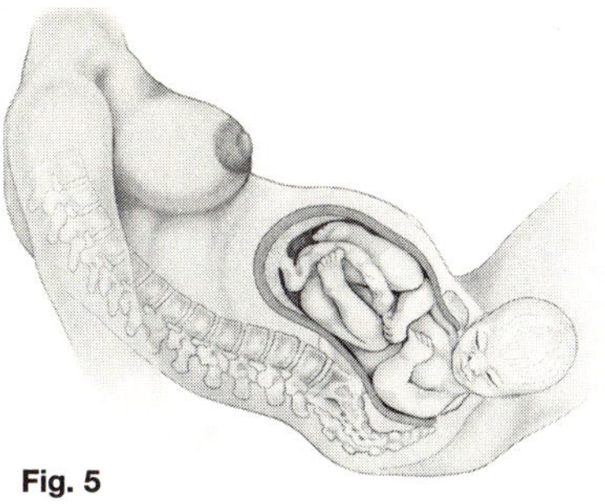

Fig. 5

When it is at the ischial spines (the bony landmarks in your pelvis), the fetal head is said to be at 0 station. The pelvis is usually divided into stations ranging from –5 (the highest) to +5 (the lowest) when delivery is about to begin. As the cervix dilates further, contractions get closer together. Membranes frequently rupture at this time, and there may be a small amount of bloody "show." Try not to bear down or push with each contraction at this time. The first stage is usually the longest of the 3 stages, and ends when the cervix is fully dilated (10 cm). Contractions come every 2-3 minutes and may last as long as 60 seconds.

Second stage: This is the expulsion stage. It begins when the cervix is fully dilated. It may last anywhere from 5 minutes to over 2 hours. The 2nd stage ends with the birth of the baby. It is at this stage that your clinician will ask you to push with each contraction.

The unique physiological changes that occur in a woman during pregnancy prepare the vagina for its elastic function. While it is normally a thin tube-shaped organ, it is now greatly distended. The baby descends further down the cervical canal and into the vagina with each contraction and bearing-down motion. First the head emerges, then shoulders, trunk, and finally feet. As the baby emerges, the clinician grasps the head and helps guide the baby through. If the umbilical cord is wrapped around the baby's neck, it is removed from this position before delivering the rest of the baby.

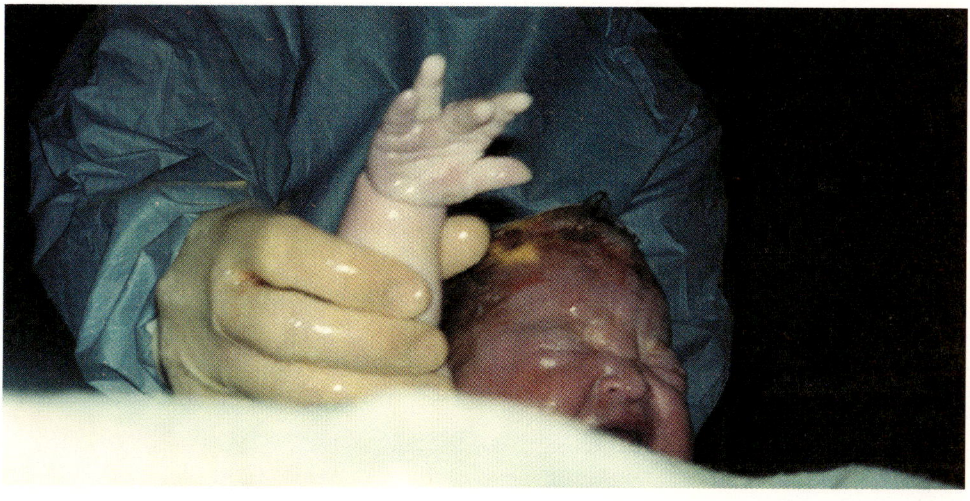

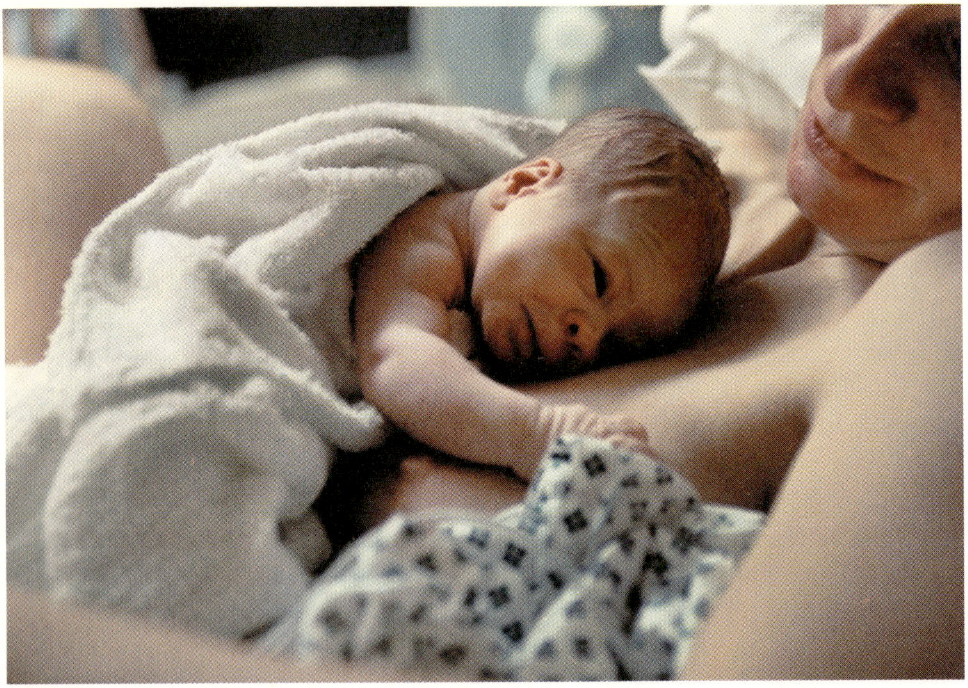

Any mucus or other amniotic residue is quickly suctioned from the baby's mouth and nose as the head emerges. The baby begins to breathe regularly and utters his/her first cry. Following the baby's delivery, mother and baby are still attached by the umbilical cord. The cord is then cut and the placenta (afterbirth) delivered.

Once the baby begins to breathe regularly and utters the first cry, he/she will be quickly dried and wrapped in blankets, or placed into a heated bassinet (or on your belly) for warmth. Drops or ointment will be put into the baby's eyes to prevent infection. Almost every jurisdiction requires by law that newborns be given this eye medication. Identification bands are placed on mother and baby before leaving the delivery room. Hand and foot prints may also be taken of baby.

The uterus will be massaged to keep it firm. The clinician will examine the vagina, cervix and the perineum to see if any repairs are needed. If you have had an episiotomy (see page 179), it will be repaired at this time.

As a part of her interest in a baby's response to birth and life on his/her own, Dr. Virginia Apgar developed a score to assess several key indicators of the baby's well-being. Practically all babies are assigned an Apgar score, taken at 1 minute after birth and again at 5 minutes as part of the monitoring process. The 5 characteristics are assigned a number between 0-2, and the Apgar score is the total of those numbers. Although the Apgar score is a good tool that assists in understanding the baby's progress at a given time, it does not by itself show how well the baby did before birth or what the future will hold. Other signs will also be checked to provide more complete information on the baby's general health.

A = appearance or color
P = pulse (heart rate)
G = grimace or reflex irritability
A = activity
R = respiration

For each sign, a score of 2 is given if the sign in the baby is normal. If a sign is missing, then a score of O is assigned. A score of 1 is given if the sign is present but below normal. As a general rule, a score of 7 or more (after 5 minutes) is considered normal; however, many doctors do not place as much significance on the Apgar score today. If the newborn shows breathing or circulation problems, doctors do not wait a full minute to take action. Also, many babies who may have lower scores at birth ultimately turn out to be healthy.

Newborn babies have very small amounts of vitamin K, which promotes normal blood clotting. For this reason, the baby may be given a shot of vitamin K. In about a week, the baby will produce sufficient quantities of vitamin K on his/her own. Standard procedures vary in hospitals, but soon after stage 2, the parents are allowed to hold the baby and can begin to establish a bond with him/her.

Third stage: Now that the baby has emerged, the mother still has one last stage in the delivery that must be completed. This stage is also called the "placental" stage because it involves delivery of the afterbirth, or placenta, the structure through which the fetus derives nourishment in order to develop. Usually it takes only a few minutes to extract the placenta and other membranes.

Episiotomy

An episiotomy is a small incision (cut) the clinician makes in the vagina and the perineum at the time of delivery. Though the vagina possesses great elasticity, there are times when the vaginal tissue is stretched so thinly that to keep the tissue from tearing, an episiotomy is performed. An episiotomy also helps relieve pressure on the baby's head.

Lochia

After delivery there is a vaginal discharge consisting primarily of blood and remnants of the uterine lining—this discharge is called lochia. The discharge will decrease in volume and turn brownish in color a few days after delivery. The amount of discharge and length of time it lasts varies from woman to woman. As a rule, the discharge becomes white or yellow and gradually stops in about 10-14 days.

Analgesics and Anesthetics

There are 2 categories of drugs/medications clinicians administer prior to or during delivery of a baby. One type known as analgesics, drugs which help relieve pain without causing a loss of consciousness. Analgesics help relax you between contractions.

Common analgesics:

1. Clinicians sometimes use narcotic drugs to reduce pain and enhance relax ation, and there may be a need to repeat the doses. A good example of such a common narcotic drug is Demerol. There are 3 possible disadvantages:
   (a) if the drug is given too early, it may slow down labor
   (b) if it is given too late, the drug may not give adequate pain relief
   (c) some women experience nausea and sleepiness.

2. Tranquilizers will relieve anxiety and alleviate nausea and vomiting. They also enhance the effect of, and thus reduce the amount of, narcotics that are needed. Examples of tranquilizers are: Atarax, Phenergan, Sparine, Thorazine, Visatril, and Valium. The possible disadvantages are that they may cause dizziness, drowsiness, dry mouth, or blurred vision.

3. The effect of barbiturates can be hypnotic and sleep-inducing. They are often given in combination with narcotics to relieve apprehension very early in labor, but they have little effect on pain. Amytal and Seconal are examples of barbiturates. One possible disadvantage is that they must not be given too close to delivery because they can cause a sleepy baby.

Clinicians must monitor all of these common medications carefully because they can cross the placenta and cause the baby to be born sleepy or with slow responses. Analgesic drugs are given in small doses and are usually avoided shortly before delivery to avoid such side effects as drowsiness or decreased ability of the mother to concentrate. And most importantly, analgesic drugs given too close to delivery can slow baby's reflexes and breathing at birth.

Anesthetics

The other category of drugs is called anesthetics. An anesthetic causes complete loss of feeling or sensation. An anesthetic can be general or regional. General anesthetics are occasionally used for cesarean deliveries or, on rare occasion, for emergency vaginal delivery. It is not given to relieve labor pains. A general anesthetic causes a state of complete unconsciousness with a total absence of pain or sensation over the entire body. It is essential that no food be eaten prior to a general anesthetic to avoid food or acid from the stomach being aspirated into the lungs or windpipe.

A regional (local) anesthetic produces a total lack of pain in a given area by interrupting the sensory nerve pathway from the region of the body where it is injected. There is no loss of consciousness with a regional anesthetic.

Common regional anesthetics

1. Epidural block: This anesthetic affects a larger area, causing a loss of sensation in the lower half of the body. The mother is awake during labor and delivery. The local anesthetic is injected into a small area in the lower back called the epidural space. If there is extensive numbness, it may interfere with the mother's ability to bear down and push, making it necessary to use forceps or vacuum extraction (see pages 183-184) to help guide the baby out. Serious complications from epidural block are rare. A "walking epidural" is a regional analgesic technique in which a woman maintains strength in her legs. Most patients prefer to stay in bed. Some however, may walk to the bathroom rather than use a bedpan. Being able to retain motor control may help during the second stage of labor.

2. Caudal block: A local anesthetic is injected into the caudal space located below the tailbone. The effect of a caudal block is the same as with an epidural block. It should be noted that not all women have a caudal space.

3. Saddle block: Spinal analgesia usually provides complete pain relief in the "blocked" area. A saddle block is a spinal block in which the level of pain relief is limited to little more than the pelvic region (saddle). Therefore, spontaneous deliveries, operative vaginal deliveries (forceps and vacuum) and episiotomies can be performed using this method of pain relief. Full operative deliveries such as cesarean sections require a higher level and dose of medication (spinal block).

4. Pudendal block: This is given shortly before delivery. The drug is injected on either side of the birth canal, numbing the perineum, should it be necessary to perform an episiotomy. It also numbs the area around the vagina and rec tum, relieving pain in these areas as the baby descends through the birth canal. Serious side effects from a pudendal block are rare. It is considered one of the safest forms of anesthesia.

5. Paracervical block: The injection of a local anesthetic into the tissue on either side of the cervix. Only a very small percentage of vaginal deliveries use this type of anesthetic any longer. Its major drawback is that it slows down the heart beat of the fetus.

Each of the methods described here has its merits and use in different situations, and there is no one ideal anesthetic for labor and delivery. Because anesthetics, like all drugs, may affect the baby, they must be administered carefully. You will want to discuss the medications and anesthetics available with your clinician to see which one is best for you.

Types of births

You should now be familiar with the basic process of a "normal" delivery. As the fetus moves down the birth canal, the top of the head becomes visible. This initial view of the head is called crowning. There may or may not be anesthesia administered by the healthcare professional, and in general, nature is allowed to proceed with the unfolding of events, with a little help from medical science. About 90 percent of all deliveries fall into the normal category. The other 10 percent of births fall into one of the following categories.

Breech birth—Instead of the head emerging first, breech-born babies emerge feet and buttocks first. In the "breech" position, the baby prefers to keep his head up out of the birth position. About 3 percent of all babies are breech-born, and clinicians can usually detect the position before the delivery. Such births may require special treatment by the clinician, but in most cases, there is no greater hardship to the mother than in a "normal" delivery, and the baby emerges satisfactorily. Doctors have been using cesarean sections more and more for breech presentations.

Sometimes the baby can be turned manually into a head-down position. This is called external version, and does not involve surgery. The clinician's hands are

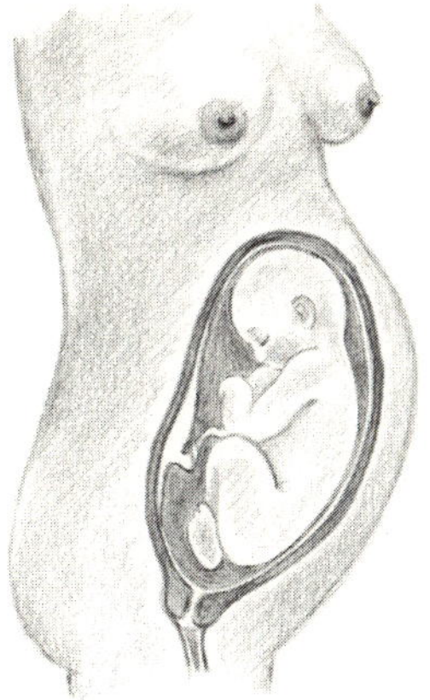

Breech Position

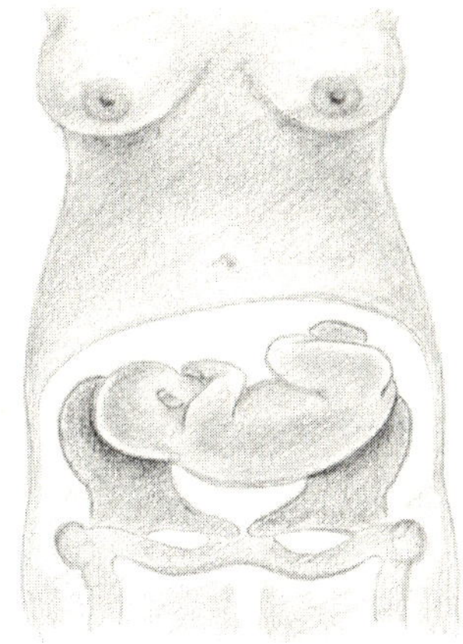

Transverse Position

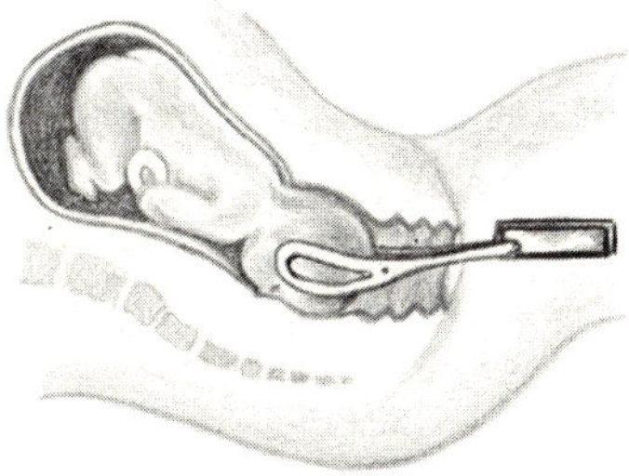

Forceps delivery

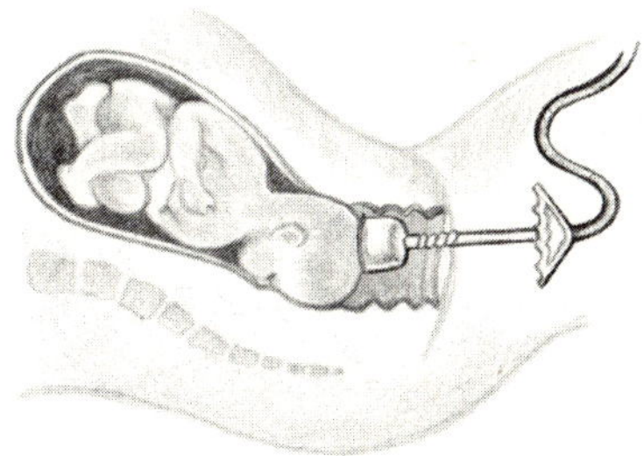

Vacuum extraction

placed at certain key points on the lower abdomen. The baby is gently pushed, almost as if baby was doing a somersault in slow motion. The clinician may give you some medication to relax the uterus. External version is done while the clinician watches the fetus with ultrasound.

Forceps delivery—Occasionally, certain physiological conditions make it difficult for a baby to push its head through the birth canal. In that case, the clinician uses a forceps to aid the baby's emergence. The forceps is a curved, tong-like instrument which is shaped to fit on each side of the baby's head. Sometimes the forceps leave a temporary mark on each side of the baby's head, but these marks disappear. There are several advantages to the use of forceps. They can relieve the mother of hours of hard, exhausting labor if her delivery proves stubborn. Forceps may also be necessary when the fetal heart rate slows or becomes irregular. An anesthetic is given prior to the use of forceps.

Vacuum extraction—The delivery of the baby can also be aided by a method called vacuum extraction. This method is widely used in the U.S. and Europe. It employs a cup-suction device which is applied to the baby's head. The situations when this method would be used are similar to those for a forceps delivery, however, it is contraindicated in preterm delivery.

Cesarean birth—A delivery of a baby through the abdomen is called a cesarean birth. In a cesarean, an incision is made in the abdominal wall. This incision may be vertical, extending from the navel to the pubic bone, or it may be transverse, extending from side to side just above the pubic hairline. This is then followed by an incision into the wall of the uterus with the baby delivered through this incision. The incision into the uterus may also be vertical or transverse. The transverse incision is preferred because less blood is lost and the incision heals with a stronger scar. There are situations, however, where a vertical incision may be necessary. The incisions into the uterus and the abdominal wall are closed with sutures or clips following the delivery of the baby and the placenta.

There are a number of reasons why a cesarean birth is indicated. These include:

- Mother's pelvis is too small for passage of the baby.
- Baby is in an abnormal position.
- There are signs the baby is in distress and must be delivered immediately.
- The mother may have medical complications making it necessary to deliver the baby as soon as possible.
- Excessive bleeding
- Baby's umbilical cord has pushed through the cervix when the membranes ruptured.
- An infection in the amniotic fluid
- Well past due date
- Intrauterine growth restriction (see pages 39)
- Macrosomia (very large baby, see page 29))

Cesarean birth is considered major surgery, and though modern surgical techniques have improved greatly, you should be aware of possible risks:

- Hospital stay and recovery time are longer.
- Greater loss of blood, sometimes requiring a transfusion
- Infection of pelvic organs
- Infection of incision
- Increased incidence of blood, clots in the legs and possibly the lungs
- Impaired bowel function

Should you have any questions or concerns regarding a cesarean birth, feel free to discuss them with your clinician prior to your time of delivery.

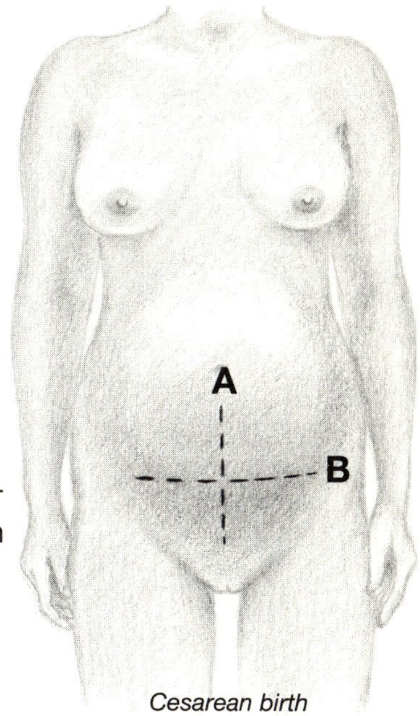

Cesarean birth
A= *Vertical incision*
B= *Transverse incision*

Vaginal birth after cesarean (VBAC)

If you have had a cesarean section in a previous birth, can you or should you attempt a vaginal delivery in your next birth? Years ago, there was a principle which said, "once a cesarean section, always a cesarean section." Because the number of cesarean deliveries in the U.S. has increased rapidly, the National Consensus of Cesarean Childbirth did a study to determine whether that old principle is medically sound, or whether a trial of labor for a subsequent delivery is a reasonable alternative. The research shows that at least 60 to 80 percent of women who have had cesarean sections in the past can safely deliver vaginally in subsequent pregnancies.

One factor in determining a vaginal birth after cesarean (VBAC) is the type of incision made in the cesarean. The exact position of a cesarean incision depends on medical considerations, and may be vertical or transverse. Doctors do advise against a vaginal delivery if a woman has had the classical or fundal vertical cesarean section previously. On the other hand, if a woman has had a low transverse cesarean, she may be advised to undergo a trial of labor for vaginal delivery. Because there are some risks involved in attempting a vaginal delivery after a previous cesarean(s), several precautionary measures should be taken:

1. It should be a singleton pregnancy (one baby). The previous cesarean should be known to be one with a low transverse uterine incision.

2. Continuous fetal monitoring should be in effect.

3. A physician competent to perform an emergency cesarean should be in the immediate area.

4. Researchers at Harvard Medical School found that women who get pregnant within 9 months of having a C-Section may be at increased risk during an attempted vaginal delivery than are women who wait longer between deliveries.

Women who underwent a cesarean delivery because of a breech position have the best probability of vaginal delivery after a previous section. How can you determine whether you are a candidate of VBAC? You and your clinician need to discuss the risks and the benefits to you and your baby of a repeat cesarean, or a trial labor for vaginal delivery. If you choose a trial of labor, it should not be attempted at home.

Preterm labor and delivery

A baby born before 37 weeks' gestation is considered preterm. The smaller and younger the baby, the greater the risk of complications. Although there have been many advances made in this area, preterm births continue to be the most important problem of pregnancy.

Preterm babies are at increased risk for breathing problems, cerebral hemorrhage, infections and feeding problems. The combination of the fetal fibronecton assay (see page 187) and the length of the cervix (as determined by your healthcare professional), help detect preterm labor delivery in those patients with symptoms of preterm labor.

Factors which can contribute to preterm birth include:

- Poor prenatal care
- A stressful pregnancy
- Past history of miscarriage and/or premature deliveries
- Multiple fetuses
- Smoking
- Uterine abnormality

Probably the most important factor is poor prenatal care. If you believe that you fall into one or more of these categories, or are otherwise at risk, discuss the issue thoroughly with your clinician. Together you can minimize your chances by working out a program for your pregnancy.

However, sometimes, despite all of your precautions, preterm contractions can take you and your clinician by complete surprise. There are times when these contractions start without any pain or forewarning. More frequently though, the first signs are a backache and a tightness around the abdomen.

The FDA has approved a test called a fetal fibronectin assay which helps clinicians decide how to manage patients with symptoms of preterm labor. When the test is negative there is a very low probability that patients will deliver in one or 2 weeks. Although many patients with a positive test will not go into labor, a negative test is very reassuring that the pateint is not in actual labor.

If you experience any of the following signs of preterm labor, you should report them to your clinician:

- Lower abdominal pain
- Increased vaginal discharge (may be blood-tinged and watery)
- Low backache
- Abdominal cramps with or without diarrhea
- Regular contractions or tightening sensation

Your clinician may ask you to come to his or her office, or go directly to the hospital, if you have one or more symptoms of premature labor. Tocolytic (to-co-li-tic) agents are drugs used to stop labor. They accomplish this by relaxing the muscles of the uterus. The clinician can administer this medication by injection, in IV fluids, or orally.

Induced labor

For medical reasons, labor is sometimes induced by the clinician. Induction of labor refers to the use of certain medications to start labor. The decision to induce labor is usually made because of concerns for the mother or fetus or when uterine contractions have not begun spontaneously and the baby is ready to be born. The initiation of labor through the use of drugs may also be indicated when labor is progressing so slowly that problems might arise for the mother or fetus. The drug most frequently used to induce labor is the intravenous administration of oxytocin.

Labor can also be induced by performing a procedure called an amniotomy. This is the artificial rupturing of the membranes (bag of water). The use of either an amniotomy or intravenous oxytocin to induce labor follows the American College of Obstetricians and Gynecologists' guidelines.

Fetal Monitoring

Your healthcare provider will be monitoring the condition of your fetus throughout your pregnancy and labor to check on the fetus' status. Because any changes in the heartbeat can signal a possible problem, the clinician monitors the baby's heartbeat frequently and regularly during labor.

Two types of monitoring can be used: auscultation and electronic fetal monitoring.

Auscultation is the term for listening to the heartbeat of the fetus. Most often the clinician uses a Doppler Ultrasound to listen to the heartbeat of the fetus. This instrument uses sound waves to create a signal that is then amplified. The clinician presses the device against the woman's abdomen, and the amplifier makes it possible for anyone in the room to hear the heartbeat.

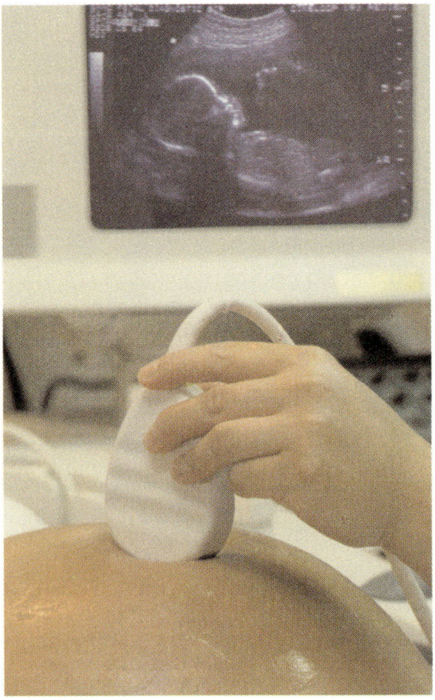

Another method of listening to the fetal heartbeat is by using a stethoscope-like instrument called a fetoscope. The clinician presses the diaphragm (round flat end) of the fetoscope against the abdomen of the woman. The heartbeat of the fetus can be heard by the one wearing the instrument earpiece.

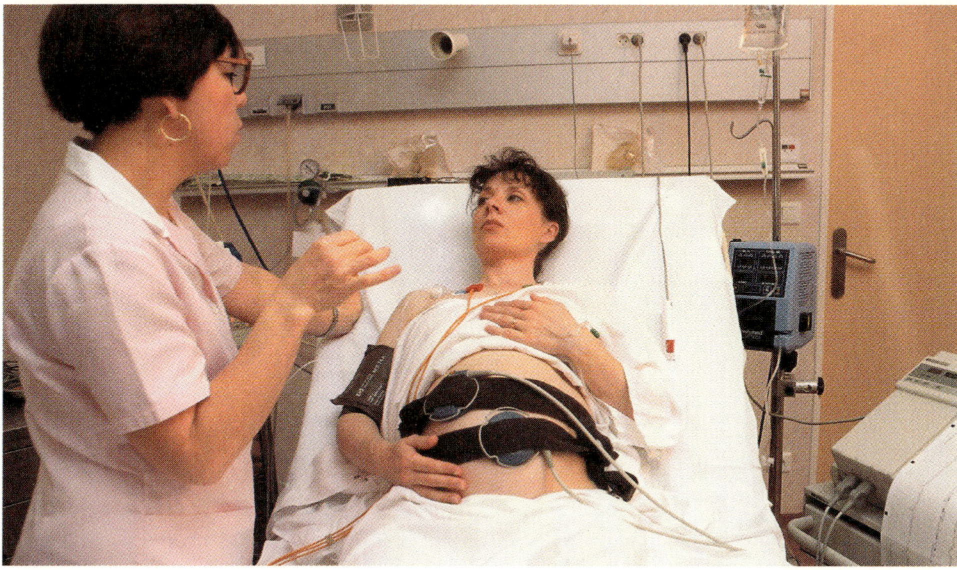

Electronic fetal monitoring measures the heartbeat of the fetus electronically. The heartbeat is recorded continuously and can be read by the clinician. The following are two types of electronic fetal monitoring:

A. External Monitoring: The clinician places 2 belts around the woman's abdomen which hold 2 instruments in place. One instrument measures fetal heart rate while the other instrument measures both the length of the uterine contractions and the length of time between the contractions).

B. Internal Monitoring: This method can be administered only after the fetal membranes (bag of water) have broken. The fetal heart rate is recorded by an instrument with an electrode that is attached to the scalp of the fetus. The clinician can also place a thin tube in the uterus to measure the strength of the uterine contractions.

Most women who have had this procedure done report only minor discomfort. Sometimes a clinician will use a combination of internal and external monitoring.

Certified Nurse-Midwives (CNM)

Nurse midwives attend births in 3 settings: the hospital, at birthing centers and at home. The vast majority of these births (94%) are in a hospital setting. The average nurse midwife has 20 years of clinical experience in maternity and public health. As a growing group of professionals, nurse-midwives are educated in 2 disciplines: nursing and midwifery. The advanced training in midwifery is obtained through accredited programs affiliated with universities across the United States. The American College of Nurse-Midwives certifies graduates by examination and individual license to become Certified Nurse-Midwives (CNM).

Nurse midwives provide the following:

- Prenatal care
- Labor and delivery
- Postpartum care
- Well-woman gynecology
- Normal newborn care
- Family planning

Nurse midwives practice in collaboration with physicians. The medical needs of the woman and the practice setting determine the degree of collaboration. The nurse midwife is especially skilled at risk-screening and will make referrals to a physician's care when necessary.

If you wish to pursue the services of a nurse-midwife and are at low risk for complications during pregnancy, think over the following points:

1. Select one who meets state requirements and has been certified by the American College of Nurse-Midwives (ACNM).

2. To find a nurse-midwife in your area or to check certification, contact the ACNM (818 Connecticut Avenue NW, Suite 900, Washington, D.C. 20006), or call 202-728-9860 or 1-888-MID-WIFE. Web site: www.midwife.org.

3. Schedule an interview appointment with a nurse-midwife in your area so that you have an opportunity to ask about her services, birth sites, fees and the physician with whom she collaborates if the need arises.

4. Nurse midwifery care offers women a choice in birth. What is important is that your birth is attended by a caring and appropriate provider of your choice.Prescriptions for medications and vitamins can be written by CNMs.

Nurse-midwifery care is covered by private insurance carriers, Medicare, Medicaid and many managed care programs. CNM services are also covered under the Civilian Health and Medical Program of the Uniformed Services and Federal Employees Health Benefit.

Chapter 19 After delivery

DURING YOUR BRIEF STAY IN THE HOSPITAL, your doctor, as well as the nurses on staff, will be able to answer any of your questions about caring for yourself and your baby when you return home. If you have particular concerns or questions in the last few weeks of your pregnancy, you may even want to write some of these down as you think of them, and put this list of questions with the personal items you're bringing to the hospital.

The uterus

There are many physical changes which occur throughout your body during pregnancy. One of the most remarkable is the change which takes place in your uterus. During the past 9 months this organ has grown, developed, and protected your new baby. Now that you have given birth, your uterus will return to its normal pre-pregnancy size much more rapidly. After delivery the uterus weighs approximately 2 1/2 pounds. By your 6-week checkup, it will weigh only 2 ounces.

After delivery of your baby and the placenta, the nurse massages the uterus to stimulate it to contract. The inability of the uterus to contract is called uterine atony. In this situation, heavy bleeding may occur. If massaging does not work, there are several medications available to the clinician to promote contraction.

As the uterus contracts, there may be occasional abdominal cramps. These are usually more noticeable with a second or third child than with a first. These cramps are called "after pains." With these contractions, the uterus is actually pushing out residual tissue which must be discharged.

This discharge includes the lining of the uterus and other cells that were created for the baby's growth. During the 1st week, this discharge may be reddish, but by the 2nd week, it may be more brownish. Eventually the discharge becomes more pale, fades to yellowish or whitish, and disappears almost completely by the end of the 3rd week. Sometimes, however, it may continue for 6 to 8 weeks before it stops.

The amount of discharge may approximate that of the last day or two of a menstrual period. During this time you should wear a sanitary pad until your clinician advises you otherwise. Do not use a tampon. Regular menstruation will start again in a few weeks if you are not nursing. If you are breastfeeding your baby, it will be much longer before menstruation resumes.

Your breasts

The uterus and the breasts have a close relationship. For example, whether your baby is premature or on time, some unknown internal signal sets off milk production in the breasts 3 days after delivery. The fluid that had been secreted earlier by the breasts was colostrum, the forerunner of the milk.

When the milk is produced there will be several obvious signs, as your breasts will become hard, heavy, full, and uncomfortable. The nursing mother will experience relief from the soreness when the baby begins to suck. For mothers who do not nurse, there may be some discomfort during the period when the milk dries up. To help relieve the discomfort, your clinician may recommend that you wear a tight supportive bra and apply ice packs to your breasts. An analgesic such as acetaminophen may be taken if your discomfort is not relieved by the tight supportive bra or the ice packs.

Smoking and your baby

In a March 8, 1995 issue of *The Journal of the American Medical Association,* it was reported that even smoking in the same room as an infant increases the risk of sudden infant death syndrome (SIDS). Breastfeeding may protect against SIDS in non-smokers but **not** in smokers. Researchers have found that breathing someone else's smoke is very dangerous. This is especially true for children.

Environmental tobacco smoke (ETS) is defined as smoke breathed out by a smoker and includes the smoke that comes from the tip of a burning cigarette. ETS has almost 4,000 chemicals in it. According to the American Academy of Pediatrics, infants and children breathe these in whenever someone smokes around them. Children who inhale ETS are at risk for many serious health problems including upper respiratory infections, ear infections and asthma. ETS can also cause problems for children later in life.

If you smoke, quit! If you must smoke, do not do it in your home. It is important not to allow anyone else to smoke in your home, or take your baby to any facility where he or she will be exposed to ETS.

The nursing mother

Almost any woman who decides to breastfeed her baby is able to do so. Breast or nipple size or shape does not affect a mother's ability to nurse her baby. The advantages of breastfeeding for both mother and baby are discussed in detail in Chapter 16.

The baby frequently is put to breast immediately after delivery.

How the breast is presented to an infant is one of the most critical factors in preventing nipple pain. Using a proper hand grasp of the breast and having the baby directly facing the breast is very important. Baby and mother must be in a comfortable position before breastfeeding begins.

Your nurse will explain how to place your baby at your breast and demonstrate techniques for keeping baby awake and interested. In order to learn to suck and develop an appetite, the nursing baby will be put to breast a few times before the milk starts to flow. After delivery, your breasts will be secreting the forerunner of breast milk—a yellowish liquid called colostrum. Colostrum (see page 154) contains certain immunological factors which protect a newborn from some types of infections.

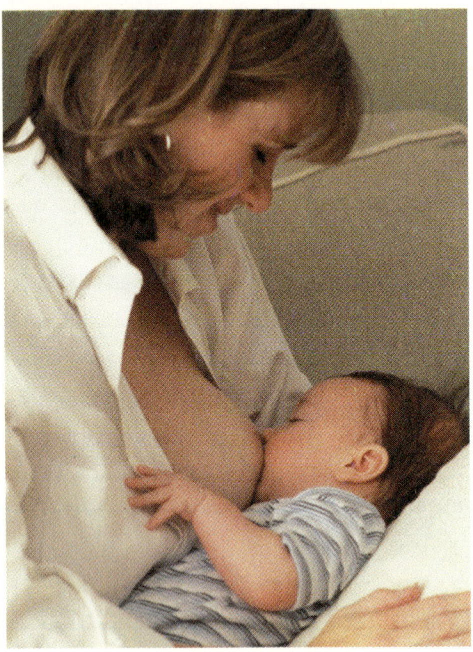

If you have the hospital rooming-in plan, you can feed your baby on demand. Let baby nurse 10 to 20 minutes on each breast. The more you nurse the more milk your breasts will produce. As your baby grows, your breasts will automatically accommodate their needs with increased milk production.

Position for breastfeeding

Proper positioning aids in your infant's grasp of the nipple, promotes effective nursing, and helps prevent sore nipples.

How to Begin

1. Hold the baby for a moment. Whisper to him or her. Feel the baby close to your breast. Take a deep breath. Relax. Remember that nursing your baby is one of the most pleasant acts of motherhood. It will be an unforgettable experience.

2. Find a comfortable position either lying down or sitting up. If lying down, take care not to fall asleep and roll over onto baby.

Breastfeed 8 to 12 times per 24-hour day.

3. Raise baby to the height of the breast and turn baby to face you. Use pillows if necessary to support the baby. Baby's and mother's abdomens should be touching.

4. Your arm supporting the infant should be held at your side as if in a sling, with your hand supporting the baby's buttocks. The baby's head, neck, and back should be in a straight line.

5. The most common and frequently recommended position for breast feeding is called the "Palmer" grasp. Support the breast with one hand with all the fingers placed under the breast and only the thumb placed above the breast. This positions the breast directly into baby's mouth and avoids having to press the breast away from baby's nose. This grasp is less likely to compress the milk ducts or cut down on the milk flow.

6. Brush infant's lower lip downward with your nipple, and when infant's mouth opens, insert the nipple and areola in as far as possible. Do not let him/her suck on just the tip or you will get sore nipples. Baby's nose and chin should touch your breast. His lips should be flanged. If the position is uncomfortable, break the suction and begin again.

7. Be sure baby's mouth covers not only the nipple but also the dark area surrounding the nipple, called the areola. The baby will not get much milk if only the nipple is grasped, and you may get sore nipples. (See page 196)

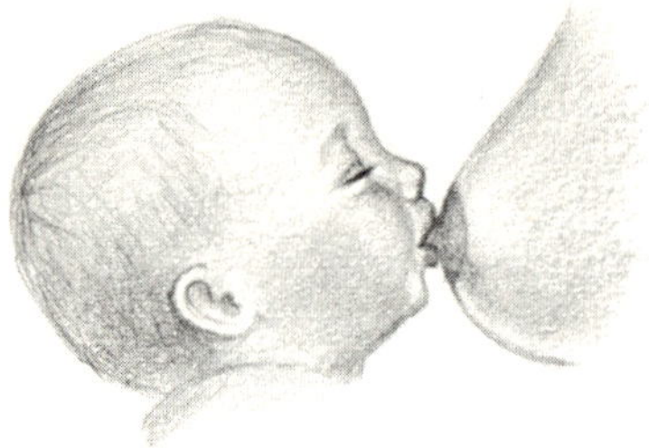

Incorrect position

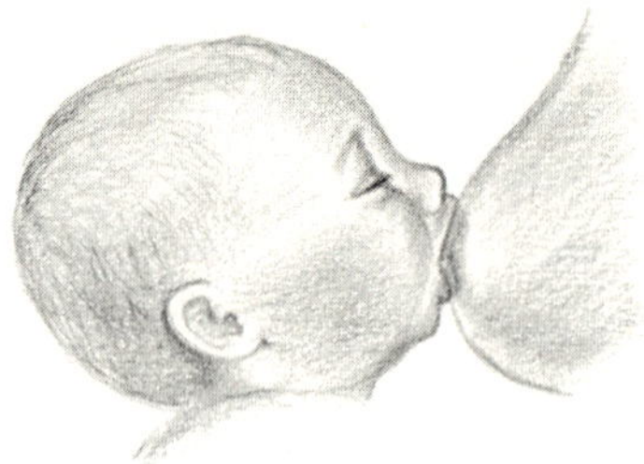

Correct position

8. Care should be taken not to let baby get chilled. Be sure baby is covered and warm.

   To stop or interrupt baby during nursing, place your finger in the corner of baby's mouth to open the jaw. This will break the suction between baby's mouth and the nipple/areola and the nipple can be withdrawn. Breastfeed 8 to 12 times per 24-hour day.

The following tips may help you during your first weeks at home:

1. Breastfeed baby from 10 to 20 minutes on one breast. This should be enough to satisfy baby's immediate hunger if sucking actively. It has been estimated that baby gets nearly 90 percent of the milk from one breast in the first 5 to 10 minutes of good, strong nursing. Do not take baby off the breast while he or she is actively nursing.

2. Take a brief break before you switch baby to the other breast. This is the time to burp baby, change the diaper, or play with baby for a moment or two.

3. Putt baby to the second breast and allow baby to nurse as long as he/she wants, within a reasonable time. It may take longer to empty the second breast as his/her first hunger pangs are over. About 20 to 30 minutes will be sufficient.

4. At the next feeding, if you are using both breasts, give the breast that was nursed last. If you started with the right breast, offer the left breast for the next feeding. Some women attach a safety pin to their bra strap to remind them which breast to use next. A few clinicians suggest that the mother first use the breast that is filled up most. This helps to relieve any discomfort of fullness for the mother right away.

5. Let baby set his own nursing pattern as long as it is not hurting the mother's breast or nipple. Newborns frequently nurse from 10 to 20 minutes.

If you discover moisture after nursing, allow air to dry the moisture rather than wiping the area dry with a tissue or towel. The routine use of ointments to the nipples, areola or breast is not recommended. Avoid soaps, alcohol and ointments that contain steroids, antibiotics, astringents or anesthetic agents on your nipples. The anhydrous lanolin, known as Lansinoh, has had all impurities and allergens removed by a special patented process, and is now recommended to relieve nipple soreness and aid in healing.

You should not be alarmed if your nipples are tender during the first few days of breastfeeding. After lactation has been established and the let-down reflex has occurred, many mothers describe an increase in fluid pressure which is relieved by the infant sucking. As a rule, nipples will adapt naturally to nursing. If, however, pain in your nipples continue, call your clinician or lactation specialist.

One of the most common causes of painful nipples is poor positioning of the baby for breastfeeding during the first few days.

In one study of nipple pain, researchers found that the single most important factor was how the breast was presented to the baby. A proper grasp of the breast and correct positioning of the infant, so that baby is facing the breast and baby's body is facing mother's body, is critical to avoiding nipple pain. Baby should not have to turn his head to begin nursing.

The best way to avoid breast engorgement is to frequently nurse your baby for lengthy periods. Nurse every 2 or 3 hours day and night, even if it's necessary to wake your baby. Nurse baby for at least 10 to 20 minutes on each breast.

If your breasts are sore after nursing, apply an ice pack to your breasts. If you continue to have a problem, contact your clinician or lactation specialist.

Although the quality of the milk produced by the breast is usually a sweet, rich substance, that milk can be affected by your diet and your medications. Excitement, anxiety or deep depression may also be reflected in the milk's quality.

Many drugs taken by the mother are passed on to the baby through the breast milk. These include:

- laxatives
- alcohol
- nicotine (from smoking)
- marijuana
- cocaine

Even a common drug like aspirin can be transmitted to the baby. Aspirin can affect clotting ability. Consequently, these substances should be eliminated while nursing. If you need to take any drugs, even non-prescription drugs, you should ask your doctor.

Women who work outside the home can start breastfeeding until they return to work. Afterwards, part-time breastfeeding can still yield benefits. Some women even arrange baby-sitting near where they work so that they can nurse in the middle of the day. Breastfeeding is considered by some healthcare providers to be so important that they encourage women to make every effort, even if it is for a short time.

There are 2 additional benefits for the nursing mother. Both the uterus and the abdomen return more quickly to normal in a nursing mother. Also, in most cases, menstruation does not resume until after the baby is weaned. Although, keep in mind, you can still become pregnant while nursing.

The American Academy of Pediatrics recommends that you nurse your baby for 1 year. Certainly, 6 weeks will give your baby an excellent start, and 2 months or more is even better. The baby will probably signal when he wants to stop nursing, but this will usually not occur for at least 1 year. By then, the need to suck may start to diminish. Weaning is really an individual matter between you and your baby, but as always, your clinician or other healthcare professional can offer practical help.

Because breasts are composed of inelastic ligamentous tissue, not muscle, your genetic makeup will determine how quickly and what shape they will return to.

A proper bra to support breasts heavy with milk is important for your comfort and to help minimize sagging. A practical feature of a nursing bra is a handy flap which can open to expose the nipple allowing you to easily feed the baby.

Should it be necessary to store your breast milk, remember that it can lose its nutritive value as well as spoil if not properly stored. In an article appearing in the January 2001 issue of the *American Academy of Pediatricians News*, pediatricians were encouraged to assure parents that refrigeration of breast milk for up to 72 hours was safe. Breast milk will keep for several weeks in a freezer if temperature is maintained below 30° F. In a deep freezer at 0° F, the milk should be able to stay for several months. Fresh breast milk should be used as much as possible, with frozen breast milk used only as a back-up.

Breast milk, when removed from the refrigerator or freezer, may appear discolored (yellow tinged, bluish green, even a little brown). This does not mean the breast milk is bad. Always check breast milk to be certain it does not smell sour or taste bad. Because breast milk does not look like cow's milk when stored, taste and smell, not color, should determine if the refrigerated breast milk is good.

Thawing breast milk

Never heat breast milk in a microwave oven:

- High temperature can destroy some of the vitamins and protective cells.
- Milk heats unevenly.
- The outside container can feel cool, but milk may be very hot and cause a burn.

Breast milk thaws quite rapidly. The best way to accomplish this is to place the container with frozen milk in a bowl under running lukewarm water.

- After it is thawed, shake bottle or container to ensure even temperature.
- Always test a few drops on your wrist to be certain milk is near body temperature.

For additional information on breastfeeding, you may want to read *Breastfeeding*, produced by the Budlong Press, the same publisher as this book, and available through your clinician.

Three ways to burp your baby

The non-nursing mother

Should you decide not to breastfeed your baby, be aware it takes approximately 14 days for the breast glands to stop producing milk. You will probably be advised to wear a tight bra and apply ice packs to your breasts to relieve any discomfort you may have.

Do NOT use a breast pump on your breasts if you are planning not to breastfeed. Pumping your breasts will only cause more milk to be produced.

If you are not breastfeeding, how do you bottle feed your baby? In the hospital, the nurse will supply a warm bottle and will show you how to position both the bottle and the baby. You will hold your baby in your arms with the same closeness of feeling as the nursing mother. A certain amount of patience is necessary to teach the bottle-fed baby how to suck on a nipple. At times, your baby will not get enough milk because the nipple holes are too small. Then you may find in the next feeding that the baby is squirted in the eyes as you bring the bottle near because the hole is too large. It's not unusual to feel frustrated and anxious as the baby cries. You can easily overcome these minor annoyances. The next time you feed, your baby will have forgotten and be sweet, docile, and cooperative. Babies are remarkably resilient and manage to survive in spite of you, the hospital staff, and everyone else.

Other concerns after delivery

Rest—Immediately after delivery, you will want to sleep. Many hospitals now allow the new mother and her baby to go home 24 hours after delivery. After a nap, your nurse will help you get out of bed, sit in a chair, or walk about.

Sterilization—Because sterilization should be viewed as a permanent or irreversible procedure, it is very important that you discuss this option with your partner and give it careful consideration. Among those women who select sterilization as a method of birth control, almost half have it done postpartum (after delivery) in the hospital and usually within a day or two of delivery.

Stitches—If you had an episiotomy, you'll have stitches to close the incision. You may feel them begin to pull and itch by the second day. They may even hurt when you walk or sit. Don't be shy about telling your clinician if your stitches are painful. Your clinician may suggest a sitz bath for relief of discomfort.

Constipation

A common complaint of pregnant women is constipation. Changes in hormones may contribute to the slow movement of food through the digestive tract. Another contributing factor may be a lack of exercise. Pressure exerted on the rectum during labor often causes the rectum to become numb. This may result in the muscles which aid in the expulsion of fecal matter becoming sluggish. The pressure during labor may cause an additional source of discomfort as a few hemorrhoids may be pushed out on the external rectal surface. Your clinician may recommend a stool softener or mild laxative to help you move your bowels without irritating the sore rectal tissues. Other steps you can take to improve regularity include:

- Daily exercise, such as a 20 to 30 minute walk is good.
- Drinking at least 8 glasses of liquid a day, including prune and other fruit juices.
- Eating high-fiber foods such as whole grain cereals and bread, as well as plenty of fruits and vegetables.

Postpartum blues

After delivery, most mothers may expect everything will be fine. The anticipation during these past months of your baby's arrival is over, and you've returned home to what you expect will be an exciting new time in your life. And it will be. Still, it's not uncommon now to experience mood swings, irritability, fatigue, agitation and symptoms that may indicate depression.

As a new mother, you may not be prepared for some of the typical discomforts or anxieties you are feeling. Your breasts are sore and you are awaken by uterine contractions. You try different positions for sitting and sleeping but still cannot get comfortable. The baby is ready to be fed but suddenly you need to go to the bathroom. As the baby cries for no apparent reason you feel helpless. Suddenly everything seems to be going wrong and you have to struggle to keep from crying yourself. This emotional storm can be caused by several factors: (1) you feel listless and lacking in energy; (2) your hormones are leveling off to find a new balance; (3) thyroid levels may drop after birth, causing dramatic mood swings; (4) the idea of learning to handle and care for a new baby seems overwhelming; (5) you hurt physically; (6) you may think that your life has changed drastically and that there are so many adjustments you will have to make; (7) you may even feel a sense of loss because you are no longer the pampered pregnant mother who is the center of attention. Instead, the baby is the center of attention and you are merely his/her food source.

Intense feelings of sadness, anxiety or despair that disrupt a new mother from functioning, are a sign of postpartum depression and should be reported to a doctor.

One very good outlet for these feelings is to talk to other parents—both new and experienced. By sharing your concerns with one another, you can be reassured that the physical and emotional problems that now seem so large will soon be manageable. In most cases, the postpartum blues go away within 2 weeks. If it lasts longer it may be postpartum depression.

Postpartum depression

Approximately 10 percent of mothers develop postpartum depression (PPD). Why some women develop this depression and others do not is not fully understood, though there are certain factors which may lead to increased risk. In many cases it is a combination of factors that may result in postpartum depression.

These factors include:

- Personal history of a mood disorder (depression) even before pregnancy

- Postpartum depression following a previous birth
- Family history of depression
- Strong anxiety feelings before giving birth
- Dissatisfaction or unhappiness with your marriage or relationship with your partner
- Social isolation
- Lack of good support from partner, family and friends

If after a week or two of the "blues", you are still feeling extreme anxiety, a sense of hopelessness, despair and/or other negative feelings, to the degree that it interferes with your daily life, you may be suffering from postpartum depression. Other symptoms of postpartum depression include:

- Disinterest in your baby or yourself
- Inability to sleep (insomnia) or the wish to sleep all the time even when baby is awake
- Loss of appetite or excessive need to eat all day
- Thoughts of harming yourself or your baby
- Feelings of guilt or hopelessness
- Panic attacks
- Extreme concerns or lack of interest in baby

Should you have any of these signs of postpartum depression, take steps immediately to get the help you need. Speak with your doctor and let him or her know what you are feeling. They have the experience and understanding to support you through this period. If necessary, he/she can refer you to the resources where you can find additional help.

Parenting is a 2-person commitment, and the father, who is the closest person to the mother, should be able to spot any distress early on. Research has shown that a supportive relationship during PPD treatment is associated with a decline in symptoms of depression. Fathers should look for changes in appetite, extreme anxiety, lack of interest in the baby, or other symptoms such as not being able to sleep or sleeping a lot more than usual. What is important is to be supportive of the new mother and encourage her to seek help.

Treatment for postpartum depression includes individual and/or group-counseling sessions, support groups, antidepressant medication and, on rare occasion, even hospitalization.

The majority of women who develop postpartum depression, if not treated, may still be depressed after 1year. The treatment for postpartum depression is highly successful once the disorder is recognized and treatment is begun.

Postpartum psychosis is the most severe type of postpartum depression. It occurs rapidly over a 24- to 72-hour period, and usually begins several days postpartum, with the greatest risk occurring within the first month after delivery. Symptoms of postpartum psychosis may include the symptoms of depression in addition to symptoms of extreme confusion, disorientation and distractibility. Prompt referral for medical/psychological evaluation and treatment is essential.

In the meantime what can you do to help take care of yourself and your baby? First recognize that you cannot do everything yourself. Most new mothers need some help the first week or two after coming home. Ask for help from family members and friends. You must get enough rest. Do not be afraid or embarrassed to ask for help in order to get that rest. Try to nap when your baby is napping. It is important to make some free-time for yourself. If you can get a sitter, take a couple of hours and have lunch out with a friend. Arrange to have some free-time with your partner.

If your postpartum blues lasts longer than a couple of weeks, or your negative feelings become worse instead of better, call your doctor or other healthcare professional for help. Postpartum depression and its debilitating effects can affect the entire family. There are hotlines and support groups that may be helpful. Your clinician can refer you to resources in your area.

Remember, the treatment for postpartum depression is highly successful once the disorder is diagnosed and treatment is begun.

Circumcision

Circumcision, one of the oldest known surgical procedures, is the practice of removing the foreskin from the penis of baby boys. In recent decades, medical views about the health benefits of circumcision have changed.

Though some studies have reported uncircumcised males may have a higher incidence of sexually transmitted diseases and that circumcision may provide some degree of protection against disease, the validity of these medical arguments has been questioned as new information becomes available. The American Academy of Pediatrics currently views circumcision, not as a medical decision, but rather as one of parental choice. Circumcision is not required by law or hospital policy. It is performed at the request of the parents.

More evidence is now accumulating that supports the reports that circumcision does offer protection against urinary tract infections, as well as cervical cancer in female partners, genital ulcer disease and HIV infection (see page 12). Complications following circumcision are rare and almost always minor according to a recent article.

Some parents want their sons circumcised for religious or cultural reasons. The procedure, if there are no contraindications, is usually performed by the doctor before the baby leaves the hospital. The penis heals within a week and very rarely are there complications.

Many hospitals offer an anesthetic cream the doctor can apply to the penis prior to circumcision, though not all doctors agree it is necessary.

Discuss circumcision with your doctor or other healthcare professional long before your due date so that you can make an informed decision. See page 218 for how to care for your baby following circumcision.

Visitors

On average, your hospital stay will last from 1 to 2 days. During that time, it's your decision whether or not you want to have visitors. Whatever your decision, it is important that you rest as much as possible. During this time you can relax with some favorite magazines or a book, read up on baby care or talk with family and friends over the telephone. If you do have visitors, you will need to take into account the hospital's visiting rules. These rules vary among hospitals. The times for visiting hours are for the good of the patient and the efficiency of the hospital. Visiting hours may be restricted to 1 or 2 hours in the afternoon or evening. Some hospitals only allow new fathers to visit maternity patients. There may also be a limit on the number of visitors allowed in a room at one time.

In many hospitals there are opportunities for new mothers to participate in demonstrations on bathing, feeding and caring for your new infant. Or you may be able to watch a movie on these subjects.

Tips on hygiene

A sponge bath at your bedside or sink will have to suffice until your doctor feels you are strong enough to take a tub bath or shower.

Use soft tissues or cotton balls to wipe yourself following urination and bowel movements. Remember, always wipe from front (vagina) to back, toward the anus (rectum)—never wipe from back to front. This is to help avoid introducing foreign bacteria into the vagina. Always put on a clean sanitary pad after using the toilet. The hospital will provide you with pads during your stay. Soiled pads should be discarded in bags specially provided for this purpose.

Chapter 20 Going home

YOUR HOSPITAL STAY will go by very quickly, usually only 1 or 2 days. Before you know it you will be getting ready to go home. So much has taken place during the past few days in the hospital that it may seem incredible that you are returning home with a new infant in your arms and a dramatically changed body.

The baby's clothes that you packed in your overnight case will be brought to you, and one of the nurses will help you dress your baby for the trip home. How many and what kind of clothes and blankets the baby needs depends on the weather conditions on the day of discharge.

Following the birth of your baby, you may have lost most of your abdomen, but chances are that your pre-pregnancy clothes will still not fit you comfortably. Most women wear the same clothes home that they wore when they entered the hospital. You and the baby will be helped to your car by the nurse and your partner. The car carrier should already be properly installed in the back seat of the car to safely transport the baby home.

If you have arranged any household help, that person should be ready and waiting for your arrival. When you first return home, it is probably a good idea to lie down and rest. Though you've been looking forward to going home, remember that your routine will change considerably with the new baby. Don't be too eager to jump back in to your regular household chores.

Family members may want to come over and welcome you back, but for your sake and the baby's, it is probably best to postpone their visits for a day or two. Your baby will be adjusting to the surroundings and will be under some strain. Loud, sharp noises may cause the baby to cry.

Your friends and family will need to understand that you and your baby need time together, and that visits can wait until you are both ready for company.

It is important not to rush things when you get home. You may feel eager to care for your baby and resume the responsibilities of your home, but it is really important for you to return slowly to your former routine. Don't feel guilty for giving yourself some short periods of rest. It's very natural to feel weak and to tire easily at this stage. Your main priorities are caring for your baby and allowing yourself adequate time for rest. Other non-essential chores can be postponed. The housework can be done by your husband or partner, along with others who can assist you in caring for the baby.

Transporting premature and low birth-weight infants

The following guidelines were issued by the American Academy of Pediatrics for transporting premature and low birth-weight infants:

- Look for either an infant-only car seat with a 3-part harness system or a convertible car seat with a 5-part harness system.
- Do not place a small baby in a car safety seat with a shield, abdominal pad or arm rest that could come in contact with the baby's face and neck during impact.
- Baby should be positioned with buttocks and back flat against the back of the car seat. Rolled-up blankets may be placed on both sides of the infant to help support his/her head and neck. A rolled-up diaper or small blanket can be inserted between the crotch strap and the baby, so that baby will not slouch forward in the car safety seat.
- Premature infants born less than 37 weeks gestation should be observed in a car safety seat before being discharged from the hospital, so that the baby can be monitored for possible breathing problems, drop in heart rate, or changes in blood oxygen levels. Check with your hospital to see if it has developed policies to include this procedure in their discharge planning process.
- Those babies with documented evidence of a decrease in blood oxygen levels, lapses in breathing, or a drop in the heart rate when placed upright in a car seat should not travel in conventional car safety seats. They should be transported in special safety devices which allow babies to be on their backs or tummies while in transport. Infant swings, seats and carriers should also be avoided for these infants.

- If heart and breathing monitors are prescribed for the baby, parents should use the equipment while traveling, using a portable, self-contained power source.

Postpartum exercises

Though you may now have lost the large abdomen, one glance in a full-length mirror will tell you that you are still a long way from your pre-pregnancy size. Your previous wardrobe will still be too tight to zip or button up. Expectations of returning immediately to non-maternity clothes are just not realistic.

The best way to get back in shape is exercise. It is important to exercise not only so that you will look better, but also to tighten and tone the muscles that were stretched during your pregnancy.

Ask your doctor how soon you can begin your postpartum exercises. Unless contraindicated, begin with simple exercises while you are in the hospital, exercising just once or twice a day, increasing gradually, and stopping before you become fatigued or strain a muscle. You should also resume the Kegel exercises (as described on pages124-126) as soon as you are able. These exercises will stimulate the flow of blood to the pelvic floor and thus promote healing.

Your diet

Write down your ideal weight and body measurements. Now take your present weight and measurements and compare them with your ideal numbers. How close are these 2 sets of measurements?

The only way to lose weight is to consume fewer calories than your body burns. A non-nursing woman burns about 2,000 calories a day. Nutritious, lower calorie meals coupled with a conscientiously followed exercise program will enable you to lose weight rapidly. In about 2 months, you should be back to your pre-pregnancy weight. Before leaving the hospital; check with your nurse for information on nutritious, low-calorie postnatal meals.

First-week exercises

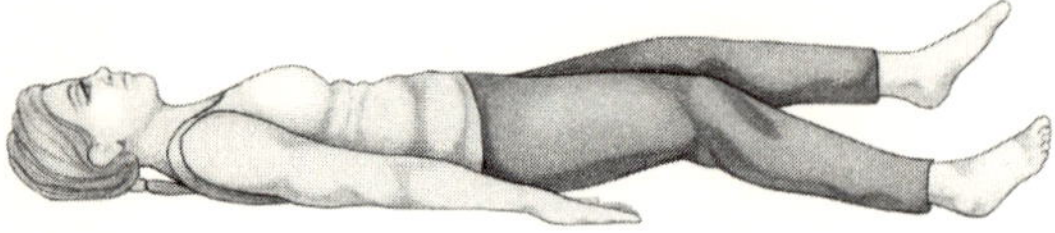

For leg raises, lie flat on your back. Raise the right foot off the bed about 6 inches, keeping the left slightly bent. Lower the right leg slowly. Do the same with the left leg. Alternate the legs. Repeat 4 to 5 times.

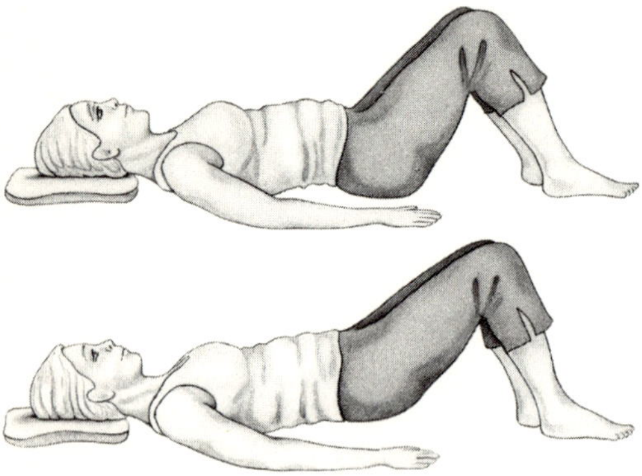

For tightening the abdominal muscles lie on your back with your head on pillow. Bend knees and keep feet flat on the floor or bed. Arch your back and push your seat against the floor. Then push your back against the floor and raise your pelvic area. Contract abdominal muscles. Relax and begin again. Repeat 4 or 5 times at first.

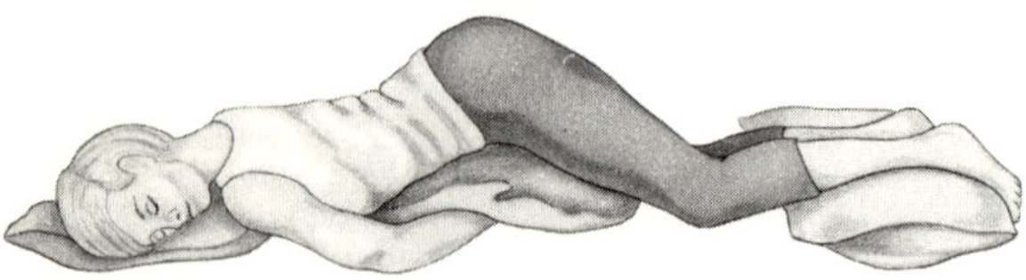

This exercise will help your uterus return to a good position. Lie stomach down, palms up, a folded blanket or pillow under your hips and another under your ankles. Turn your face to one side and fall asleep if you can during this "exercise."

Second-week exercises

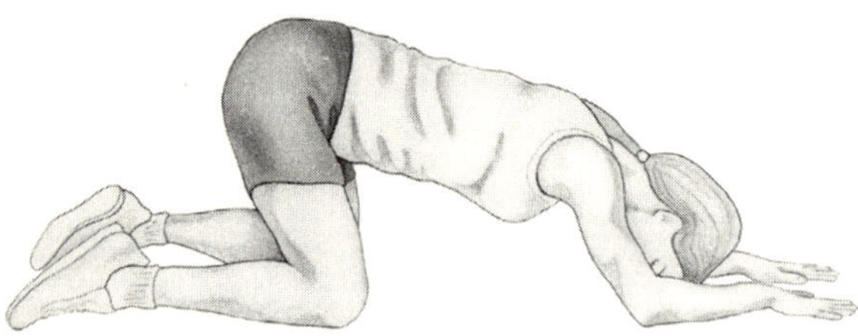

This exercise helps the uterus to return to its normal size and position. Keep your forehead on the floor. Lean on your elbows and knees and arrange them so they are together. Pull your back upward, contract your buttocks, and pull in your abdomen. Relax and breathe deeply. Try to assume this position every morning and evening for about 5 minutes.

For abdominal muscle tone, get down on your hands and knees with feet slightly apart, head parallel to the floor. Gently pull in abdominal muscles and round your back like a cat. Hold for a second, then let the abdominal muscles sag completely, hollowing the back. Repeat several times.

Third-week exercises

For trunk muscles, get on hands and knees keeping the back as straight as possible. Turn your head to the right and look toward your feet. As you turn, contract your right trunk muscles and stretch the left ones. Straighten the body, rest a minute, then repeat in the opposite direction.

Walking is still one of the best exercises. About the beginning of the 3rd week, you can take a walk out of doors, but do make an effort to do a lot of walking about the house before then. Walk with the abdomen pulled in, chin high, and swing the arms.

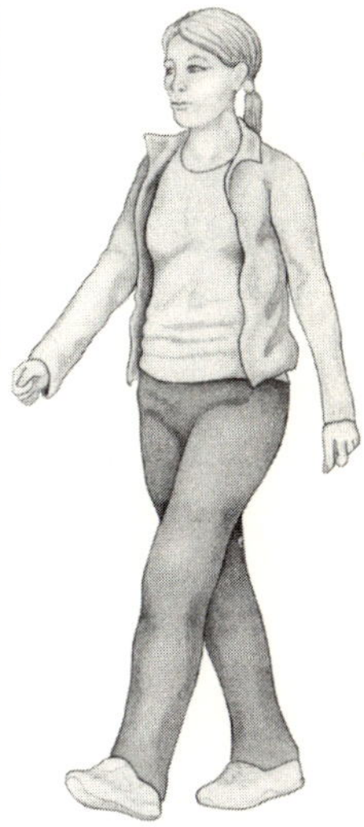

Fourth-week exercises

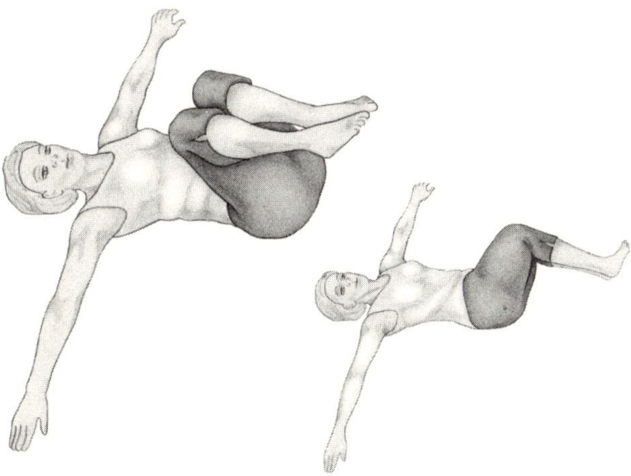

For general muscle tone, posture, and vigor, lie flat on your back with knees to chest, arms straight out at sides. Keep shoulders flat and twist the pelvic area until the left knee touches the floor. Keep both legs together. Return to central position. Rest. Twist to the right until right knee touches floor.

Swimming

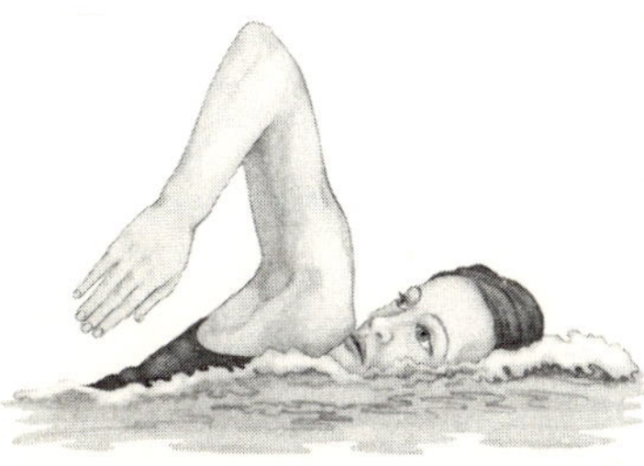

Swimming is very helpful in regaining abdominal muscle tone. Increase time gradually and adjust to your capacity. Do not rush schedule.

Exercise for your breasts

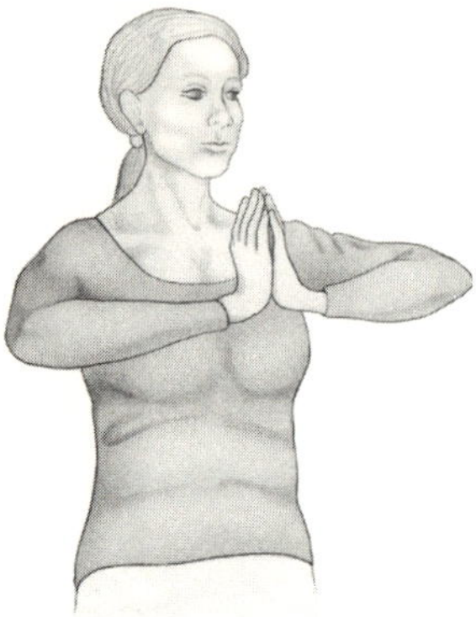

Breasts have no muscle tissue, they are formed of glands and fatty tissue. Exercise of any kind cannot firm them up. However, the prominence and contour of the breasts are helped by strengthening the pectoral muscles upon which the breasts rest.

With arms semi-outstretched, place your hands together while opposing each other and push firmly. This isometric exercise causes the pectoral muscles to stand out.

Return of menstruation

The uterus returns to its normal size in approximately 6 weeks. If you are not nursing, your menstrual period may resume 7 to 9 weeks after delivery, although it is not unusual for it to take a little longer. Your first period may be somewhat erratic, lasting for a longer or shorter period of time than is usual for you. It may also be heavier or lighter than you've experienced in the past. Your system will regulate itself in a month or two and return to what is normal for you. It is not unusual for women who suffered from severe menstrual cramps (dysmenorrhea) before becoming pregnant to experience less discomfort during menstruation after the baby is born.

You should be aware that your ovaries may begin to function before menstruation begins. This means you can become pregnant before your first menstrual period if you engage in intercourse without using birth control. You should use a reliable form of birth control 3 to 4 weeks after delivery if you are going to have sexual relations and do not want to become pregnant.

If you are breastfeeding your baby, your menstrual periods may be delayed for several months or possibly not resume until you stop breastfeeding. It is still possible, however, to get pregnant while you are nursing your baby. Breastfeeding is not a reliable form of birth control.

Sexual relations

A few weeks after delivery, you will need to see your clinician for a postpartum checkup. It is often a good idea to refrain from sexual relations until you have this checkup. The reason is that your internal organs are still sensitive. You may be sore, and your uterus is still in the process of shrinking. You will probably also be experiencing some vaginal discharge.

Although the postpartum period lasts for 6 weeks, many couples resume sexual relations before it is over. The resumption of sexual relations is neither harmful nor dangerous, depending on your physical condition and frame-of-mind. Remember, you are not immune from pregnancy during the postpartum period. If you are going to resume a sexual relationship, you should use a reliable form of contraception, provided you have no religious or moral objections to birth control devices. If you used a diaphragm or a cervical cap prior to your pregnancy and wish to continue to use either of these forms of contraception again, you must be remeasured since most frequently there is a size change following delivery.

The postpartum period is also a good time to discuss with your partner your plans for other babies. You and your husband need to decide how you want your babies to be spaced. You must allow your body time to regain its strength and give your reproductive organs a rest before you conceive again. It will take about 3 months for you to feel more like you did before becoming pregnant. For most women, a wait of 1 1/2 to 2 years between births is best.

If you and your partner have engaged in unprotected sex, contact your healthcare professional right away to discuss emergency contraception. A high dosage of birth control pills taken within 72 hours of sex, followed by a second dose 12 hours later, lowers the risk of pregnancy by approximately 75 percent. Another emergency contraception protocol is to have your clinician insert an IUD after unprotected sex. Emergency contraception works by preventing ovulation, preventing a fertilized egg from implanting in the uterus or blocking fertilization. The high dose of birth control pills may cause nausea, bloating and breast tenderness for a day or two. If you do not get your period within 3 weeks, take a home pregnancy test and contact your physician.

Your healthcare provider is the best source for advice for any questions about birth control or resuming sexual relations.

Other forms of contraception include:

- Birth control pills (oral contraceptives): The most popular method of contraception, the pill, which contains synthetic female hormones, prevents ovulation. A new birth control pill called Seasonale® was cleared for market use by the FDA.

Seasonale is an extended cycle contraceptive pill designed to reduce the number of menstrual periods from 13 to 4 periods per year. Seasonale is a 91-day regimen taken daily (84 days of pills which contain the hormones levonorgestrel and esthinly estradiol, followed by 7 days of inactive pills).

There may be increased incidence of breakthrough bleeding or spotting. Risks associated with other types of contraceptive pills such as blood clots, stroke and heart attack are the same for this extended use contraceptive. Women who take Seasonale or any other contraceptive containing hormones are advised not to smoke.

- Intrauterine devices (IUD): This is a small plastic device inserted into the uterus (usually at the first postpartum checkup or during a menstrual period) to prevent the sperm from fertilizing the egg. Currently there are 2 IUDs that are approved by the Food and Drug Administration (FDA) in the U.S. One IUD, the Para Gard T380A, contains copper but does not contain any hormones. A second IUD, called MIRENA, was recently approved by the FDA. It contains a hormone. All are contraindicated in the presence of pelvic inflammatory disease (PID) or in women with a history of pelvic inflammatory disease.

- Barrier methods of contraception: This method prevents sperm from coming in contact with the egg: includes the diaphragm, cervical cap, condom, female condom, and contraceptive gel and cream which contain a chemical that kills sperm. Contraceptive gels/creams are more effective when used in conjunction with other barrier-type devices.

- Sterilization: This is most frequently performed in women following delivery. It is called tubal ligation, and involves either cutting or placing a clip around the fallopian tubes. Sterilization in a man is called a vasectomy. In this procedure, the tubes through which the sperm travels (vas deferens) are sealed so that sperm cannot be released during sexual relations. A new, less invasive procedure not requiring an incision has been cleared by the FDA.

- Depo-Provera®: A hormone injection that protects against pregnancy for 3 months by preventing egg cells from ripening and being released from the ovary. It does not contain estrogen.

- Chewable oral contraceptive is a spearmint-flavored version of 1 of the combination oral contraceptives, and can be chewed or swallowed. It will carry the same risks and warnings as the regular contraceptive pills.

- Contraceptive patch has been cleared by the FDA. The Patch looks like a square band-aid. It is applied to the upper torso or arms, but never on the breasts. The Patch is changed on the same day each week for 3 weeks. The 4th week is PATCH-FREE. It carries the same risks and warnings as does the contraceptive pills.

- Emergency contraception. There are 2 methods of emergency contraception:

  a. the emergency contraceptive pill called "the morning after pill" which must be taken with in 72 hours of unprotected sexual intercourse; although less effective, the emergency contraceptive has been shown to work up to 120 hours after unprotected sex.

  b. an intrauterine device (IUD) which should be inserted into the uterus by a physician

- Nuva Ring® is a vaginal ring containing hormones that is inserted into the vagina for 3 weeks, followed by 1 week ring-free, allowing for a withdrawal bleed.

This text is intended for a broad-based patient population and does not represent the teachings or beliefs associated with Catholic healthcare. If you have religious or moral objections to birth control devices, please disregard this section and other references to birth control measures in this text.

The postpartum checkup

The postpartum examination is similar to the examination which you had when you became pregnant; however, this time the clinician will be checking for other factors. Three of the main areas which your clinician will check are:

- Whether your organs have returned to their normal size

- Whether your vaginal stitches have dissolved

- Whether the cervix has healed

Symptoms and signs to report after delivery:

- Fever over 100.4°F (38°C)
- Bleeding heavier than a menstrual period
- Swelling and tenderness in your legs
- Chest pain and/or cough
- Nausea and vomiting
- Burning, pain, urgency (frequent, strong desire to void) on urination
- Painful, hot and tender breasts
- Perineal pain and tenderness that does not subside

Some advice about your first weeks at home

1. It is a good idea to stay around the house for the first week or so.
2. 1 nap a day is desirable, 2 if possible.
3. Consult with your clinician about how soon you can drive a car.
4. If you are not nursing your baby and your breasts are having trouble drying up, use ice packs. Ask your clinician about medication if your breasts become painful.
5. In a few weeks, you may again experience baby "blues." You are especially likely to become cross and irritable if you allow yourself to become overtired. However, this condition is perfectly normal. You will know when it is happening to you, and you will know that it passes.
6. Before you attempt to get pregnant again, it is a good idea to give your body a few months to rest. During this time, your body can rebuild its store of nutrients.

Chapter 21 The beginning of motherhood

BEING A MOTHER PROVIDES A GREAT DEAL of pleasure, but also requires a great deal of work. It is important to know ahead of time about some of the circumstances that will occur in the first few weeks and months of motherhood.

Baby's weight

The first week after bringing your baby home, you may notice that your baby looks thinner than at birth. Your first reaction may be to question whether or not your feeding him/her enough.

You shouldn't worry, it's not unusual for babies to lose weight during their first week of life. Your baby will be back to his/her birth weight in another week, and after that will continue to grow rapidly.

Baby's sleeping position

The American Academy of Pediatrics now recommends that all healthy infants be placed on their backs to sleep rather than on their stomachs. Unless there are special medical conditions requiring your baby to sleep on his or her stomach, always put your baby to sleep on his/her back. If special conditions exist, discuss the situation with your physician before placing your baby to sleep on his/her stomach. Studies have found that infants who sleep on their stomachs have a higher incidence of sudden infant death syndrome (SIDS). While awake and under your watchful eyes, you can allow your baby play time on his/her stomach.

The soft spot

When observing your baby closely, you will notice what looks like a soft spot at the top of the head. This soft spot is known as a fontanelle. This skeletal separation of the baby's skull allows the head to conform to the shape of the vaginal canal during delivery. After birth, the head may even look quite elongated rather than round. In a few months, this will change as the head rounds out and the fontanelle begins to close. By 2 years of age, this soft spot will be completely closed. You must take added precautions that your baby does not fall or receive blows to the head that would cause serious and permanent injury. It is perfectly safe to wash baby's head when he/she is being bathed.

Do not be alarmed if you see some black and blue marks on your baby's head after delivery. The forces of labor put a great deal of pressure on the baby's head. Forceps or vacuum delivery can also leave bruises. These black and blue marks usually disappear in a couple of days.

How to care for the umbilical cord and circumcision

When your baby was born, the clinician severed the umbilical cord and now a small stump remains attached to the baby's navel. The first day or two after birth, this stump will begin to shrivel and start to dry up. Sometime between the 7th and 8th day, it will drop off. Until it does drop off, it will be attached to the baby. You should simply allow nature to take its course. When bathing the baby, you should keep the area clean by removing crusty material. If necessary, you can use baby oil to soften the crusty area.

The circumcision heals naturally and complications following a circumcision are rare. After the procedure is completed, the penis is wrapped with a gauze square saturated with vaseline or other suitable cream. The gauze usually falls off the penis by itself. If it does not fall off, do not pull on it, just squeeze some warm water on the gauze to loosen it. Check with your clinician as to the care of the circumcised or uncircumcised penis.

Birth certificate

When your baby is born, the clinician signs a birth certificate which is then filed with the appropriate agency in your city or town. The law in the United States and Canada require that every baby born is registered in this way at birth. About 4 weeks after you return home, you will receive a certified copy of the birth certificate. Because this is a very important document, you should check it carefully for accuracy as soon as you receive it. Check that names are spelled correctly and that dates are right. If you find any inaccurate information, you should have it corrected at once. The longer you wait, the more difficult it will be to correct any errors. Place the birth certificate somewhere that is safe. It is also a good idea to have a copy made. This certificate will be needed when your child registers for school as well as for other occasions.

Enjoying your baby

Learn to enjoy your role as a new parent now that your baby is off to a good start in life. Reading books and articles on child care can help you reduce many of the fears or anxieties you may have about raising your baby. They will help you know

what to expect at different steps in your baby's development. Your doctor will help you with information on how frequently your baby needs to be examined, when immunization programs must be started, and any other important issues about your baby's development and health. The booklet, *A Doctor Discusses the Care and Development of Your Baby*, covers the first 18 months of a baby's development. It is published by Budlong Press, the publisher of this book, and is available through your doctor.

Appendix

How to handle emergency childbirth

Late in pregnancy, expectant mothers often take trips after making sure that medical care is nearby. At other times, pregnant mothers and their families go camping or take boating trips to isolated areas, and thus increase their chances of a do-it-yourself baby delivery.

The following set of guidelines are a step-by-step approach to delivering your baby on your own. These guidelines have been recommended by leading experts, and most of the advice is directed to the father. However, the mother should also be acquainted with these steps and be fully prepared for an emergency.

1. Attempt to get help. You must first make sure that there is no way to get to the hospital on time. If going to the hospital is out of the question, you should call your clinician, or call an ambulance to come to your aid.

2. Do not panic. This rule applies to both parents. Remember: pregnancy is a normal condition, and childbirth is the natural culmination of that process.

3. Help make the mother comfortable. A pregnant woman who is about to deliver will be most comfortable and safe when she is lying down. Place her on a bed, a floor (in a camper), or on the seat of a car. Depending on the time available, you should place paper or a clean sheet or towel underneath her in order to absorb the excess fluid expelled during delivery. If the mother prefers, however, she can sit up or even assume a squatting position. At this time, the mother should practice her prenatal relaxation exercises. If the mother has an urge to empty her bladder or bowel, she should use a bed pan or a basin. She should not use the toilet.

4. Thoroughly wash your hands. Use plenty of soap and water to help prevent infection. Do not try to clean any area of the mother's body, including the vaginal entrance.

5. Allow the baby to come out naturally. When the baby enters the birth canal, nature will prevail, forcing the mother to bear down until the baby is delivered. During labor, the mother should try to relax, breathing as normally as possible. If the mother becomes tense, the contractions will be less effective in dilating the cervix and delivery may be delayed. You may hear the mother scream if her contractions are extremely painful, but do not let her screams "rattle" you. Keep "cool!" The father should not pull, push, tug or interfere in any way with the delivery. The baby should then be allowed to emerge onto a clean towel or sheet. Sometimes in bearing down, the mother may have a bowel movement. Take the feces and cover or remove it to avoid contaminating the baby.

   If you were unable to reach your healthcare provider and trouble develops, you should help the mother to lie down or place her in the most comfortable position in your car, and take her to the nearest help available.

6. If the baby emerges in the unbroken sac, you should break that sac. Usually the sac will already have broken spontaneously, but if not, use your fingernail, a pin, the tip of a scissor, or a knife to break it open. **Warning:** be very careful not to injure the baby inside the sac. Once the sac is broken, wipe the sac away from the baby's head so that normal breathing can start.

7. Clean off the baby's face, using a clean handkerchief, towel, or even a dish towel. Do not use paper towels for this step because a paper towel could tear and small pieces could become lodged in the baby's nostrils or mouth, and then be inhaled into the baby's lungs. Using the towel, wipe the baby's face and head, including the nose and mouth. By wiping off the baby's face, you will be removing any thick mucus that could be inhaled into the baby's lungs.

8. Be careful with the umbilical cord. After the baby emerges, the cord should be left slack, especially if it is still pulsating, to allow the blood to continue to flow into the baby. The umbilical cord extends from the baby's navel to the after birth. During pregnancy, this is the baby's lifeline for food and oxygen. Make sure that the cord is not wrapped around the baby's neck. You do not have to cut the cord immediately after the baby is born. When the clinician arrives later, he or she can do this. However, if no medical assistance is

available, you should take a piece of clean string or strong twine and tie the cord tightly in two places. Then take a pair of clean scissors or a knife and cut the cord between the two ties.

9. Do not dispose of the afterbirth. Usually the afterbirth, which is attached to the umbilical cord, will be expelled from the mother without assistance. You should not pull on the umbilical cord to remove the afterbirth because you might prematurely break the cord. When the afterbirth emerges, you should place it in a basin or on a newspaper. The clinician will want to examine it to make sure nothing has been left inside the mother.

10. Place the baby as close to the mother as possible. The mother's body is the best place to keep the baby warm. If you find that the umbilical cord is long enough, you should place the baby on the mother's arm or next to her breast. Whether or not nursing takes place, it will actually help the mother if the baby sucks at her nipple. The reason is that the sucking causes the uterus to contract, which then helps to expel the afterbirth more quickly. On the other hand, you may find that the umbilical cord is short. In that case, remove or cover the fluid between the mother's legs and place the baby there.

11. Place a cover over the baby. If nothing else is available, use a warm blanket or coat. The baby's head should also be covered because the baby can lose a great deal of body heat through his/her head. Be careful not to block the baby's mouth and nose so that he/she can breathe normally.

12. Begin massaging the mother's abdomen. By applying gentle massage to the abdomen where the uterus is located, you can help to prevent excessive bleeding, even if the afterbirth has been expelled. Locate the uterus by placing a cupped hand just between the pubic hair and the belly button.

13. Complete the delivery by cleaning the mother and making her warm and comfortable. However, do not attempt to clean the baby. The cheesy coating on its skin protects the baby, and this coating should be allowed to remain for a while. Make sure the baby is warm. While you and the mother are waiting for the clinician, you can relax and enjoy your success.

Family Medical History

Detailed family medical records are helpful in diagnosing and treating potential health problems, especially those that recur in some families. For your clinician's reference, note any serious diseases in your family. The list below should be consulted when filling out the form. When you have completed the form, discuss it with your clinician.

Is there any history in your family of:

Allergies	Hearing defects	Sickle cell anemia
Arthritis	Heart defects	Tay-Sachs disease
Cancer	Hemophilia	Visual defects
Diabetes	Hypertension	Other recurring family diseases
Epilepsy	Mental retardation	

Name	Birth date	Blood type and Rh	Disease History	Medications

Mother ____________________

____

Her mother ____________________

____

Her father ____________________

____

Father ____________________

____

His mother ____________________

____

His father ____________________

____

Other Children ____________________

____

____

Calorie counter

The calories listed are average amounts, and although the caloric content of individual foods may vary, your diet should average to the correct number of calories if you use the listed figures. Bear in mind that your diet must supply enough of all of the important food elements: vitamins, minerals, proteins, etc. The best diet is the one your clinician recommends. Be sure you follow it.

Calories in one gram of:		
	carbohydrate	**4 calories**
	fat	**9 calories**
	protein	**4 calories**

T. = Tablespoon

Calories	
A	
424	Almonds (1-1/2 cup)
108	Angel food cake (2" slice)
76	Apple (1 average size)
124	Apple juice (1 cup)
331	Apple pie (4" slice)
184	Applesauce, sweetened (1 cup)
18	Apricot (1 large)
97	canned in syrup (4 halves + 2 T. juice)
10	dried (1 half)
22	Asparagus (6 spears)
200	Asparagus soup, creamed (1 cup)
279	Avocado (1/2 med. size)
B	
50	Bacon, Canadian, fried (1 slice)
119	Banana (1 large)
108	Beans baked (1/3 cup)
9	green (1/3 cup)
76	kidney (1/3 cup)
50	lima-young, fresh
191	Bean soup (1 cup)
	Beef:
200	pot roast (1 slice)
200	prime rib (1 slice)
300	steak (1 serving)
252	Beef and vegetable stew (1 cup)
23	Beets (1/3 cup)
350	Berry pie (1 slice)
	Berries:
72	Blackberries canned in syrup (1/3 cup)
27	fresh (1/3 cup)
28	Blueberries (1/3 cup)
82	canned in syrup (1/3 cup)
30	water packed (1/3 cup)
33	Raspberries, black, fresh (1/3 cup)
23	red, fresh (1/3 cup)
85	frozen (3 oz. pkg.)
33	water-packed (1/3 cup)
27	Strawberries, fresh (1/2 cup)
100	frozen (3 oz.)
129	Biscuits, baking powder (1)
116	Bologna (1 slice)
9	Bouillion (1 cup)
	Bread:
60	Cracked wheat (1 slice)
50	French (1 slice)
65	Raisin (1 slice)
57	Rye (1 slice)
64	White (1 slice)
55	Whole wheat (1 slice)
17	Broccoli (1/3 cup)
100	Brownies (one)
150	Buns, hamburger (one)
50	Butter (1 average pat)
C	
36	Candy, hard (one piece)
37	Cantaloupe (1/2)
105	Carbonated beverages (cola-type) (1 glass)
15	Carrots (1/3 cup)
164	Cashew nuts (1 oz.)
17	Catsup (1 T.)
10	Cauliflower, cooked (1/3 cup)
55	Cereals, cooked (1/3 cup)
	Corn meal
	Cream of Wheat
	Farina
	Hominy Grits
	Rolled Oats
	Wheat, whole
	Cereals, dry:
117	Bran Flakes (1 cup)
96	Corn Flakes (1 cup)
28	Grape Nuts (1 T.)
39	Rice, puffed (1 cup)
39	Rice flakes (1 cup)
133	Rice Krispies (1 cup)
100	Shredded Wheat (1 large size)
	Cheese:
104	Blue (1 oz.)
85	Camembert (1 oz.)
113	Cheddar (1 oz.)
90	Cottage (1/3 cup)
56	Cream (1 T.)
100	Edam (1" cube)
97	Limburger (1 oz.)
104	Roquefort (1 oz.)
105	Swiss (1 oz.)
40	Cherries, canned in syrup (1/3 cup)
5	Chestnuts (one)
	Chicken:
50	breast, roasted (1 slice)
50	broiled (1 average piece)
200	canned, boned (1/3 cup)
50	liver (one)
75	Chicken soup or consomme (1 cup)
150	noodle soup (1 cup)
100	with rice soup (1 cup)
133	Chicken salad (1/3 cup)
17	Chili sauce (1 T.)
143	Chocolate bar, milk, plain (1 oz.)
151	with almonds (1 oz.)
150	Chocolate cake (1 slice)
100	Chocolate creams (one)
100	Chocolate fudge sauce (1 T.)
185	Chocolate milk (1 cup)
75	Chocolate chip cookies (1)
42	Chocolate syrup (1 T.)
200	Chop suey, meat and vegetables (1 cup)
124	Cider (1 cup)
92	Clams (4 oz.)
200	Clam chowder (1 cup)
150	Coconut cake with icing (1 average slice)
0	Coffee, black
100	with sugar or cream (1 cup)
100	Coffee cake (1 slice)
34	Cole slaw (1/3 cup)
25	Collards (1/3 cup)
100	Cookie, plain (one)
56	Corn, canned (3 oz.)
84	on cob (one ear)
159	Corn bread or muffin (one)
125	Cooking oil (1 T.)
50	Crab meat (1/2 cup)

Calories	
40	salad (1/3 cup)
	Crackers:
14	Graham (1 small)
100	Matzoth (one)
17	Pretzel (one)
20	Ry-Krisp (one)
33	Saltines (1 double)
17	Soda (one)
18	Cranberries (1/3 cup)
208	sauce (1/3 cup)
30	Cream, light (1 T.)
49	sour, heavy (1 T.)
50	whipped (1 T.)
150	Cream puff (one)
33	Cream sauce (1 T.)
1	Cucumber, raw (1 slice)
200	Cup cake, iced (one)
150	Cup cake, plain (one)
266	Custard pie (1 slice)
100	Pudding (1/3 cup)
D	
79	Dandelion greens, cooked (1 cup)
168	Dates, pitted (1/3 cup)
20	whole (one)
136	Doughnut (one)
E	
250	Eggnog (1 cup)
100	Eggs (1 egg)
50	Evaporated milk (2 T.)
F	
100	Figs, canned in syrup (1/3 cup + 2 T. juice)
57	dried (one)
56	Fig Newton cookies (one)
78	Flounder (4 oz.)
228	Foundation cake (1 slice)
124	Frankfurter (one)
100	French roll (one)
59	French salad dressing (1 T.)
82	Frog legs (4 oz.)
200	Fruit cake (2" x 1/2" pc.)
60	Fruit cocktail, canned,
60	solids & liquid (1/3 cup)
116	Fudge, plain (1 piece)
G	
66	Gefilte fish (1/3 cup)
155	Gelatin, plain (1 cup)
80	Ginger Ale (1 cup)
20	Ginger snap (one)
90	Gingerbread (1 slice)
34	Grapes, seedless (1/3 cup)
115	Grape juice (1 glass)
43	Grapefruit, canned sweetened (1/3 cup)
50	Grapefruit, fresh (one-half)
297	juice, frozen concentrate (6 oz. can)
25	Gravy, brown (1 T.)
17	meat (1 T.)
H	
158	Haddock, fried (1 serving)
100	smoked (1 serving)
228	Halibut steak, broiled (1 serving)
339	Ham, smoked or cooked (3 oz.)
400	Hamburger on bun (one)
119	Hominy, cooked (1 cup)
62	Honey (1 T.)
50	Honeydew melon (1 average slice)
I	
167	Ice cream, plain (1 scoop)
300	Ice cream soda (1 glass)
J	
55	Jams and jellies (1 T.)
50	Jello (1/3 cup)
K	
15	Kale (1/3 cup)
120	Kidney, beef (3 oz.)
89	lamb (3 oz.)
97	pork (3 oz.)
41	Kohlrabi, raw, diced (1 cup)
L	
350	Lamb, rib chops, broiled (1)
230	roast leg (1 slice)
126	Lard (1 T.)
20	Lemon (one)
4	Lemon juice (1 T.)
302	Lemon meringue pie (1 slice)
133	Lentils (1/3 cup)
7	Lettuce (3 leaves)
19	Lime (one)
120	Liver, calf (1 serving)
150	Liverwurst (1 serving)
78	Lobster, canned (3 oz.)
66	salad (1/3 cup)
250	Luncheon meat (3 oz.)
M	
155	Macaroni and cheese (1/3 cup)
50	Macaroons (one)
154	Mackerel, canned (3 oz.)
500	Malted milk with ice cream (1 large glass)
87	Mango (one)
200	Maple sugar (1 square)
50	Maple syrup, pure (1 T.)
100	Margarine (1 T.)
55	Marmalades (1 T.)
20	Marshmallows (one)
100	Mayonnaise (1 T.)
25	Melba toast (1 slice)
	Milk:
86	Buttermilk, cultured (1 glass)
87	Skim (1 glass)
166	Whole (1 glass)
33	Skim, powdered (1 T.)
40	Whole, powdered (1 T.)
341	Minced pie (1 slice)
50	Mints, chocolate (one)
45	Molasses (1 T.)
134	Muffins (one)
9	Mushrooms, canned (1/3 cup)
300	soup, creamed (1 cup)
N	
100	Nectarine, fresh (one)
107	Noodles (and spaghetti) (cooked) (1 cup)
O	
50	Oatmeal cookies, plain (1)
7	Olive, green (one)
125	Olive oil (1 T.)
50	Onions, raw (one)
4	small, green (one)
100	Onion soup (1 cup)
106	Orange, fresh (1 large)
300	Orange juice, frozen Concentrate (6 oz. can)
108	Orange juice, fresh or canned, unsweetened (1 glass)
120	Ovaltine, skim milk (1 glass)
200	Oxtail soup (1 cup)
14	Oysters, raw (one)
100	Oyster soup, creamed (1 cup)
250	stew, 6-8 oysters (1 cup)
P	
59	Pancakes (one)
1	Parsley (1 T.)
94	Parsnips, boiled (1 cup)
79	Peaches, canned in syrup (2 halves)
46	fresh (one)
89	frozen (4 oz.)
50	Peanuts, shelled, roasted (1 T.)
50	Peanut brittle (1 piece)
92	Peanut butter (1 T.)
95	Pears, fresh (one)
58	syrup packed (1/3 cup)
25	water packed (1/3 cup)
48	Peas, canned (1/3 cup)
37	fresh or frozen (1/3 cup)
141	Pea soup (1 cup)
52	Pecans (1 T.)
16	Peppers (one)
250	Pepper-pot soup (1 cup)
15	Pickles, dill, large (one)
22	sweet (one)
15	relish, sweet (1 T.)

Calories	
95	Pineapple, canned in syrup (1 slice + juice)
44	fresh (1 slice)
97	frozen (4 oz.)
121	juice, canned (1 glass)
33	Pistachio nuts (1 T.)
29	Plums (one)
200	Plum pudding (1 slice)
54	Popcorn, plain (popped) (1 cup)
310	Pork chop (1 serving)
350	Pork roast (1 slice)
75	Pork sausage (one)
6	Postum (1 cup)
97	Potatoes, baked (one)
118	boiled (one)
18	French fries (one)
160	fried (1/3 cup)
157	hash brown (1/3 cup)
53	mashed (1/3 cup)
25	new (one)
200	sweet, baked (one)
75	canned (1/3 cup)
11	Potato chips (one)
66	Potato salad (1/3 cup)
200	Potato soup (1 cup)
200	Pound cake (1 slice)
4	Pretzel (one)
20	Prunes, dried (one)
161	sweetened (1/3 cup)
170	juice, canned (1 glass)
263	Pumpkin pie (1 slice)

R

150	Rabbit (1 hind quarter)
1	Radishes (1/3 cup)
143	Raisins (1/3 cup)
300	Raisin pie (1 slice)
128	Rhubarb, stewed (1/3 cup)
100	Rice, boiled (1/2 cup)
133	Rice pudding, custard (1/3 cup)
300	Rich cake (1 piece)
100	Rolls, French (one)
50	Root Beer (1 small glass)
100	Roquefort salad dressing (1 T.)
100	Russian salad dressing (1 T.)
17	Rutabaga (1/3 cup)

S

204	Salmon, baked or broiled (1 steak)
140	canned (3 oz.)
200	loaf (1/3 cup)
350	Sandwiches (cheese, chicken, egg, tuna, ham or other meat between 2 slices bread with mayonnaise or butter)
150	Sardines, canned in oil (1)
100	tomato sauce (one)
39	Sauerkraut (1 cup)
340	Sausage, pork (4 oz.)
30	Scallops (one)
250	Scotch broth (1 cup)
191	Shad (4 oz.)
118	Sherbet (1/3 cup)
40	Shortbread (one)
125	Shortening (1 T.)
10	Shrimp, dry packed (one)
83	jumbo, fried (one)
33	salad (1/3 cup)
125	Smelt, fried (one)
250	Sole, fried (1 serving)
218	Spaghetti, canned (1 cup)
15	Spinach, cooked (1/3 cup)
150	Sponge cake (1 slice)
11	Squash, summer, cooked (1/3 cup)
30	Squash, winter, cooked (1/3 cup)
88	Succotash (1/3 cup)
16	Sugar, cane or beet (1 teaspoon)
27	lump (one)
51	brown (1 T.)
31	powdered (1 T.)
223	Swordfish, broiled (1 steak)
57	Syrup, maple or corn (1 T.)

T

35	Tangerine, fresh (one)
100	Tapioca pudding (1/3 cup)
50	Tartar sauce (1 T.)
0	Tea, unsweetened
50	Thousand Island salad dressing (1 T.)
50	Tomato juice, canned (1 glass)
5	sauce (1 T.)
90	soup (1 cup)
15	Tomatoes, canned (1/3 cup)
30	raw (one)
50	Tortillas (one)
300	Trout (1 serving)
	Tuna:
169	canned, no oil (3 oz.)
247	canned in oil (3 oz.)
100	salad (1/3 cup)
304	Turkey (4 oz.)
14	Turnips cooked - greens (1/3 cup)

V

100	Vanilla pudding (1/3 cup)
25	Vanilla wafers (one)
150	Veal cutlet, broiled (one)
75	roast (1 slice)
225	Vegetable beef soup (1 cup)
40	Vegetable juice (1 glass)
82	Vegetable soup (1 cup)
60	Vienna sausage, canned (1 oz.)
0	Vinegar

W

216	Waffles (one)
49	Walnuts, halves (1 T.)
45	Watermelon (1 slice)
115	White fish, steamed (portioned)
198	Wild rice (1/3 cup)

Y

24	Yeast (1 oz.)

Z

33	Zwieback (1 slice)

Comparative Prenatal Weight Gain Chart

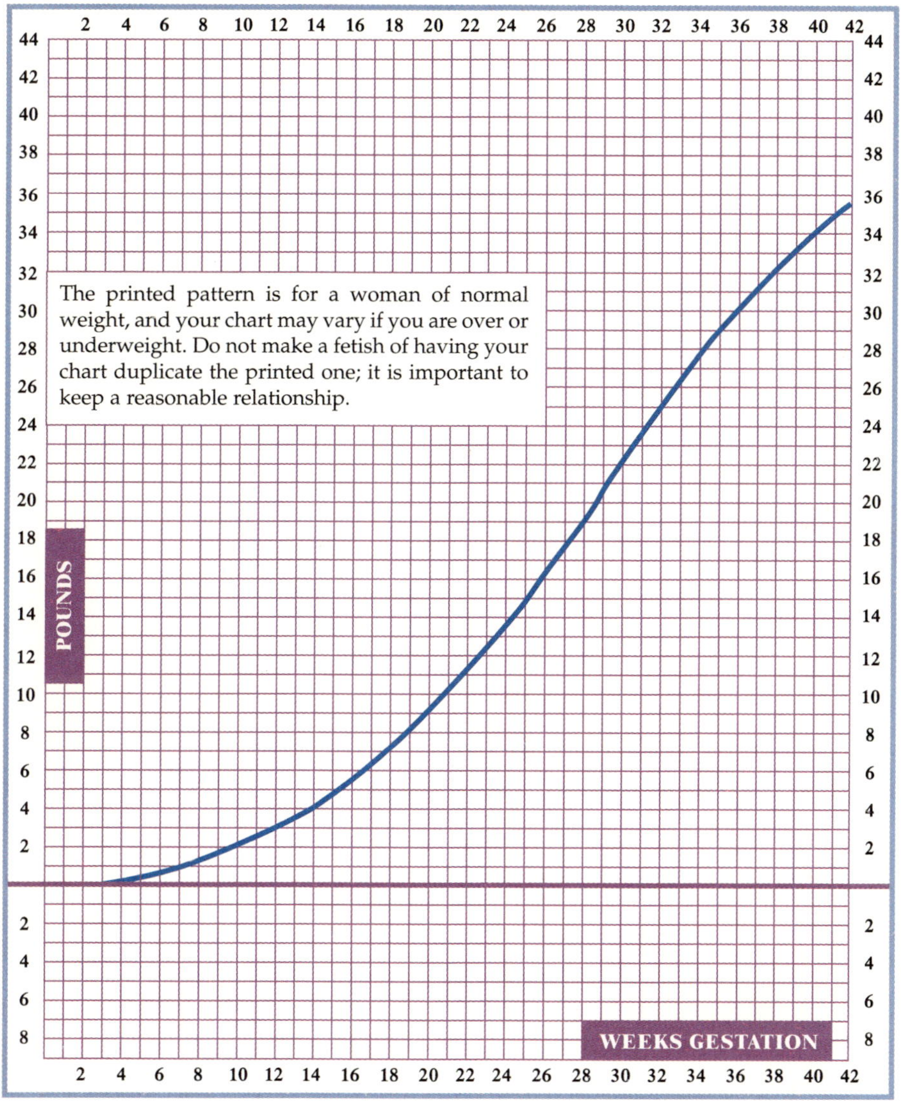

The Appearance of a Healthy Week-Old Baby

THE LEGS are most often seen drawn up against the abdomen in pre-birth position. Extended legs measure shorter than you'd expect compared to the arms. The knees stay slightly bent, and legs are more or less bowed.

THE FACE will disappoint you unless you expect to see pudgy cheeks, a broad, flat nose with a mere hint of a bridge, a receding chin, undersized lower jaw.

THE TRUNK may startle you in some normal detail: short neck; small, sloping shoulders; swollen breasts; large, rounded abdomen; umbilical stump (future navel); slender, narrow pelvis and hips.

WEIGHT, unless well above the average of 7 or 8 lbs., will not prepare you for how really tiny a newborn is. Top to toe measure is anywhere between 19" and 21."

ON THE SKULL you will see or feel two most obvious soft spots or fontanelles. One is above the brow; the other is close to the crown of the head in back.

THE SKIN is thin and dry. You may see veins through it. Fair skin may be rosy-red temporarily. Downy hair is not unusual.

A DEEP FLUSH spreads over the entire body if baby cries hard. Veins on head swell and throb. You will notice no tears as tear ducts do not function yet.

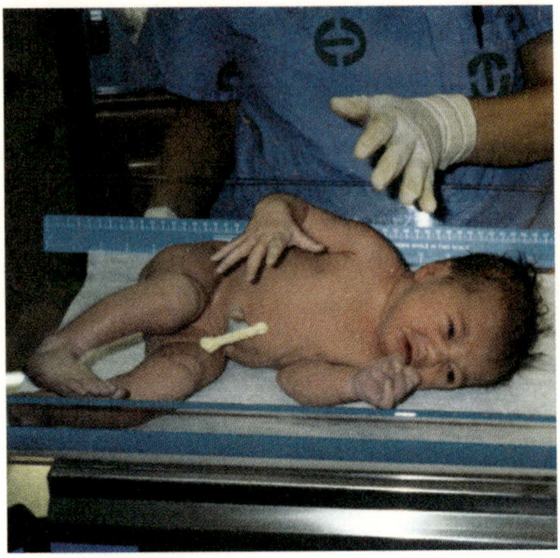

THE FEET look more complete than they are. X-ray would show only one real bone of the heel. Other bones are now cartilage. Skin is often loose and wrinkly.

EYES appear dark blue, have a blank starry gaze. You may catch one or both turning or turned to crossed or wall-eyed position.

THE HANDS, if you open them out flat from their characteristic fist position, have finely lined palms, tissue-paper-thin nails, dry, loose-fitting skin, and deep bracelet creases at wrist.

GENITALS of both sexes will seem large (especially scrotum) in comparison with the scale of, for example, the hands to adult size.

THE HEAD usually strikes you as being too big for the body. Immediately after birth, it may be temporarily out of shape, lop-sided or elongated, due to pressure.

Agents Known to be Harmful to the Fetus

Agents	Why or How Used	Effects on Fetus
Accutane	Cystic acne.	Abnormalities during developmental stage. Increased risk of miscarriages.
Alcohol	Social reasons, dependency.	Mental retardation. Abnormal growth pattern. Fetal alcohol syndrome (FAS).
Androgens	To treat endometriosis.	Genital abnormalities.
Anticoagulants	Prevent blood clotting. To treat thromboembolism (clots that can block blood vessel).	Increased risk of bleeding. Abnormalities in bones, cartilage, eyes, central nervous system defects.
Antithyroid drugs	To treat hyperthyroidism.	Enlarged or underactive thyroid condition.
Anticonvulsants	To treat epilepsy.	Mental and growth retardation, developmental abnormalities and neural tube defects (spina bifida or anencephaly).
Chemotherapy	To treat cancer or severe psoriasis (a skin condition).	Increase in incidence of miscarriage and birth defects.
Soriatane	Topical agents used to treat psoriasis.	Abnormal changes in cervix and uterus of female fetus. Possible effect on male and female fertility.
Diethylstilbestrol (DES)	Was used in the 1940s and 1950s to help prevent miscarriages and preterm labor. Also used in treating problems with menstruation, menopause, and breast cancer. Also used to stop the production of milk.	Abnormal changes in cervix and uterus of female fetus. Possible effect on male and female fertility.
Isotretinoin	See Accutane.	
Lead	Used in manufacture of and in paint, printing, glasses, ceramics, and pottery glazing.	Increased incidence of stillbirths and miscarriages.
Lithium	To treat depression.	Congenital heart defects.
Mercury (Organic)	From eating contaminated food.	Brain disorders.
Streptomycin	An antibiotic to treat tuberculosis or other infections.	Hearing loss.
Tetracycline	Antibiotic to treat various types of infections.	Affects development of tooth enamel.
Thalidomide	At one time used as a sedative to treat sleep disorders and "morning sickness."	Limb reduction, absence of limb.
X-Ray therapy	To treat medical disorders including cancer	Retardation, mental or physical growth.

Abortion: The premature expulsion from the uterus of an embryo or nonviable fetus. The main types are: (1) induced, (2) spontaneous, more commonly called miscarriage, (3) therapeutic (to save the life or health of the mother).

Abruptio placentae: The premature separation of the placenta from the inner wall of the uterus.

Accutane: A drug used to treat severe acne and known to cause birth defects. This drug should not be used during pregnancy, or for a month prior to becoming pregnant.

Active labor: The second phase of the first stage of labor, the cervix dilates from 4 to 8 centimeters.

Acupressure: Application of pressure using the fingertips, on specific parts of the body for the relief of nausea, pain and fatigue.

Alpha-fetoprotein (AFP): A protein produced by the fetus that is present in the amniotic fluid and in the mother's blood. An elevation in AFP levels aids in prenatal diagnosis of neural tube defects in the fetus.

Amenorrhea: Absence of menstruation.

Amniocentesis: A procedure in which a needle is inserted through the abdomen into the amniotic sac to remove a small amount of amniotic fluid surrounding the fetus, for testing.

Amniotic fluid: The fluid surrounding the fetus in the amniotic sac in the mother's uterus, whose main purpose is to cushion the fetus, protecting it against injury.

Analgesic: An agent that alleviates pain without causing loss of consciousness.

Anencephaly: One type of neural tube defect that occurs when the brain and head of the fetus do not develop normally.

Anesthesia: An agent that induces loss of feeling or sensation. A general anesthesia induces a state of unconsciousness with total absence of feeling or sensation over the entire body. Regional or local anesthesia produces a lack of feeling or sensation in a part of the body by interrupting the conductivity from the sensory nerve for a given region of the body.

Antepartum: The time between conception to birth; also called prenatal.

Antibody: A protein in the blood produced in reaction to foreign substances such as bacteria and viruses that cause infections.

Antibiotics: Drugs that kill microorganisms.

Antigens: Substances such as proteins or microorganisms which are capable, under appropriate conditions, of inducing an immune response and causing the production of antibodies.

Apgar Rating: A numerical expression of the condition of a newborn infant taken 1 minute and again 5 minutes after birth, to assess the newborn's responses to life.

Ausculation: A method of listening to fetal heartbeat during labor, either with a special stethoscope or use of a Doppler ultrasound device.

Autoimmune Diseases: Diseases that can occur when the body's immune system goes askew and, instead of protecting the body, attacks and injures the body's own tissues. Autoimmune diseases are usually chronic. How these diseases may affect a pregnancy depends on the specific disorder. The 3 most common autoimmune diseases are systemic lupus erythematosus (SLE), rheumatoid arthritis and antiphospholipid.

Autoimmune Disorder: Loss of function or destruction of normal tissue as a result of an immune response to one's own body cells.

Bilirubin: The breakdown of red blood cells which can cause jaundice.

Biophysical Profile: An assessment of fetal heart rate, fetal body movement, fetal muscle tone, and the amount of amniotic fluid surrounding the fetus. The heart rate is determined by the non-stress test. Ultrasound is used for the other measurements.

Birth canal: The passageway from the uterus through which the baby is born.

Blood Pressure: The heart pumps oxygen-rich blood through the arteries to all parts of the body. The blood is returned to the heart through the veins. Blood pressure is read as 2 numbers. For example, if the blood pressure is 120/80, the top number (120) indicates the pressure in the arteries when the heart contracts; this is called systolic pressure. The lower number here (80) is the pressure in the arteries when the heart is at rest and is called the diastolic pressure.

Braxton-Hicks Contractions: False labor pains.

Breech Presentation: The buttocks or the feet of the baby are positioned at the top of the birth canal.

Carcinogens: Compounds known to cause cancer.

Carrier: A person who has an abnormal gene of a recessive disorder is a carrier of the disorder. A carrier may have no signs of the disorder but can pass the gene on to his or her children. Only females can be carriers of X-linked recessive traits.

Cerebral Palsy: A defect of motor power and coordination, related to damage in the brain.

Chancre: An infectious sore caused by syphilis and appearing at the site of infection.

Chloasma: The brownish blotches that appear around the eyes and nose during pregnancy.

Chorioamnionitis: Inflammation of the membrane surrounding the fetus.

Chorionic Villi Sampling (CVS): Cells from the microscopic, finger-like projections that make up the placenta are withdrawn, either by a needle inserted through the abdomen, or a catheter inserted through the vagina and cervix into the edge of the placenta. These cells are then placed in a special culture and grown so that their genetic makeup can be analyzed.

Chromosome Disorders: Chromosome disorders can be either inherited or, as in the majority of cases, the result of an error in the developing egg or sperm. Extra, missing or incomplete chromosomes usually result in serious health problems.

Chromosomes: Structures that are located inside each cell in the body, and contain the genes that determine a person's physical makeup.

Coagulation: Clotting of blood.

Colostrum: The liquid substance secreted by the breasts a few days prior to and after delivery, that precedes the flow of breast milk.

Congenital Defect: A defect that exists at or before birth, regardless of the cause of the defect.

Contraction Stress Test: A test in which mild contractions of the mother's uterus are induced, and the fetus' heart rate in response to the contraction is recorded using an electronic fetal monitor.

Corticosteroids: Hormones used in the treatment of arthritis and other medical conditions.

Cystic Fibrosis: A disorder that strikes in childhood, whereby the lungs produce thick, sticky mucus that clogs the bronchial tubes and leads to lung infections. It is possible to test for carriers of this disease.

Doula: Greek word meaning to "mother the mother."

Down's Syndrome: This is a genetic disorder caused by the presence of an extra Chromosome 21 (normally there are 2 Chromosomes 21; in Down's syndrome, there are 3). It is characterized by mental retardation, abnormal features of the face, and medical problems such as heart defects. Multiple marker screening test can measure the levels of the protein alpha-fetoprotein and the hormones human chorionic gonadatropin and estriol in the mother's blood in prenatal testing for this disorder.

DNA (Deoxyribonucleic Acid): A chemical that contains the genetic code for the entire body. Chromosomes are made up of DNA material. There are approximately 3 billion pairs of DNA in a human body.

Duchenne Muscular Dystrophy: This is an X-linked disease that causes the muscles to weaken. It is one of the most severe of the muscle dystrophies and affects almost only boys. Carriers of this disease can be tested prenatally.

Ectopic Pregnancy: A pregnancy where the fertilized egg is implanted and grows somewhere other than the inside of the uterus, usually in one of the fallopian tubes.

Edema: Swelling caused by the retention of fluid.

Effacement: The thinning and softening of the cervix.

Electronic Fetal Monitoring: A procedure recording the heartbeat of the fetus and uterine contractions by the use of special instruments.

Encephalopathy: A disorder (swelling) of the brain

Endometriosis: A condition in which tissue similar to that normally found in the uterus is found outside the uterus, usually on the ovaries, fallopian tube and other pelvic structures.

Epidural Block: One type of anesthesia that numbs the lower half of the body.

Episiotomy: A surgical incision into the perineum and vagina to widen the vaginal opening, thus helping to prevent tearing during delivery.

Estrogen: A female hormone produced in the ovaries.

Fetal Alcohol Syndrome (FAS): This syndrome is diagnosed when a baby, whose mother was known to have abused alcohol, is found to have growth retardation (defined as very low birth weight, length and/or head circumference), abnormalities of the central nervous system (such as irritability in infancy, hyperactivity in childhood, delayed development or impaired intellect), and an abnormally small head.

Fetal Monitoring: See Electronic Fetal Monitoring.

Fibroids: Benign (non-cancerous) growths that form on the inside of the uterus, on its outer surface, or within the uterine wall itself.

Follicle - Stimulating Hormone (FSH): A hormone secreted by the pituitary gland that helps an egg to mature and be released by the ovary.

Forceps: Special instrument sometimes used in delivery. The instrument is placed around the baby's head to help guide it out of the birth canal.

Fragile X: The most common inherited cause of mental retardation. The gene is on the X-chromosome. Normal women may be carriers of this disease.

Gene: A gene is a segment of the DNA molecule which is coded to pass along specific characteristics. Each gene has a specific function and position on the chromosome. Each human being has approximately 50,000 to 100,000 genes. Scientists know the role of only a small number of human genes.

Genome: A full set of genes is called a human genome. It is the genome that controls all aspects of human growth, development, and function.

Gestation: Pregnancy

Hemophilia: The lack of a substance in the blood that helps the blood clot. It affects only males, but women are the carriers of this gene. Testing can detect carriers and male fetuses that are affected.

Human Chorionic Gonadotropin (hCG): A hormone produced by the placenta after a fertilized egg has developed and implanted into the wall of the uterus.

Huntington Chorea: A nerve disorder which leads to uncontrollable movements and mental decline. The gene can be carried by either parent. It is usually diagnosed in middle age. There is a test to determine which family members have inherited the disease.

Hydramnios: A condition in which there is an excess amount of amniotic fluid in the sac surrounding the fetus.

Insulin: A hormone that controls the levels of glucose (sugar) in the blood.

Ionizing radiation: The radiation used to X-Ray the internal organs.

IU: International Unit of measurement.

Jaundice: A yellowish appearance to the skin and whites of the eyes (conjunctiva) due to a buildup of bilirubin in the blood.

Kegel Exercises: Perineal exercises to strengthen the muscles surrounding the openings of the urethra, vagina, and anus.

Lanugo: Fine hair that sometimes grows on a baby's back and shoulders at birth; it disappears in 1 or 2 weeks.

Laparoscopy: A surgical procedure which uses a thin instrument with a light at one end to visually examine the pelvic organs.

Lightening: The term given to describe the fetus' head when it moves down in the uterus pressing against the cervix and bladder. The fetus has "dropped" into a birthing position.

Linea Nigra: The dark line which runs from the top of the abdomen to the bottom during pregnancy. The line slowly fades after delivery.

Lochia: The vaginal discharge that occurs the first week or two after childbirth.

Luteinizing Hormone (LH): A hormone produced by the pituitary glands, which helps the egg to mature so that it can be released by the ovary.

Macrosomia: A condition in which a fetus grows too large. It is often associated with a mother who is diabetic or in a post-term pregnancy.

Maternal Serum Screening: A group of blood tests that check for substances linked with certain birth defects.

Meconium: The dark green gelatinous material, that is a mixture of secretions from the intestinal tract mixed with some amniotic fluid, that builds up in a growing fetus and is excreted shortly after birth.

Miscarriage: The spontaneous loss of a pregnancy, usually prior to 20 weeks gestation.

Multifactorial Disorders: Disorders/diseases believed to be caused by a mix of genetic and environmental factors are known as multifactorial inheritance. Sometimes these defects can be surgically corrected. Examples of a multifactorial disorder are cleft palate, hare lip.

Multiple Gestation: A pregnancy where more than 1 fetus is growing in the uterus.

Mutagens: Compounds which change the genetic material in the body cells.

Neural Tube Defects (NTD): A birth defect which results from the improper development or closure of the spinal cord or the brain.

Nitrosamine: Potent carcinogen.

Nonionizing Radiation: The radiation from color TV, video display screens and microwave ovens.

Non-Stress Test: A test performed by placing a monitor over a patient's abdomen, and recording fetal movements and the fetal heart rate occurring in relationship to the movements.

OSHA: The Occupational Safety and Health Administration.

Oxytocin: A hormone administered intramuscularly or intravenously, to induce or increase the force of contractions in labor.

Palmer Grasp: The most frequently recommended hand position for breastfeeding.

Paracervical Block: A local anesthetic injected into the tissues around the cervix to relieve pain.

Pellagra: A disease due to a deficiency of Vitamin B_3 (Niacin).

Perineum: The area located between the vagina and the anus.

Phenylketonuria (PKU): An inborn condition in which the body is unable to use phenylalanine properly, resulting in an accumulation of amino acids in the body fluid.

Pica: The compulsive eating of nonfood items such as dirt, clay, cornstarch; more common during pregnancy.

Pituitary Gland: A gland located at the base of the brain, that secretes hormones that cause the egg to mature and be released during ovulation.

Placenta: The tissue which connects the fetus and mother, and provides nourishment to the fetus; it also takes waste from the fetus.

Placenta Previa: The placenta rests very low in the uterus, partially or entirely covering the cervical opening.

Polydactyly: This disorder results in a baby being born with extra fingers and/or toes. It is easily corrected by surgery.

Postterm Pregnancy: A pregnancy that extends beyond 42 weeks' gestation.

Preeclampsia: A complication of pregnancy in which high blood pressure, retention of fluid (edema), and protein in the urine are present.

Preterm Delivery: Birth prior to 37 weeks' gestation.

Progesterone: A female hormone produced in the ovaries, whose function is to prepare the uterus for the reception and development of the fertilized egg by maintaining the intrauterine environment for sustaining a pregnancy.

Pudenal Block: A regional or local anesthetic injected into the perineum to relieve pain during delivery but not labor.

Pyelonephritis: A kidney infection.

Quickening: The first feeling of life felt by a pregnant woman.

Recessive Disorders: A genetic disorder where a gene from each parent is necessary in order to cause the disorder.

Recommended Daily Dietary Allowance (RDA): Nutritional standards determined by a committee of the National Academy of Science.

Respiratory Distress Syndrome (RDS): A condition of some preterm babies in which the lungs are not fully developed.

Sickle Cell Anemia: A blood disorder where the red blood cells become "crescent" shaped rather than the normal round shape. These crescent or sickle-shaped blood cells get caught in the blood vessels, cutting off oxygen to the tissues (causing a great deal of pain). Occurs almost exclusively in African-Americans. About 1 in 10 African-Americans are carriers of this disorder but do not have the disease themselves. Both parents must be carriers or have the disease to have a child with this disorder. The test for this disorder can be detected during early pregnancy.

Spina Bifida: A neural tube defect due to the improper closure of the spinal canal.

Spinal Block: A form of anesthesia that numbs the lower half of the body.

Stillbirth: Delivery of a baby who has died before delivery.

Sudden Infant Death Syndrome (SIDS): The sudden death of an infant with no apparent cause.

Systemic Lupus Erythematosus (SLE): This is a group of connective tissue disorders, primarily affecting women aged 20 to 40 years, that can affect the entire body, including the skin, nervous system, joints and kidneys. Though it doesn't seem to interfere with fertility, it does appear to increase the risks of miscarriage, premature birth and stillborn births. Physicians advise women with lupus to wait for a remission before getting pregnant.

Tay-Sachs disease: This disorder is caused by the absence of a chemical needed for normal brain function. It causes severe mental retardation, blindness, seizures and death before 5 to 7 years of age. It is found primarily in persons of Eastern European Jewish descent. There is a test to detect the gene that carries this disorder.

Teratogens: Compounds that can cause structural changes during a fetus' development.

Thalassemia: This genetic disease causes anemia and can lead to liver and heart problems. One type, beta thalassemia, is more common in those of Mediterranean descent. Another type, alpha-thalassemia, occurs most frequently in those of Asian descent. Carrier testing of the parents and prenatal testing of the fetus can be done.

Toxoplasmosis: A disease caused by a 1-celled organism, which often exists in the intestinal tracts of cats and some farm animals such as pigs, sheep and cattle. It usually causes only minor symptoms in adults but can seriously damage a fetus.

Transducer: A device that emits sound waves and translates the echoes into electrical signals.

Trimester: Pregnancy divided into 3-month segments: 1st, 2nd, 3rd trimesters.

Trisomy: The presence of an extra chromosome in a cell which should normally have two chromosomes (it would then have 3 chromosomes). Down's syndrome is an example; instead of having 2 Chromosomes 21, it has 3.

Tubal Sterilization: A method of female sterilization in which the fallopian tubes are closed by tying, banding, clipping or sealing the ends with an electric current.

Ultrasound: A test in which sound waves are used to examine internal structures. During pregnancy, it can be used to examine the fetus.

Vacuum Extraction: A special cup-like device, which is attached to a baby's head by suction, to help ease the baby out of the birth canal.

Vasectomy: A method of male sterilization in which a portion of the vas deferens is removed.

Vernix: The whitish, cheesy coating covering a newborn.

Zygote: A cell produced by the union of a sperm pronucleus and an egg pronucleus when fertilization is completed until first cleavage.

**10 Most popular boy's names.*

Aaron
Abbott
Abdul
Abel
Abraham
Adair
Adam
Addison
Adrian
Alan
Alastair
Albert
Alden
Aldrick
Alec
Alex
Alexander
Alfred
Allan
Allard
Allen
Alonzo
Alphonse
Alvin
Amos
Andre
* Andrew
Angelo
Antonio
* Anthony
Archer
Aristotle
Arlin
Armand
Arne
Arnold
Arthur
Ashby
Asher
Ashley
Augustin
Austin
Avery

Baldwin
Barnabas
Barnaby
Barnett
Barney
Barret
Barry
Bart
Barth
Basil
Baxter
Benjamin
Bennett
Benson
Benton
Bernard
Bertram
Bjorn
Blaine
Blair
Blake
Borden
Boris
Boyce
Boyd
Bran
Brad
Bradford
Bradley
Brady
Brandon
Brendan
Brent
Brett
Brian
Broderick
Bronson
Brooks
Bruce
Bryan
Burgess
Byron

Caleb
Caldwell
Calvin
Cameron
Carey
Carl
Carleton
Carlin
Carlos
Carmine
Carroll
Carson
Carter
Carver
Cary
Casey
Cecil
Cedric
Chad
Chadwick
Chandler
Charles
Charlton
Chen
Chester
Christian
* Christopher
Clarence
Clark
Claude
Clay
Clayton
Clement
Clifford
Clifton
Clint
Clinton
Clyde
Cody
Colby
Cole
Colin
Conan
Conrad
Cordell
Corey
Cornelius
Cornell
Cort
Cory
Courtney
Craig
Crawford
Culver
Curtis
Cyril
Cyrus

Dale
Dalton
Damian
Damon
Dana
* Daniel
Darby
Darius
Darnell
Darrel
Darren
Darryl
Dave
David
Davis
Dean
Delaney
Demetrius
Dennis
Derek
Desmond
Devin
Devlin
Dewey
Dexter
Dillon
Dominick
Donald
Donovan
Douglas
Doyle
Drake
Drew
Duane
Duncan
Dustin
Dwight
Dylan

Earl
Edgar
Edmund
Edward
Edwin
Elden
Eli
Elias
Ellery
Elliott
Ellsworth
Elmer
Elmo
Elston
Elton
Elvis
Elwood
Emanuel
Emerson
Emery
Emil
Emilio
Emmett
Enoch
Enrico
Ephraim
Eric
Erin
Ernest
Errol
Erskine
* Ethan
Eugene
Evan
Everett
Ezra

Fabian
Farley
Felix
Ferdinand
Fergus
Ferris
Fitzgerald
Fletcher
Floyd
Flynn
Forrest
Foster
Francis
Frank
Franklin
Frazer
Frederick
Freeman
Fremont
Fulton

Gabriel
Galen
Galvin
Gareth
Garner
Garrett
Garrick
Garth
Garvin
Gary
Gaston
Gavin
Gaylord
Geno
Geoffery
George
Gerald
Gerard
Gideon
Gilbert
Giles
Gino
Giovanni

Glenn
Goddard
Godfrey
Gordon
Grady
Graham
Granger
Grant
Gregor
Gregory
Griffen
Griffith
Gunther
Gustave
Guy

Hadley
Hakeem
Hal
Hale
Haley
Harold
Harper
Harrison
Harry
Hart
Hartley
Harvey
Harwood
Hashim
Haslett
Hayes
Hayward
Haywood
Heath
Hector
Henry
Herbert
Herman
Hernando
Hilliard
Hilton
Hobart
Hogan
Holden
Horace
Horton
Howard
Hoyt
Hubert
Hugh
Hugo
Humphrey
Hunter
Hyatt
Hyman

Ian
Igor
Ingram
Ira
Irving
Irwin
Isaac
Isaiah
Isadore
Ivan

Jack
Jackson
* Jacob
Jacques
Jamie
James
Jamal
Jan
Jared
Jarred
Jarvis
Jason
Jasper
Jay
Jed
Jedidiah
Jefferey
Jefferson
Jeremy
Jerome
Jesse
Jethro
Jody
Joel
John
Jonah
Jonathan
Jordan
Jose
* Joseph
* Joshua
Juan
Julian
Justin

Kale
Kane
Kareem
Karl
Keanne
Keenan
Keir
Keith
Kelby
Kelly
Kelsey
Kelvin
Kendall
Kendrick
Kennedy
Kenneth
Kent
Kenton
Kerry
Kerwin
Kevin
Killian
Kimball
Kingsley
Kirby
Kirk
Kit
Kristopher
Kurt
Kyle

Laird
Lambert
Lamont
Lance
Langston
Lars
Lawrence
Lawton
Lazarus
Lee
Leif
Leigh
Leighton
Leland
Leo
Leon
Leonard
Leroy
Leslie
Lester
Levi
Lewis
Lincoln
Lindsay
Lionel
Llewellyn
Lloyd
Logan
Loren
Lorne
Louis
Lowell
Lucas
Lucian
Luciano
Lucius
Ludwig
Luke
Luther
Lyle
Lyndon
Lynn

Mackenzie
Malcolm
Mallory
Manfred
Manuel
Marc
Marcus
Marcel
Mario
Marion
Mark
Marlin
Marlon
Marlow
Marshall
Martin
Marvin
Mason
Matt
* Matthew
Maurice
Max
Maximillian
Maxwell
Melvin
Merrill
Merrick
Meyer
Michael
Mike
Miles
Millard
Milo
Milton
Mischa
Mitchell
Monroe
Monte
Montgomery
Morgan
Morley
Morris
Mortimer
Morton
Murdock
Murray
Myron

Nathan
Nathaniel
Neal
Ned
Neil
Nels
Nelson
Nevin
Newton
Nicholas
Nick
Niels
Nigil
Noah
Noble
Noel
Nolan
Norbert
Norman
Norris
Norton

Odell
Ogden
Olin
Oliver
Omar
Oren
Orlando
Orrin
Orson
Orville
Oscar
Osgood
Osmond
Otis
Otto
Owen

Pace
Paddy
Palmer
Parker
Parnell
Patrick

Patton
Paul
Pembroke
Penn
Percival
Percy
Perry
Peter
Peyton
Phillip
Pierce
Pierre
Porter
Powell
Prentice
Prescot
Preston

Quentin
Quincy
Quinlan
Quinn

Radcliffe
Rafferty
Raleigh
Ralph
Ramon
Ramsay
Rand
Randall
Randolph
Raphael
Raul
Ravi
Ray
Raymond
Raynard
Redford
Reed
Regan
Reginald
Remington
Reuben
Rex
Reynard
Reynold
Rhett
Richard
Richmond
Riley
Riodan
Roarke
Robert
Robin
Rock
Rockwell
Rod
Roderick
Rodney
Rodrigo
Roger
Roland
Rolf
Ronald
Rory
Roscoe
Ross
Rowland
Roy
Royce
Rudolph
Rudyard
Rupert
Russ
Russell
Rutherford
Ruthledge
Ryan

Salim
Salvatore
Sampson
Sam
Samuel
Sanders
Sandor
Sanford
Sargent
Saul
Sawyer
Schuyler
Scott
Seamus
Sean
Sebastian
Selby
Seth
Seward
Seymour
Shane
Shannon
Shawn
Sheffield
Shelby
Sheldon
Shelley
Sheridan
Sherman
Sherwin
Sherwood
Sidney
Siegfried
Silas
Simon
Sinclair
Slade
Sloan
Solomon
Spencer
Stacey
Stanford
Stanley
Staton
Stephen
Sterling
Steven
Stewart
Stuart
Sumner
Sven
Sylvester

Tab
Tad
Talbart
Talbot
Tanner
Taylor
Tate
Templeton
Terence
Terrill
Terry
Thatcher
Thaddeus
Theobald
Theodore
Thomas
Thor
Thorton
Thorpe
Thurston
Timmy
Timothy
Titus
Tobias
Toby
Todd
Tony
Torrance
Townsend
Tracy
Travis
Tremain
Trent
Trevor
Troy
Tucker
Tully
Turner
Tyler
Tyrone

Ulysses
Upton
Uriel

Vail
Van
Vance
Vaughn
Vern
Vernon
Victor
Vincent
Vinson
Virgil
Vladimir

Walden
Walker
Wallace
Walter
Ward
Warner
Warren
Wayne
Webb
Webster
Wendell
Wesley
Weston
Wilbur
Wiley
Willard
William
Winfield
Winslow
Winston
Woodrow
Woody
Wyatt
Wynn

Xavier

Yale
Yancy
York
Yuri
Yves

Zachariah
Zachary
Zane
Zeke

*10 Most popular girls names.

Abra
Ada
Abby
* Abigail
Adair
Adara
Addi
Adelaide
Adele
Adelle
Adrienne
Afton
Agatha
Agnes
Aileen
Aimee
Ainsley
Alaina
Alamanda
Alanna
Alberta
Alesia
Alexa
Alexandra
Alexandria
* Alexis
Alfreda
Ali
Alice
Alicia
Alida
Alidia
Allegra
Allie
Allison
Allyn
Alma
Almira
Althea
Alvina
Alyssa
Amanda
Amber
Amée
Amelia
Amelina
Amy
Anastasia
Andi
Andra
Andrea
Andrianna
Angela
Angeline
Angelique
Anita
Ann
Anna
Annabel
Annamarie
Annette
Antoinette
April
Ariela
Arlene
Arlinda
* Ashley
Astrid
Athena
Aubrey
Audrey
Audrianna
Augustina
Aurelia
Aurora
Ava
Avis
Aviva

Babette
Barbara
Bambi
Barrie
Beatrice
Beatrix
Becky
Belinda
Belita
Benita
Bernadette
Bernadine
Bernice
Beryl
Beth
Bethany
Betsy
Bette
Betty
Beulah
Beverly
Bianca
Billie
Birdie
Blair
Blakely
Blanche
Bliss
Blythe
Bonita
Bonnie
Brandy
Brenda
Briana
Bridget
Brigitte
Brittany
Brooke

Caitlin
Calla
Callie
Camilia
Camille
Candace
Candice
Candide
Candra
Candy
Caprice
Cara
Carey
Cari
Carina
Carla
Carleen
Carlotta
Carmela
Carmelina
Carmelita
Carmen
Carol
Carole
Caroline
Carolyn
Caryn
Carrie
Casey
Cassandra
Cassie
Catherine
Cathy
Celeste
Celia
Celina
Chandra
Channa
Charity
Charlene
Charlotte
Charmaine
Chasity
Chastity
Chelsea
Cherice
Cheryl
Chloe
Chloris
Chrissy
Christie
Christina
Christine
Chrystine
Christy
Cicely
Cindy
Claire
Clara
Clarissa
Claudette
Claudia
Claudine
Clementina
Coleen
Colette
Collen
Constance
Cora
Cordelia
Coretta
Corey
Corliss
Cornelia
Corrine
Courtney
Crissey
Crista
Cristina
Crystal
Cybil
Cynthia

Daisy
Dale
Dahlia
Dalila
Dana
Daniella
Danielle
Danyelle
Daphene
Daphnie
Darcie
Darcy
Daria
Darla
Davita
Dawn
Dayna
Deanne
Deborah
Debra
Dede
Dedra
Deidre
Deirdre
Delia
Della
Demitria
Denise
Desiree
Deva
Devin
Diana
Diane
Dianna
Dinah
Dionne
Dixie
Dodie
Dolores
Dominique
Dona
Donna
Donielle
Doreen
Doris
Dorothea
Dorothy
Dory
Drew
Dulcie
Dyan
Dyna

Eartha
Ebony
Eden
Edith
Edna
Edwina
Eileen
Elana
Elaine
Eleanor
Electra
Elise

Elissa
Eliza
* Elizabeth
Elke
Ella
Ellen
Ellie
Elly
Eloise
Elsa
Elvira
Elyse
Elysia
Emelyne
* Emily
Emma
Enid
Erma
Ernestine
Erica
Erin
Estelle
Esther
Ethel
Etta
Eugenia
Eunice
Eva
Evangeline
Eve
Evelina
Evelyn
Evonne

Faith
Fallon
Farrah
Fay
Felicia
Fern
Fiona
Flora
Florence
Frances
Francine
Francisca
Frederica
Frida

Gabriella
Gabrielle
Gail
Gay
Gayle
Genevieve
Georgeanne
Georgetta
Georgia
Georgiana
Geraldine
Gerri
Gertrude
Gigi
Gilda
Gillian
Gina
Ginger
Ginny
Giselle
Gladys
Glenna
Glenda
Gloria
Glynis
Golda
Grace
Gracie
Greer
Gretchen
Guinevere
Gwen
Gwendolyn
Gwyneth
Gwynne

Haley
Hailey
* Hannah
Harriet
Hazel
Heather
Heidi
Helen
Helena
Henrietta
Hilary
Hilda
Hildegarde
Hillary
Hollis
Holly
Hope
Hortense

Ida
Ilene
Imogene
Ina
Ines
Inga
Ingrid
Irene
Iris
Irma
Isabel
Isadora
Ivory
Ivy

Jacelyn
Jaclyn
Jacqueline
Jamie
Jan
Jane
Janet
Janice
Janine
Janis
Jasmine
Jean
Jeanine
Jeanette
Jena
Jennie
Jennifer
Jenny
Jessica
Jewel
Jill
Jillian
Jinny
Joan
Joanna
Joanne
Jocelyn
Jodie
Joelle
Johanna
Jolene
Jordan
Josephine
Josie
Joy
Joyce
Juanita
Judi
Judith
Julia
Juliane
Julie
Julietta
June
Justine

Kaitlyn
Kala
Kameko
Kara
Karen
Kari
Karisa
Karla
Karleen
Karylin
Kate
Katherine
Kathleen
Kathryn
Kathy
Katie
Katrina
Katy
Kay
Kayla
Kelley
Kelsey
Kendra
Kim
Kimberly
Kira
Kirby
Kirsten
Koressa
Krista
Kristin
Kristina
Kristi

Lana
Lani
Lara
Larissa
Laura
Lauralee
Laurel
Lauren
Lauryn
Laverne
Lavinia
Leah
Leandra
Leanora
Lee
Leigh
Leila
Lena
Lenore
Leona
Leslie
Letitia
Libby
Lila
Lilith
Lillian
Lily
Linda
Lindsey
Linette
Linnae
Lisa
Liza
Lois
Lola
Loni
Lora
Loreen
Lorelei
Lorelle
Loretta
Lorna
Lorraine
Louisa
Louise
Lucia
Lucille
Lucinda
Lucy
Luella
Lydia
Lynn
Lynne
Lynnette

Maddy
Madeline
Mae
Madelina
* Madison
Mady
Magdaline
Maisie
Mallory
Mandy
Manon
Marcella
Marcia
Marcy
Margaret
Margo
Margot
Marguerte
Maria
Marianna
Marianne

Maribel
Marie
Mariel
Marietta
Marily
Marion
Marilyn
Marisa
Marissa
Marjorie
Marlene
Marla
Marlo
Marni
Marsha
Martha
Marti
Martina
Mary
Maryann
Marybeth
Marylou
Matilda
Maud
Maude
Maureen
Maurita
Mavis
Maxine
May
Meara
Megan
Meghann
Meghin
Melanie
Melba
Melinda
Melissa
Melody
Melva
Mercedes
Meredith
Merele
Merrill
Mia
Michaela
Michele
Mildred
Millicent
Minerva
Mindy
Minna
Miranda
Miriam
Mitzi
Modesta
Mollie
Molly
Mona
Monica
Monique
Morgan
Morgana
Moria
Muriel
Myra
Myrna

Nadia
Nadine
Nancy
Nanette
Nani
Naomi
Nara
Natalie
Natasha
Nettie
Nicole
Nikki
Nina
Nita
Noel
Nola
Nona
Nora
Noreen
Norma

Odelia
Odette
Olga
Olive
Olivette
* Olivia
Opal

Paige
Pamela
Pat
Patience
Patrice
Patricia
Paula
Paulette
Pauline
Pearl
Penelope
Penny
Phedra
Phoebe
Phylis
Pia
Pier
Piper
Polly
Portia
Priscilla
Prudence
Prudy

Rachel
Rae
Ramona
Randee
Randi
Rani
Raquel
Raynell
Raven
Reba
Rebecca
Regan
Regina
Remy
Renata
Renee
Rhea
Rhoda
Rhonda
Rhonna
Rica
Rita
Rikki
Riva
Roanna
Roberta
Robin
Robyn
Rona
Rochelle
Rorie
Rosa
Rosalie
Rosalind
Rose
Rosemarie
Rosemary
Rowena
Roxanne
Ruby
Ruth
Ruthann
Ryann

Sabina
Sabrina
Sally
* Samantha
Sandra
Sara
Sarah
Sarena
Sasha
Selina
Selma
Shandra
Shani
Shanna
Shannon
Shari
Sharon
Sharri
Shawn
Sheena
Sheila
Shelly
Sherry
Sheryl
Shirley
Shoshana
Sibyl
Silvia
Simone
Sondra
Sonya
Sophia
Sophie
Stacy
Stella
Stephanie
Susan
Suzanne
Suzette
Sybil
Sydney
Sylvia

Tabitha
Taffy
Tallulah
Tamara
Tami
Tammy
Tanya
Tara
Tasha
Tatum
Teresa
Terese
Tess
Tessa
Thelma
Therese
Tiffany
Tilda
Tina
Terri
Toby
Toni
Tracy
Tricia
Trina
Trish
Trudy
Tuesday

Una
Ursula

Valerie
Venessa
Velma
Vera
Veronica
Vicki
Vicky
Victoria
Viola
Violet
Virginia
Vivian

Wanda
Wendy
Whitney
Whilhelmina
Wilma
Wilona
Winifred
Winna
Winona
Wynee
Wynn

Yetta
Yoko
Yolanda
Yoshiko
Yvette
Yvonne

Zelda
Zena
Zoe
Zsa Zsa

A

C

O

T

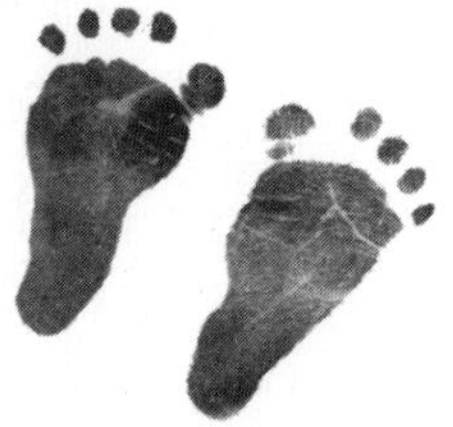

OTHER BOOKS IN THIS SERIES:

PREGNANCY

PREGNANCY AND CHILDBIRTH*

A DOCTOR DISCUSSES NUTRITION DURING PREGNANCY AND BREASTFEEDING

BREASTFEEDING

A DOCTOR DISCUSSES YOUR LIFE AFTER THE BABY IS BORN
The Postpartum Period

A DOCTOR DISCUSSES THE CARE AND DEVELOPMENT OF YOUR BABY

A DOCTOR DISCUSSES MENOPAUSE AND CURRENT ESTROGEN GUIDELINES

A DOCTOR'S APPROACH TO SENSIBLE DIETING AND WEIGHT CONTROL

**Available in Spanish*

BUDLONG MINIBOOKS:

A GUIDE TO BREAST HEALTH CARE-HOW TO EXAMINE YOUR BREASTS*

STD's AND VAGINITIS

OSTEOPOROSIS-THE SILENT STALKER*

**Available in Spanish*

BUDLONG PRESS, A CooperSurgical Company • Trumbull, CT 06611